# 200 Best
# Sheet Pan
# Meals

## Quick & Easy Oven Recipes
## One Pan, No Fuss!

# Camilla V. Saulsbury

*Robert*
**ROSE**

**For complete cataloguing information, see page 240.**

*Disclaimer*
The recipes in this book have been carefully tested by our kitchen and our tasters. To the best of our knowledge, they are safe and nutritious for ordinary use and users. For those people with food or other allergies, or who have special food requirements or health issues, please read the suggested contents of each recipe carefully and determine whether or not they may create a problem for you. All recipes are used at the risk of the consumer.

We cannot be responsible for any hazards, loss or damage that may occur as a result of any recipe use.

For those with special needs, allergies, requirements or health problems, in the event of any doubt, please contact your medical adviser prior to the use of any recipe.

Design and production: Daniella Zanchetta/PageWave Graphics Inc.
Editor: Sue Sumeraj
Recipe editor: Jennifer MacKenzie
Proofreader: Kelly Jones
Indexer: Gillian Watts
Photographer: Colin Erricson
Associate photographer: Matt Johannsson
Food stylist: Michael Elliott
Prop stylist: Charlene Erricson

Cover image: Pork Chops with Roasted Apples, Pearl Onions and Thyme (page 34)

The publisher gratefully acknowledges the financial support of our publishing program by the Government of Canada through the Canada Book Fund.

Published by Robert Rose Inc.
120 Eglinton Avenue East, Suite 800, Toronto, Ontario, Canada M4P 1E2
Tel: (416) 322-6552 Fax: (416) 322-6936
www.robertrose.ca

Printed and bound in Canada

1 2 3 4 5 6 7 8 9 MI 24 23 22 21 20 19 18 17 16

# Contents

# Introduction

**Dinnertime, and the cooking is easy** — it's what every hungry home cook dreams of right around 6 p.m. But turning that dream into reality? Sometimes it feels like a magic wand is the only way to make it happen.

I have a solution, and it's even better than a magic wand: sheet pan meals.

Using a sheet pan (plus a hot oven!) is one of the easiest and swiftest techniques for getting dinner — and breakfast, brunch, lunch and dessert — to the table. Your oven does most of the work, while you spend time with family, a good book or your favorite lounge chair, all of which make the method particularly appealing on busy weekdays.

Much like using a slow cooker, sheet pan cooking is largely a set-it-and-forget-it cooking method. Most of the (minimal) effort comes primarily before the actual cooking begins. Foods are simply prepared — chicken, fish or cuts of meat are sprinkled or rubbed with seasonings, vegetables are cut up, oil is drizzled, salt and pepper are shaken — and then everything bakes, broils or roasts, mostly hands-free, until the entire meal emerges from the oven with crisp-tender textures and oven-intensified flavors.

This streamlined approach to crafting entire meals in one fell swoop is what makes this collection of recipes so exciting. It's going to get you through every season, and countless meals, whether you're pulling together a last-minute weeknight meal, casually entertaining at home, looking for new inspiration for some of your favorite vegetables and proteins or would like some fresh ideas for fuss-free breakfasts, snacks and desserts.

I know I am not supposed to pick favorites, but this book is filled with so much irresistible, easygoing goodness that I have to wear my heart on my sleeve: this is one of my favorite projects, ever. What I like most about it is that it includes classic and often humble ingredients and recipes and makes them new, exciting and easier to prepare. For example, turning Thanksgiving dinner on its head with an all-in-one sheet pan dinner (turkey, stuffing, vegetables and cranberries included!) that is bound to get a double-take (and double helpings!) on a weeknight. Or taking otherwise complicated or time-consuming dishes such as fajitas, butternut squash risotto or eggplant Parmesan and presenting them in a new repertoire of simplified recipes. Even ground beef gets irresistible new spins such as Middle Eastern Kefta and Sizzling Eggplant, Soy-Glazed Beef Patties with Roasted Snow Peas, and Streamlined Meatloaves with Cheddar Roasted Broccoli.

And then there's my biggest weakness of all: Sheet Sweets, my chapter devoted to desserts made entirely on a sheet pan. Think Sheet Pan Cheesecake, Graham Cracker Toffee, Browned Butter Rice Crispy Treats and so much more. For someone who has always maintained that dessert should be one of the major food groups, I rest my case.

Welcome to the world of sheet pan meals!

# Sheet Pans 101

## Choosing the Best Pans

The starting point for all great sheet pan meals is choosing and using the right kind of pan. But which kind is best? It can be confusing, especially since the terms "sheet pan," "cookie sheet" and "baking sheet" are often used interchangeably in recipes. But there are some important differences that will determine whether your creation is a success.

The good news is that, once you know the criteria for choosing the right kind of pan, the selection process is a snap. Here's a checklist for guiding your choice:

- **Size:** Choose a pan that measures 18 by 13 inches (45 by 33 cm). This is the standard size for a half sheet pan — so named because these pans are half the size of a standard commercial-size sheet pan. Most ovens have interior racks that measure 22 inches (55 cm) wide, which means this pan size maximizes the use of interior space while still leaving enough room around it for hot air to circulate.

- **Edges:** The pan should have 1-inch (2.5 cm) high rolled edges, also known as the "lip." This feature is fairly standard for half sheet pans.

- **Metal construction:** For optimal cooking, as well as pan longevity, opt for aluminum or stainless steel pans. Both types conduct heat quickly and uniformly, plus they are durable and easy to clean. Aluminum pans are more affordable than stainless steel pans, but they also vary more in metal thickness. Opt for pans that are labeled "heavy-gauge" or "double-sided aluminum"; they are the longest lasting and least likely to warp at high temperatures.

### A British Original

The French may have cornered the market in rich, elaborate, time-intensive sauces, but when it comes to fresh, modern meals, it's the British who first crafted the perfect antidote: tray bakes. A tray bake is simply a sheet pan preparation by a different moniker: a "tray" is the British equivalent of a sheet pan, and "bake" refers to the fuss-free method of baking the elements of an entire meal (think meat and two veg) on said tray to make a fast, fresh, fuss-free meal. Tray bakes also encompass a range of easy-peasy British desserts, including cakes, brownies, puddings and cookie bars, all baked on a tray and cut into pieces — perfect for a crowd, make-ahead lunch-box treats and so much more.

## Sheet Pans to Avoid

Now that you know what is best, it is worth taking a moment to review the types of pans that are not suitable — for a variety of reasons — for sheet pan meals.

### Rimless and Low-Edge Cookie Sheets

Cookie sheets are perfect: for cookies. The rimless or low-edge design offers the advantage of a large surface area (ideal for maximizing the total number of cookies per sheet), while the lightweight construction is ideal for baking cookies evenly and swiftly. But this construction makes cookie sheets unsuitable for sheet pan meals. The low or complete lack of edges means that ingredients and juices can roll right off the pan, and the thinness of the pan can lead to uneven cooking as well as warping at higher temperatures.

## Jelly Roll Pans

Jelly roll pans are deceptive: they typically have a 1-inch (2.5 cm) lip and generally look like a sheet pan. However, they are smaller in both length and width, which means that a majority of the recipes in this collection will overcrowd or overflow the pan. In addition, jelly roll pans are typically thinner than sheet pans, making them likely to warp at heat settings higher than 400°F (200°C).

## Nonstick Sheet Pans

Nonstick sheet pans are typically darker in color than standard sheet pans, which means that baked goods, in particular, brown faster. While they may be easier to clean than standard sheet pans, nonstick pans can vary significantly in quality, and all nonstick cookware must eventually be replaced because the finish wears off over time.

In addition, nonstick sheet pans have specialized coatings that can leach perfluorinated chemicals (PFCs) into foods. While the U.S. Environmental Protection Agency (EPA) maintains that products made with PFCs (such as Teflon-coated sheet pans and frying pans) pose no health risk, research indicates that when these products break down, they can release a variety of chemicals that have been linked to birth defects and myriad health problems, including thyroid disease and infertility.

## Insulated Sheet Pans

These pans may be labeled as baking sheets or cookie sheets, but they look similar to sheet pans in that they typically have a 1/2- to 1-inch (1 to 2.5 cm) lip and feel heavier than less expensive cookie sheets thanks to the weight of the insulating layers. Insulated pans are best for delicate cookies because they regulate heat to prevent cookies from browning too quickly. This function, however, makes them unsuitable for sheet pan meals: they significantly slow down overall cooking time and prevent foods from browning and caramelizing.

### No-Scrub Method for Cleaning Sheet Pan Buildup

No matter how fastidious your cleaning methods, it is inevitable that your favorite sheet pan will eventually accumulate some greasy grime buildup, most often in the corners and on the underside of the pan. Luckily, a simple, low-cost, no-heavy-scrubbing solution exists, and it involves only two ingredients: baking soda and hydrogen peroxide. Here's how it works:

1. Sprinkle a thin, even layer of baking soda over the area of the pan in need of gunk removal.
2. Lightly sprinkle the baking soda with hydrogen peroxide.
3. Sprinkle the same area with a second light layer of baking soda. Let the pan stand for at least 3 hours, or as long as 12 hours. Lightly rub away the baking soda mixture with a soft, damp towel, and voila! No more gunk!
4. Wash the pan with regular dish detergent and rinse to remove any remaining baking soda mixture.

## Silicone Sheet Pans

Silicone sheet pans should be avoided because the maximum recommended temperature is 428°F (220°C), and many of the recipes in this collection require higher temperatures. Once silicone sheet pans are heated beyond their maximum temperature, they have the potential for melting and omitting fumes from undisclosed additives.

# Best Practices for Sheet Pan Meals

## Read the Recipe and Follow the Instructions

Sheet pan meals are easy to prepare, but no matter how simple, the instructions are important for the success of the recipe.

Take the time to read through the recipe in its entirety before beginning, then gather the needed ingredients and equipment.

## Position the Oven Rack in the Center of the Oven

Unless otherwise noted in the recipe, position the oven rack in the center of the oven. Setting the rack in this position promotes the most even cooking, baking and browning on all areas of the sheet pan.

## Preheat the Oven

Preheat to the temperature specified in the recipe. It typically takes 10 to 20 minutes (depending on the oven manufacturer) to heat the oven to the desired temperature. Often, this is just the amount of time needed to prep the ingredients for the recipe.

## Line and Spray the Pan

All but a few recipes in this book specify lining the pan with either parchment paper or foil and then lightly spraying the paper or foil with nonstick cooking spray. This takes no more than a minute or two to accomplish and serves a dual function. First, it prevents the food from sticking to the pan. Second, it makes cleanup a breeze: simply scrunch up and toss away the used paper or foil after cooking. You will still need to wash the pan to remove any residual oil and cooking juices, but absolutely no scrubbing is required.

Note that when the oven temperature is 400°F (200°C) or below, parchment or the choice of foil or parchment are given as options; for temperatures exceeding 400°F (200°C), foil is the only option. Most parchment paper brands recommend using the product at temperatures lower than 425°F (220°C).

## Vegetables: Size Matters

Be sure to follow the instructions for cutting and adding vegetables to the sheet pan. In general, vegetables are cut to equal sizes when they are roasted at the same time. Softer vegetables such as tomatoes and zucchini need less time in the oven, so they will often be added to the sheet pan later than starchier vegetables such as carrots and potatoes.

## Proteins Need Their Rest

Once cooking is complete, allow meats and poultry to rest, on average, 5 minutes for poultry and at least 10 minutes for larger cuts of meat. This gives the juices in the proteins time to redisperse, resulting in moist and tender meats.

## Use a Rack on the Pan When Instructed

A very small number of recipes require the use of a metal rack set directly on top of the sheet pan. This allows air to circulate around the food positioned on the rack, for even browning and crisping. Choose a sturdy, oven-safe metal rack that fits snugly inside the sheet pan.

## Pay Attention to Cooking Times

The majority of recipes in this book have ingredients added to the pan at staggered times. Longer-cooking items are added first, followed by ingredients that require less overall cooking time. Be sure to follow the directions for adding ingredients at the indicated times.

Check for doneness of the foods on the sheet pan, using the method described in the recipe, when the minimum cooking time in the recipe has elapsed. If the ingredients are not ready, check again in 1 minute. Continue to check every minute until the foods are done.

# The Sheet Pan Pantry

**Most of the recipes** in this book can be made with a minimal list of fresh ingredients (a protein and one or two vegetables) coupled with ingredients — salt, pepper, spices, soy sauce — you already have in your pantry. My focus in developing the recipes in this collection was to use a minimum number of readily available ingredients to maximize both taste and convenience in one fell swoop. Here are some of the most commonly used ingredients, which I recommend keeping at the ready for a variety of sheet pan meals.

## Frozen Fruits and Vegetables

Keeping a selection of frozen fruits and vegetables in the freezer is a great way to make quick and simple sheet pan meals. In addition to its convenience, frozen produce can sometimes be more nutritious than fresh. When fresh fruits and vegetables are shipped long distances, they rapidly lose vitamins and minerals thanks to exposure to heat and light; by contrast, frozen fruits and vegetables are frozen immediately after being picked, ensuring that all of the vitamins and minerals are preserved.

Some varieties to keep on hand include:

• berries (such as blueberries and cranberries)
• broccoli florets
• chopped greens (spinach, Swiss chard, mustard greens)
• chopped or pearl onions
• chopped peppers and onions
• corn
• petite peas
• shelled edamame

## Shelf-Stable Tomato Products
### Diced Tomatoes

Canned diced tomatoes can replace diced fresh tomatoes in most recipes. Stock up on tomatoes with chiles, too, as they add a peppery accent to a wide range of sheet pan meals.

## Marinara Sauce

Jarred marinara sauce — a highly seasoned Italian tomato sauce made with onions, garlic, basil and oregano — is typically used on pasta and meat, but it is also a great pantry staple for creating sheet pan meals. For the best tomato flavor and the most versatility, choose a variety with minimal ingredients that is low in sodium and free of sweeteners and preservatives.

## Sun-Dried Tomatoes

Sun-dried tomatoes are a flavorful and nutritious way to add an extra bit of zest to your recipes. Look for organic sun-dried tomatoes, which are often processed at a lower temperature than most commercial varieties, preserving some of the nutrients.

## Chunky Tomato Salsa

Like marinara sauce, ready-made chunky salsa — rich with tomatoes, peppers, onions and spices but low in calories — packs tremendous flavor and makes a great accompaniment to a range of sheet pan meals.

# Soybean Products

Two soybean products — tofu and tempeh — are used in several recipes in the Meatless Meals chapter. They are usually available in well-stocked grocery stores.

## Tofu

Tofu, or bean curd, is made from soybeans that have been cooked, made into milk and then coagulated. The soy milk curdles when heated, and the curds are skimmed off and pressed into blocks.

All of the recipes in this collection were tested with refrigerated tofu. While shelf-stable tofu is convenient, the flavor and texture are markedly inferior. Tofu can be found in extra-firm, firm and soft varieties in the refrigerated section of the supermarket. For optimal results, be sure to use the variety specified in the recipe.

## Tempeh

Tempeh (pronounced *TEM-pay*) is a traditional Indonesian food. It is made from fully cooked soybeans that have been fermented with a mold called rhizopus and formed into cakes. Some varieties have whole grains added to the mix, creating a particularly meaty, satisfying texture. Tempeh, like tofu, takes on the flavor of whatever it is marinated with and also needs to be stored in the refrigerator.

# Eggs and Dairy

Eggs and dairy products come into play with a number of sheet pan meals, especially in the Sheet Sweets and Breakfast and Brunch chapters.

## Dairy Milk

All of the recipes calling for milk were tested with lower-fat (2%) milk. However, any fat level can be used in its place.

## Eggs

The recipes in this book were tested with large eggs. Select clean, fresh eggs that have been handled and refrigerated properly. Do not use dirty, cracked or leaking eggs, or eggs that have a bad odor or unnatural color when cracked open; they may have become contaminated with harmful bacteria, such as salmonella.

## Yogurt

All of the recipes in this collection call for plain yogurt or plain Greek yogurt. Greek yogurt is a thick, creamy yogurt similar in texture to sour cream.

## Shredded and Grated Cheeses

Ready-to-use cheeses are handy for a range of sheet pan meals, from breakfast to dinner and beyond. They save the steps of shredding or grating cheese and subsequently cleaning a grater. In addition, shredded and grated cheeses are easy to freeze. Here are the varieties used most often throughout the book:

- shredded Cheddar cheese
- shredded Italian cheese blend
- grated Parmesan cheese

## Ricotta Cheese

Ricotta is a rich fresh cheese with a texture that is slightly grainy but still far smoother than cottage cheese. For the best texture and flavor, opt for regular or lower-fat (not nonfat) varieties when making the recipes in this collection.

# Fats and Oils

## Olive Oil

Olive oil is the fat used most in this collection. It is a monounsaturated oil that is prized for a wide range of cooking preparations. I recommend using plain olive oil (simply labeled "olive oil"), which contains a combination of refined olive oil and virgin or extra virgin oil. The subtle nuances of extra virgin olive oil are not very noticeable after cooking in the oven.

## Vegetable Oil

"Vegetable oil" is a generic term used to describe any neutral plant-based oil that is liquid at room temperature. You can use a vegetable oil blend, canola oil, light olive oil, grapeseed oil, safflower oil, sunflower oil, peanut oil or corn oil.

## Butter

Butter quickly picks up off-flavors during storage and when exposed to oxygen, so once the carton or wrap is opened, place it in a sealable plastic food bag or other airtight container. Store it away from foods with strong odors, especially items such as onions and garlic.

If you use butter only occasionally, I recommend storing it in the freezer. Wrap entire sticks, or use a method I developed in my student days: cut the butter into 1-tbsp (15 mL) pats and place them on a cookie sheet lined with plastic. Place in the freezer for 30 to 60 minutes, until frozen, then place the frozen pats in an airtight container. The butter can be frozen for up to 6 months. Remove pats of butter as needed and thaw in the refrigerator or at room temperature.

I don't recommend margarine as a replacement for butter because it is lacking in flavor. If you do use margarine in any of the baking recipes, it is important to use 100% vegetable oil varieties in stick form. Margarine spreads — in tub or stick form — contain a significant amount of water, which will alter the results of the recipe.

## Unrefined Virgin Coconut Oil

Virgin coconut oil can be used in a few recipes in this collection, often as an alternative for butter. It is semisolid at room temperature. It is simple to scrape out a teaspoon (5 mL) or tablespoon (15 mL) of coconut oil, but when a larger amount is needed for a recipe, it is easier to melt the coconut oil before measuring. It does not harm the oil to be warmed to a liquid state, so you can quickly liquefy the entire jar. To do this, simply hold the sealed jar under warm running water, or place it in a bowl of warm water, until there is enough liquid coconut oil to measure out.

## Toasted Sesame Oil

Toasted sesame oil has a dark brown color and a rich, nutty flavor. It is used sparingly, mostly in Asian recipes, to add a tremendous amount of flavor.

## Nonstick Cooking Spray

A number of recipes in this collection call for the use of nonstick cooking spray, which helps keep foods from sticking to the sheet pan or the sheet pan lining (either foil or parchment paper). It may seem odd to spray the liner, but it really works: the cooked food is much easier to remove when the liner is sprayed, and cleanup from lining the pan is far simpler than when you just spray the pan.

# Flours

## All-Purpose Flour

Made from a blend of high-gluten hard wheat and low-gluten soft wheat, all-purpose flour is fine-textured flour milled from the inner part of the wheat kernel and contains neither the germ nor the bran. All-purpose flour comes either bleached or unbleached; these can be used interchangeably.

## Whole Wheat Pastry Flour

A fine-textured, soft wheat flour, whole wheat pastry flour can be used interchangeably with all-purpose flour in most recipes. Most, but not all, whole wheat pastry flours include the wheat germ; for optimum nutrition, select a variety that includes 100% of the wheat berry.

In several recipes in this book, I suggest substituting whole wheat pastry flour as an alternative to all-purpose flour. It is extremely important not to substitute regular whole wheat flour instead; the results will be coarse, leaden and possibly inedible.

You can find whole wheat pastry flour at well-stocked supermarkets and at natural food stores. Store it in a sealable plastic food bag in the refrigerator.

# Leavening Agents

## Baking Powder

Baking powder is a chemical leavening agent made from a blend of alkali (sodium bicarbonate, known commonly as baking soda) and acid (most commonly calcium acid phosphate, sodium aluminum sulfate or cream of tartar), plus some form of starch to absorb any moisture so a reaction does not take place until a liquid is added.

## Baking Soda

Baking soda is a chemical leavener consisting of bicarbonate of soda. It is alkaline in nature and, when combined with an acidic ingredient, such as buttermilk, yogurt, citrus juice or honey, it creates carbon dioxide bubbles, giving baked goods a dramatic rise.

# Sweeteners

## Granulated Sugar

Granulated sugar (also called white sugar) is refined cane or beet sugar, and is the most common sweetener used in this book. Once opened, store granulated sugar in an airtight container in a cool, dry place.

## Brown Sugar

Brown sugar is granulated sugar with some molasses added to it. The molasses gives the sugar a soft texture. Light brown sugar (also known as golden yellow sugar) has less molasses and a more delicate flavor than dark brown sugar. Once opened, store brown sugar in an airtight container or a sealable plastic food bag to prevent clumping.

## Confectioners' (Icing) Sugar

Confectioners' (icing) sugar (also called powdered sugar) is granulated sugar that has been ground to a fine powder. Cornstarch is added to prevent the sugar from clumping together. It is used in recipes where regular sugar would be too grainy.

## Honey

Honey is plant nectar that has been gathered and concentrated by honeybees. Any variety of honey may be used in the recipes in this collection. Unopened containers of honey may be stored at room temperature. After opening, store honey in the refrigerator to protect against mold. Honey will keep indefinitely when stored properly.

## Maple Syrup

Maple syrup is a thick liquid sweetener made by boiling the sap from maple trees. It has a strong, pure maple flavor. Maple-flavored pancake syrup is just corn syrup with coloring and artificial maple flavoring added, and it is not recommended as a substitute for pure maple syrup. Unopened containers of maple syrup may be stored at room temperature. After opening, store maple syrup in the refrigerator to protect against mold. Maple syrup will keep indefinitely when stored properly.

# Fresh Herbs

Fresh herbs add both flavor and color to sheet pan meals. Cilantro, chives and parsley — either flat-leaf (Italian) or curly — are readily available and inexpensive, and they store well in the produce bin of the refrigerator, so keep them on hand year round. Basil, mint and thyme are best in the spring and summer, when they are in season in your own garden or at the farmers' market.

# Flavorings

Here are my top recommendations for the flavorings to keep in your pantry, all of which can elevate your sheet pan meals to delicious new heights.

## Salt

All of the recipes in this collection were tested using common table salt. An equal amount of fine sea salt can be used in its place.

## Black Pepper

Black pepper is made by grinding black peppercorns, which have been picked when the berries are not quite ripe and then dried until they shrivel and their skin turns dark brown to black. Black pepper has a strong, slightly hot flavor, with a hint of sweetness.

## Ground Spices and Dried Herbs

Spices and dried herbs can turn the simplest of meals into masterpieces. They should be stored in light- and air-proof containers, away from direct sunlight and heat, to preserve their flavors.

Co-ops, health food stores and mail-order sources that sell herbs and spices in bulk are all excellent options for purchasing very fresh organic spices and dried herbs, often at a low cost.

With ground spices and dried herbs, freshness is everything. To determine whether a ground spice or dried herb is fresh, open the container and sniff. A strong fragrance means it is still acceptable for use.

Note that ground spices, not whole, are used throughout this collection. Here are my top picks for a wide variety of sheet pan meals:

- black pepper
- cayenne pepper (also labeled "ground red pepper")
- cinnamon
- cumin
- curry powder (any heat level, but mild is the most versatile)
- dried dillweed
- ginger
- Italian seasoning
- nutmeg
- pumpkin pie spice
- rubbed sage
- thyme

## Hot Pepper Sauce

Hot pepper sauce is a spicy condiment made from chile peppers and other common ingredients, such as vinegar and spices. They come in countless heat levels and flavors, so pick the multipurpose sauce that best suits your taste buds.

## Sriracha

Sriracha is a multipurpose hot sauce made from red chile peppers, garlic, vinegar, salt and sugar. It is hot and tangy, with a slight sweetness that distinguishes it from other hot pepper sauces. Sriracha is often served as a condiment in Thai, Vietnamese and Chinese restaurants, but it can be used in a wide range of cuisines and preparations.

## Citrus Zest

"Zest" is the name for the colored outer layer of citrus peel. The oils in zest are intense in flavor. Use a zester, a Microplane-style grater or the small holes of a box grater to grate zest. Avoid grating the white layer (pith) just below the zest; it is very bitter.

## Cocoa Powder

Select natural cocoa powder rather than Dutch-process for the recipes in this collection. Natural cocoa powder has a deep, true chocolate flavor; it also tends to be less expensive. The packaging should state whether it is Dutch-process, but you can also tell the difference by sight: if it is dark to almost black, it is Dutch-process; natural cocoa powder is much lighter and is typically brownish red in color.

## Vanilla Extract

Vanilla extract adds a sweet, fragrant flavor to dishes, especially baked goods. It is produced by combining an extraction from dried vanilla beans with an alcohol and water mixture. It is then aged for several months.

## Almond Extract

Almond extract is a flavoring manufactured by combining bitter almond oil with ethyl alcohol. It is used in much the same way as vanilla extract. Almond extract has a highly concentrated, intense flavor, so measure with care.

## Miso

Miso is a sweet, fermented soybean paste usually made with some sort of grain. It comes unpasteurized and in several varieties, from golden yellow to deep red to sweet white. It can be made into a soup or a sauce or used as a salt substitute.

## Thai Curry Paste

Available in small jars, Thai curry paste is a blend of Thai chiles, garlic, lemongrass, galangal, ginger and wild lime leaves. It is a fast and delicious way to add Southeast Asian flavor to a broad spectrum of recipes in a single step. Panang and yellow curry pastes tend to be the mildest. Red curry paste is medium hot, and green curry paste is typically the hottest.

## Mustard

Mustard adds depth of flavor to a wide range of dishes. It is most commonly used in this collection for salad dressing because it facilitates the emulsification of oil and vinegar. I recommend either Dijon mustard or brown mustard for their versatility.

## Vinegars

Vinegars are multipurpose flavor powerhouses. Delicious in vinaigrettes and dressings, they are also stealth ingredients for use at the end of cooking time to enhance and balance the natural flavors of dishes. Store vinegars in a dark place, away from heat and light.

Cider vinegar — inexpensive and versatile — is an excellent multipurpose choice. It is made from the juice of crushed apples. After the juice is collected, it is allowed to age in wooden barrels. Red and white wine vinegars, produced by fermenting wine in wooden barrels, are also good multitasking options.

## Ready-to-Use Chicken Broth

Ready-made chicken broth is used in a few recipes in this collection. Opt for broths that are all-natural, reduced-sodium (you can always add more salt) and MSG-free. Look for brands made from chickens raised without hormones or antibiotics.

For convenience, look for broths in Tetra Paks, which typically come in 32-oz (1 L), 48-oz (1.5 L) and occasionally 16-oz (500 mL) sizes. Once opened, these can be stored in the refrigerator for up to 1 week. You can also freeze small amounts (2 tbsp to $\frac{1}{4}$ cup/30 to 60 mL) in ice-cube trays. Once frozen, simply pop out the cubes and store them in an airtight bag for up to 6 months (thaw in the microwave or the refrigerator).

## Basil Pesto

Basil pesto is an Italian sauce that is traditionally made from basil, garlic, pine nuts, olive oil and cheese. It adds tremendous flavor to recipes in one simple step. Look for it where pasta and marinara sauce are shelved in the supermarket, or in the refrigerated section, near fresh pastas.

# Measuring Ingredients

**Accurate measurements** are important for sheet pan meals to achieve the right balance of flavors in any recipe. So take both time and care as you measure.

## Measuring Dry Ingredients

When measuring a dry ingredient, such as flour, cocoa powder, sugar, spices or salt, spoon it into the appropriate-size dry measuring cup or measuring spoon, heaping it up over the top. Slide a straight-edged utensil, such as a knife, across the top to level off the extra. Be careful not to shake or tap the cup or spoon to settle the ingredient, or you will have more than you need.

## Measuring Moist Ingredients

Moist ingredients, such as brown sugar, coconut and dried fruit, must be firmly packed in a measuring cup or spoon to be measured accurately. Use a dry measuring cup for these ingredients. Fill the measuring cup to slightly overflowing, then pack down the ingredient firmly with the back of a spoon. Add more of the ingredient and pack down again until the cup is full and even with the top of the measure.

## Measuring Liquid Ingredients

Use a clear plastic or glass measuring cup or container with lines up the sides to measure liquid ingredients. Set the container on the counter and pour the liquid to the appropriate mark. Lower your head to read the measurement at eye level.

# 25 Extra-Simple Pantry Meals

# Baked Eggs in Holes

Some salt, pepper and butter are all it takes to bring together fresh eggs and your favorite sliced bread into the easiest, most satisfying dinner – or breakfast, brunch or lunch – ever. Gussy it up with toppings, if you like, or savor the minimalism.

**Tip**

If adding a sprinkle of cheese for a topping, add it during the last minute of cooking time.

- Preheat oven to 375°F (190°C)
- 18- by 13-inch (45 by 33 cm) rimmed sheet pan, lined with parchment paper or foil and sprayed with nonstick cooking spray

| | | |
|---|---|---|
| 2 tbsp | unsalted butter, softened | 30 mL |
| 6 | large slices multigrain or white sandwich bread | 6 |
| 6 | large eggs | 6 |
| | Salt and freshly cracked black pepper | |

**Suggested Toppings**

Shredded, grated or crumbled cheese (such as Cheddar, Parmesan or goat cheese)

Chopped fresh herbs

Diced or sliced avocado

Chopped tomato

Salsa

1. Spread butter on both sides of each bread slice and place on prepared pan. Using a 2- to $2\frac{1}{2}$-inch (5 to 6 cm) cookie cutter or glass, cut a round from the center of each bread slice. Bake in preheated oven for 5 minutes.

2. Remove pan from oven and turn bread over. Carefully crack 1 egg into the center of each bread slice. Season with salt and pepper. Bake for 7 to 9 minutes, rotating pan halfway through, until egg whites are set but yolks are still runny. Using a large pancake lifter, transfer each serving to a plate. Serve immediately with any of the suggested toppings, as desired.

# Roasted Home Fries with Oven-Fried Eggs

The secret to irresistible roasted home fries is an extra-hot oven, a drizzle of good olive oil and a final sprinkle of fresh herbs. The accompanying oven-fried eggs add protein and a silky sauce (the runny yolk) in one fell swoop.

## Tip

The hash can be made without the eggs. Skip step 3 and increase the roasting time in step 2 to 16 to 25 minutes.

## Variation

Add 1 chopped bell pepper (red, green or yellow) when stirring the hash in step 2.

- Preheat oven to 500°F (260°C)
- 18- by 13-inch (45 by 33 cm) rimmed sheet pan, lined with foil and sprayed with nonstick cooking spray

| | | |
|---|---|---|
| 2 lbs | russet or gold potatoes, diced | 1 kg |
| 1 | large onion, coarsely chopped | 1 |
| 2 tbsp | olive oil | 30 mL |
| | Salt and freshly cracked black pepper | |
| 4 | large eggs | 4 |
| 1/2 cup | packed fresh parsley, cilantro or basil leaves, chopped | 125 mL |

1. On prepared pan, toss together potatoes, onion, oil, 1 tsp (5 mL) salt and 1/2 tsp (2 mL) pepper. Spread in a single layer. Roast in preheated oven for 12 minutes.

2. Remove pan from oven and stir the hash. Roast for 10 to 15 minutes or until potatoes are fork-tender.

3. Remove pan from oven and stir the hash. Make 4 evenly spaced wells in the hash. Crack the eggs into the wells and season with salt and pepper. Roast for 6 to 10 minutes or until egg whites are opaque.

4. Sprinkle with parsley and serve.

# Broccoli Cheddar No-Crust Quiche

I love any variation of quiche, but I'm extremely partial to this broccoli incarnation because it's so darned easy, which means I can make it almost anytime. Incorporating cottage cheese keeps the dish far leaner than heavy cream versions, plus it ups the overall cheese flavor.

## Storage Tip

Store leftover quiche squares in an airtight container in the refrigerator for up to 3 days. Serve cold or at room temperature, or warm in the microwave at 70% power for 45 to 75 seconds.

## Variation

*Goat Cheese and Roasted Pepper Quiche:* Replace the broccoli with 1 jar (12 oz/340 mL) roasted red bell peppers, drained and chopped, and replace the Cheddar cheese with 4 oz (125 g) crumbled soft goat cheese.

- Preheat oven to 350°F (180°C)
- 18- by 13-inch (45 by 33 cm) rimmed sheet pan, lined with parchment paper or foil and sprayed with nonstick cooking spray

| | | |
|---|---|---|
| 2 | packages (each 12 oz/375 g) frozen chopped broccoli, thawed and squeezed dry | 2 |
| 2 cups | shredded sharp (old) Cheddar cheese | 500 mL |
| 8 | large eggs | 8 |
| ½ tsp | salt | 2 mL |
| ¼ tsp | freshly ground black pepper | 1 mL |
| 2 | containers (each 16 oz/500 g) cottage cheese | 2 |

1. Spread broccoli in an even layer on prepared pan. Sprinkle with Cheddar cheese.

2. In a large bowl, whisk together eggs, salt, and pepper until blended. Stir in cottage cheese until blended. Pour evenly over broccoli and cheese.

3. Bake in preheated oven for 35 to 40 minutes or until center is just set and top is golden brown. Using parchment to lift quiche, transfer quiche to a wire rack and let cool for 20 minutes before cutting into squares.

# Spanish Tortilla with Potatoes and Roasted Peppers

My version of tortilla Española – a rustic omelet made with fried potatoes and eggs – makes extra-quick work of the potato component by using kettle-cooked potato chips. After all, they are just fried potatoes, and once they have had a quick soak in the egg mixture, they plump up to delicious perfection.

## Storage Tip

Store leftover tortilla squares in an airtight container in the refrigerator for up to 3 days. Serve cold or at room temperature, or warm in the microwave at 70% power for 45 to 75 seconds.

- Preheat oven to 450°F (230°C)
- 18- by 13-inch (45 by 33 cm) rimmed sheet pan, lined with foil and sprayed with nonstick cooking spray

| | | |
|---|---|---|
| 12 | large eggs | 12 |
| 2 | bags (each 5 oz/142 g) kettle-cooked potato chips, coarsely crushed | 2 |
| 1 | jar (12 oz/340 mL) roasted red bell peppers, drained and coarsely chopped | 1 |
| 1½ cups | chopped green onions (about 1 bunch) | 375 mL |
| 1 tbsp | olive oil | 15 mL |
| 1 cup | grated manchego, Romano or Parmesan cheese | 250 mL |

1. In a large bowl, whisk eggs until blended. Stir in potato chips and let stand for 10 minutes. Stir in roasted peppers.

2. Meanwhile, on prepared pan, toss green onions with oil. Spread in a single layer. Roast in preheated oven for 5 minutes.

3. Remove pan from oven and pour egg mixture evenly over onions. Sprinkle with cheese. Bake for 15 to 20 minutes or until eggs are just set (the eggs will continue to cook from the heat of the pan). Let cool on pan on a wire rack for 10 minutes before cutting into squares. Serve warm or let cool completely.

# Double Cheese–Stuffed Zucchini with Basil Crumb Topping

---

**Makes 4 servings**

I'm skipping the meat here in favor of cheese times two, baked into zucchini vessels for a seriously satisfying dinner. A crisp panko and Parmesan topping is the final touch atop the best (and simplest!) meatless meal you've had in a while.

## Variations

Add ½ cup (125 mL) crumbled cooked bacon or ¾ cup (175 mL) chopped ham to the ricotta mixture.

Add ½ cup (125 mL) chopped roasted red bell peppers or ¼ cup (60 mL) chopped drained oil-packed sun-dried tomatoes to the ricotta mixture.

- Preheat oven to 400°F (200°C)
- 18- by 13-inch (45 by 33 cm) rimmed sheet pan, lined with parchment paper or foil

| | | |
|---|---|---:|
| 4 | zucchini, halved lengthwise | 4 |
| 1½ cups | ricotta cheese | 375 mL |
| ¾ cup | grated Parmesan cheese, divided | 175 mL |
| ½ cup | packed fresh basil leaves, chopped, divided | 125 mL |
| 1 cup | panko (Japanese bread crumbs) | 250 mL |
| 1 tbsp | olive oil | 15 mL |

1. Using a metal spoon, scoop and scrape out seeds from each zucchini half.

2. In a small bowl, combine ricotta, ½ cup (125 mL) Parmesan and half the basil until blended. Pack into hollowed-out zucchini, dividing equally.

3. In another small bowl, combine the remaining Parmesan, the remaining basil, panko and oil. Sprinkle over ricotta mixture. Place zucchini on prepared pan.

4. Bake in preheated oven for 35 to 40 minutes or until zucchini are tender and topping is golden brown.

# Spaghetti Squash with Pesto and Chickpeas

In recent years, spiralized vegetable "pastas" have taken center stage, but there is nothing like the original: spaghetti squash, roasted and then raked into golden "noodles." Here, it is complemented with pesto and chickpeas for an ultra-easy weeknight repast.

## Tip

An equal amount of white beans (such as cannellini, navy or Great Northern beans) can be used in place of the chickpeas.

## Variations

*Black Bean and Queso Spaghetti Squash:* Replace the chickpeas with black beans and use 1 cup (250 mL) salsa plus 1 tbsp (15 mL) olive oil in place of the pesto. Instead of Parmesan, sprinkle the finished dish with crumbled queso fresco or mild feta cheese.

*Spaghetti Squash Marinara:* Use an equal amount of marinara sauce plus 1 tbsp (15 mL) olive oil in place of the pesto.

- Preheat oven to 450°F (230°C)
- 18- by 13-inch (45 by 33 cm) rimmed sheet pan, lined with foil

| | | |
|---|---|---|
| 1 | spaghetti squash (about 2 lbs/1 kg) | 1 |
| ¾ cup | basil pesto | 175 mL |
| 1 | can (14 to 19 oz/398 to 540 mL) chickpeas, drained and rinsed | 1 |
| ½ cup | grated Parmesan cheese | 125 mL |

1. Cut squash in half lengthwise and remove seeds. Place squash, cut side down, on prepared pan. Roast in preheated oven for 35 to 45 minutes or until a knife is easily inserted into squash. Remove from oven, leaving oven on, and let squash cool for 5 to 10 minutes or until squash is cool enough to handle.

2. Scoop squash pulp out onto sheet pan. Using a fork, rake squash into strands. Add pesto and chickpeas, tossing to coat. Spread in an even layer. Return pan to oven for 5 to 8 minutes or until warmed through. Serve sprinkled with Parmesan.

# Parmesan Polenta with Roasted Mushrooms

The inspiration for this recipe came from a bowl of creamy polenta with wild mushrooms I had the pleasure of eating at a restaurant in the heart of California wine country. This weeknight interpretation relies on ready-to-use polenta and more humble mushrooms, but the result is still sophisticated and surprisingly substantial.

## Tip

If mushrooms are especially large, cut them into quarters.

## Variation

Add 2 cloves garlic, minced, with the mushrooms in step 1.

- Preheat oven to 450°F (230°C)
- 18- by 13-inch (45 by 33 cm) rimmed sheet pan, lined with foil and sprayed with nonstick cooking spray

| | | |
|---|---|---|
| 1 lb | white or cremini mushrooms, trimmed and halved | 500 g |
| 3 tbsp | olive oil, divided | 45 mL |
| | Salt and freshly cracked black pepper | |
| 1 | roll (17 oz/482 g) prepared plain polenta | 1 |
| $^2/_3$ cup | grated Parmesan cheese | 150 mL |
| | Chopped fresh flat-leaf (Italian) parsley or basil | |

1. On prepared pan, toss mushrooms with 2 tbsp (30 mL) oil, $^1/_4$ tsp (1 mL) salt and $^1/_4$ tsp (1 mL) pepper. Spread in a single layer. Roast in preheated oven for 10 minutes.

2. Meanwhile, cut polenta crosswise into $^1/_2$-inch (1 cm) slices. Brush one cut side of slices with the remaining oil and season with salt and pepper.

3. Remove pan from oven and stir mushrooms. Arrange polenta slices, seasoned side up, in between the mushrooms. Sprinkle slices with cheese. Bake for 10 to 13 minutes or until mushrooms are brown and polenta slices are golden brown.

4. Serve polenta with mushrooms, sprinkled with parsley.

# California Fish Tacos with Cucumber and Pineapple

While pork, beef and chicken tacos are more familiar – and I've never met a meaty taco I didn't like – why not give fish tacos, a popular favorite from my home state of California, a try? They are as easy as can be when made on a sheet pan. Topped with succulent pineapple and crunchy cucumber, they are a dazzling departure.

## Tips

Other mild, lean white fish, such as orange roughy, snapper, tilapia, tilefish or striped bass, may be used in place of the cod.

Thawed frozen diced pineapple may be used in place of the fresh pineapple.

## Variation

Substitute diced mango for the pineapple.

- Preheat broiler, with rack set 4 to 6 inches (10 to 15 cm) from the heat source
- 18- by 13-inch (45 by 33 cm) rimmed sheet pan, lined with foil and sprayed with nonstick cooking spray

| | | |
|---|---|---|
| 4 | skinless cod fillets (each about 6 oz/175 g) | 4 |
| 1 tbsp | olive oil | 15 mL |
| 1 tsp | chipotle chile powder | 5 mL |
| 1/4 tsp | salt | 1 mL |
| 1 cup | diced fresh pineapple | 250 mL |
| 8 | 6-inch (15 cm) corn tortillas | 8 |
| 1 cup | diced cucumber | 250 mL |

**Suggested Accompaniments**

Fresh cilantro leaves

Lime wedges

Guacamole

1. Place fish on prepared pan, spacing evenly. Lightly brush both sides of fish with oil, then sprinkle with chile powder and salt. Broil for 3 minutes.

2. Open oven door and scatter pineapple around fish. Close door and broil for 1 to 3 minutes or until fish is opaque and flakes easily when tested with a fork. Flake fish into small pieces.

3. Fill tortillas with fish, broiled pineapple and cucumber. Serve with any of the suggested accompaniments, as desired.

# Butter-Roasted Salmon and Cauliflower

**Makes 4 servings**

Tired of the same old broiled salmon? Try this butter-roasted version – it just may be the best you've ever tasted. The equally buttery cauliflower that roasts alongside will very likely rock your world as well.

## Tip

An equal amount of olive oil can be used in place of the butter.

Broccoli florets can be used in place of the cauliflower.

- Preheat oven to 450°F (230°C)
- 18- by 13-inch (45 by 33 cm) rimmed sheet pan, lined with foil and sprayed with nonstick cooking spray

| | | |
|---|---|---|
| 6 cups | cauliflower florets | 1.5 L |
| 4 tbsp | unsalted butter, divided | 60 mL |
| ½ tsp | salt, divided | 2 mL |
| ½ tsp | freshly cracked black pepper | 2 mL |
| 4 | pieces skinless salmon fillet (each 6 oz/175 g) | 4 |

**Suggested Accompaniments**

Chopped fresh flat-leaf (Italian) parsley

Lemon wedges

1. On prepared pan, toss cauliflower with half each of the butter, salt and pepper. Spread in a single layer. Roast in preheated oven for 12 minutes.

2. Remove pan from oven and stir cauliflower. Nestle fish among the cauliflower, spacing evenly. Brush fish with the remaining butter and season with the remaining salt and pepper. Roast for 9 to 12 minutes or until cauliflower is browned and fish is opaque and flakes easily when tested with a fork. Serve with the suggested accompaniments, as desired.

# Lemon-Pepper Tilapia with Roasted Asparagus

Here, skinless tilapia fillets and asparagus roast side by side with garlic, lemon and a touch of olive oil. It's simple, healthy and altogether delicious.

## Tip

Other mild, lean white fish, such as orange roughy, snapper, cod, tilefish or striped bass, may be used in place of the tilapia.

## Variation

An equal amount of trimmed green beans can be used in place of the asparagus.

- Preheat oven to 425°F (220°C)
- 18- by 13-inch (45 by 33 cm) rimmed sheet pan, lined with foil and sprayed with nonstick cooking spray

| | | |
|---|---|---|
| 1 lb | asparagus, ends trimmed | 500 g |
| 3 tbsp | olive oil, divided | 45 mL |
| | Salt and freshly cracked black pepper | |
| 3 | cloves garlic, minced | 3 |
| 2 tbsp | finely grated lemon zest | 30 mL |
| 4 | skinless tilapia fillets (each 6 oz/175 g) | 4 |
| | Lemon wedges | |

1. Place asparagus on prepared pan. Drizzle with 1 tbsp (15 mL) oil and season with salt and pepper. Toss to coat, then spread in a single layer. Roast in preheated oven for 10 minutes.

2. Meanwhile, in a small cup, combine garlic, lemon zest, $3/4$ tsp (3 mL) pepper, $1/2$ tsp (2 mL) salt and the remaining oil.

3. Remove pan from oven and nestle fish among the asparagus, spacing evenly. Rub lemon-pepper mixture evenly over fish. Roast for 6 to 9 minutes or until asparagus is tender-crisp and fish is opaque and flakes easily when tested with a fork. Serve with lemon wedges.

# Salt and Pepper Shrimp with Green Rice

**Makes 4 servings**

The rich meatiness of shrimp makes it an ideal partner for sprightly cilantro and ginger rice.

## Tip

If packaged frozen rice is not available, substitute 4 cups (1 L) cooled cooked brown or white rice.

## Variations

For a subtle tropical flavor, replace the vegetable oil with an equal amount of melted virgin coconut oil.

*Salt and Pepper Shrimp with Rice Verde:* Replace the ginger with 2 cloves garlic, minced, and replace the cilantro with flat-leaf (Italian) parsley. Use lemon wedges in place of the lime wedges.

- Preheat oven to 450°F (230°C)
- 18- by 13-inch (45 by 33 cm) rimmed sheet pan, lined with foil and sprayed with nonstick cooking spray

| | | |
|---|---|---|
| 1 lb | frozen large shrimp, thawed, peeled and deveined | 500 g |
| 3 tbsp | vegetable oil, divided | 45 mL |
| 1¼ tsp | salt, divided | 6 mL |
| ¾ tsp | freshly ground black pepper | 3 mL |
| 2 | packages (each 12 oz/375 g) frozen brown or white rice, thawed | 2 |
| 2 tsp | ground ginger | 10 mL |
| 1½ cups | packed fresh cilantro leaves, chopped | 375 mL |
| | Lime wedges | |

1. On prepared pan, toss shrimp with 1 tbsp (15 mL) oil, ¾ tsp (3 mL) salt and pepper. Spread in a single layer on one side of the pan.

2. On the other side of the pan, toss rice with the remaining oil, ginger and the remaining salt. Spread in an even layer.

3. Roast in preheated oven for 10 to 12 minutes or until shrimp are firm, pink and opaque. Add cilantro to the rice, tossing to combine.

4. Serve shrimp with rice and lime wedges alongside.

# Crispy Chicken Thighs with Roasted Carrots and Fresh Mint

**Makes 4 servings**

Roasting is perhaps the ultimate quick and easy dinner technique. And this recipe is a total winner for its minimalism, great looks and even better taste.

**Tip**

An equal amount of cilantro or flat-leaf (Italian) parsley can be used in place of the mint.

- Preheat oven to 400°F (200°C)
- 18- by 13-inch (45 by 33 cm) rimmed sheet pan, lined with parchment paper

| | | |
|---|---|---|
| 8 | bone-in skin-on chicken thighs, patted dry (about 2 lbs/1 kg total) | 8 |
| | Salt and freshly cracked black pepper | |
| 1 | package (1 lb/500 g) peeled baby carrots | 1 |
| 1½ tbsp | olive oil | 22 mL |
| 1 cup | packed fresh mint leaves, chopped | 250 mL |

1. Place chicken thighs on prepared pan, spacing evenly. Season with ¾ tsp (3 mL) salt and ¼ tsp (1 mL) pepper. Roast in preheated oven for 20 minutes.

2. Meanwhile, in a medium bowl, toss carrots with oil. Season with salt and pepper.

3. Remove pan from oven and arrange carrots around the chicken. Roast for 20 to 25 minutes or until carrots are fork-tender, chicken skin is crispy and an instant-read thermometer inserted in the thickest part of a chicken thigh registers 165°F (74°C). Serve sprinkled with mint.

# Apricot-Dijon Chicken Tenders with Rosemary Roasted Potatoes

*1/27/17*

**Makes 4 servings**

A small amount of olive oil and a few bold flavors (apricot preserves, Dijon mustard and fresh rosemary) make this chicken and potatoes meal a winner.

## Tips

If you don't have fresh rosemary on hand, you can use 1½ tsp (7 mL) dried rosemary.

In place of the miniature potatoes, you can use 1 lb (500 g) regular red- or yellow-fleshed potatoes, cut into 1-inch (2.5 cm) cubes.

- Preheat oven to 425°F (220°C)
- 18- by 13-inch (45 by 33 cm) rimmed sheet pan, lined with foil and sprayed with nonstick cooking spray

| | | |
|---|---|---|
| 1 lb | miniature red- or yellow-fleshed potatoes, halved crosswise | 500 g |
| 2 tbsp | olive oil, divided | 30 mL |
| | Salt and freshly cracked black pepper | |
| 3 tbsp | apricot preserves or jam | 45 mL |
| 2 tbsp | Dijon mustard | 30 mL |
| 1 lb | boneless skinless chicken breast tenders, patted dry | 500 g |
| 1 tbsp | minced fresh rosemary leaves | 15 mL |

1. Place potatoes on prepared pan. Drizzle with half the oil and season with salt and pepper. Toss to coat, then spread in a single layer.

2. In a medium bowl, combine preserves, mustard, the remaining oil, and ¼ tsp (1 mL) each salt and pepper. Add chicken, turning to coat. Nestle chicken among the potatoes, spacing evenly. Sprinkle potatoes and chicken with rosemary.

3. Roast in preheated oven for 20 minutes. Open oven door, stir potatoes and turn chicken pieces over. Close door and roast for 10 to 15 minutes or until potatoes are tender and chicken is no longer pink inside.

# Chicken and Cannellini Marinara

A bout in a hot oven transforms plump, acidic tomatoes into luscious, caramelized, sweet bites of heaven. Add some chicken and white beans near the end of the cooking time and you'll have your new go-to dinner in no time.

## Variation

An equal amount of canned chickpeas can be used in place of the cannellini beans.

- Preheat oven to 400°F (200°C)
- 18- by 13-inch (45 by 33 cm) rimmed sheet pan, lined with parchment or foil and sprayed with nonstick cooking spray

| | | |
|---|---|---|
| 1 | can (28 oz/796 mL) whole peeled tomatoes, with juice | 1 |
| 3 | cloves garlic, roughly chopped | 3 |
| 3 tbsp | olive oil, divided | 45 mL |
| 1 lb | boneless skinless chicken breasts, cut into 1-inch (2.5 cm) pieces | 500 g |
| 1 | can (14 to 19 oz/398 to 540 mL) cannellini (white kidney) beans, drained and rinsed | 1 |
| | Salt and freshly cracked black pepper | |

**Suggested Accompaniments**

Torn fresh basil leaves

Grated Parmesan cheese

1. Place tomatoes and their juice on prepared pan. Using your hands, roughly tear each tomato into 1-inch (2.5 cm) strips. Add garlic to pan and drizzle tomatoes and garlic with 2 tbsp (30 mL) oil. Roast in preheated oven for 45 minutes.

2. Remove pan from oven and stir tomatoes. Add chicken, beans and the remaining oil, stirring to combine. Roast for 12 to 17 minutes or until chicken is no longer pink inside. Season to taste with salt and pepper. Serve with the suggested accompaniments, as desired.

# Handheld Chicken Pot Pies

Here's an easy supper that takes the flavor of chicken pot pie and reconfigures it into portable turnovers that kids (from 2 to 90) will love.

## Variation

*Handheld Chicken and Artichoke Pot Pies:* Use an equal-size package of frozen artichoke hearts, thawed, drained and chopped, in place of the peas and carrots.

- Preheat oven to 400°F (200°C)
- 18- by 13-inch (45 by 33 cm) rimmed sheet pan, lined with parchment paper

| | | |
|---|---|---|
| ²⁄₃ cup | spreadable garlic-and-herb cheese (such as Boursin) | 150 mL |
| 3 tbsp | milk | 45 mL |
| ¼ tsp | freshly cracked black pepper | 1 mL |
| 1 | package (10 oz/300 g) frozen peas and carrots, thawed and drained | 1 |
| 2 cups | chopped cooked chicken or turkey | 500 mL |
| 2 | refrigerated rolled pie crusts (15-oz/435 g package) | 2 |

1. In a large bowl, whisk together cheese, milk and pepper until blended. Stir in peas and carrots and chicken.

2. On a cutting board, cut each pie crust in half. Spoon chicken mixture over one side of each half-circle, leaving a ¹⁄₂-inch (1 cm) border. Using your fingertip, wet the border with water. Fold crust over filling, pressing to seal edges. Make three 1-inch (2.5 cm) slits in top of each. Transfer pies to prepared pan.

3. Bake in preheated oven for 15 to 18 minutes or until crust is golden brown. Let cool on pan for at least 5 minutes before serving.

# Chicken Sausages with Cumin Roasted Acorn Squash

**Makes 4 servings**

When it comes to a family-pleasing dinner, few things beat a pan of roasted sausages for ease and appeal. A sprinkle of cumin adds a Mediterranean touch to the accompanying slices of acorn squash.

**Variation**

Other varieties of fully cooked chicken, turkey or pork sausages can be used in place of the chicken and apple sausages.

- Preheat oven to 400°F (200°C)
- 18- by 13-inch (45 by 33 cm) rimmed sheet pan, lined with parchment paper

| | | |
|---|---|---|
| 2 | acorn squash | 2 |
| 3 tbsp | olive oil, divided | 45 mL |
| 2 tsp | ground cumin | 10 mL |
| $\frac{1}{2}$ tsp | salt | 2 mL |
| $\frac{1}{4}$ tsp | freshly cracked black pepper | 1 mL |
| 4 | fully cooked chicken and apple sausages | 4 |

1. Trim off ends of squash, then cut each squash in half lengthwise. Scrape out and discard seeds. Cut squash halves crosswise into $\frac{3}{4}$-inch (2 cm) slices.

2. On prepared pan, toss squash with 2 tbsp (30 mL) oil, cumin, salt and pepper. Spread in a single layer. Roast in preheated oven for 20 minutes.

3. Remove pan from oven and turn squash pieces over. Nestle sausages among the squash, spacing evenly. Brush sausages with the remaining oil. Roast for 15 to 20 minutes or until sausages are browned and squash is lightly browned and tender.

# French Bread Pizzas

**Makes 4 pizzas**

A blend of soft, crunchy and melty textures combined with a parade of potential toppings makes these playful pizzas an irresistible option any night of the week.

## Variation

Replace the marinara sauce with an equal amount of prepared alfredo sauce or ½ cup (125 mL) prepared pesto sauce.

- Preheat oven to 450°F (230°C)
- 18- by 13-inch (45 by 33 cm) rimmed sheet pan, lined with foil

| 1 | loaf (about 16 oz/ 500 g) French bread | 1 |
|---|---|---|
| 2 tbsp | olive oil | 30 mL |
| 1 cup | marinara sauce | 250 mL |
| 2 cups | shredded mozzarella cheese | 500 mL |

**Suggested Toppings**

Sliced pepperoni
Crumbled cooked Italian sausage
Diced ham
Chopped roasted chicken
Anchovies
Thinly sliced bell peppers
Thinly sliced onions
Sliced olives

1. Cut bread in half horizontally, then vertically, to create 4 pieces. Brush cut sides of bread with oil. Place bread, cut side up, on prepared pan. Bake in preheated oven for 3 to 5 minutes or until lightly browned.

2. Spread ¼ cup (60 mL) marinara sauce on each bread piece and top with ½ cup (125 mL) cheese. Top with any of the suggested toppings, as desired. Bake for 5 to 8 minutes or until cheese melts and toppings are hot.

# Herbed Pork Tenderloin with Garlic Roasted Broccoli

**Makes 4 servings**

This pork and vegetable combination gets the garlic and herb treatment, turning readily available pork tenderloin and broccoli into an extra-special meal.

## Variation

An equal amount of cauliflower florets or 1 lb (500 g) trimmed green beans can be used in place of the broccoli.

- Preheat oven to 400°F (200°C)
- 18- by 13-inch (45 by 33 cm) rimmed sheet pan, lined with parchment paper or foil

| | | |
|---|---|---|
| 5 cups | small broccoli florets | 1.25 L |
| 3 | cloves garlic, minced | 3 |
| 3 tbsp | olive oil, divided | 45 mL |
| 1/2 tsp | salt, divided | 2 mL |
| 1 | pork tenderloin (about 1 lb/500 g), trimmed | 1 |
| 2 tsp | dried herbes de Provence or Italian herb blend | 10 mL |
| 1/4 tsp | freshly ground black pepper | 1 mL |

1. On prepared pan, toss broccoli with garlic, 2 tbsp (30 mL) oil and 1/4 tsp (1 mL) salt. Spread in a single layer, then clear a space for the tenderloin.

2. Brush pork with the remaining oil and sprinkle with herbes de Provence, pepper and the remaining salt. Rub seasoning all over pork, turning to coat. Place tenderloin in the cleared space on the pan.

3. Roast for 20 to 25 minutes or until broccoli is browned and an instant-read thermometer inserted in the thickest part of the tenderloin registers 145°F (63°C) for medium-rare. Transfer pork to a cutting board and let rest for 5 to 10 minutes before slicing across the grain.

# Pork Chops with Roasted Apples, Pearl Onions and Thyme

Why relegate onions to the background? Here, wedges of tart-sweet apples and a sprinkle of thyme conspire to make charming pearl onions costars with meaty pork chops.

## Variations

For chops that have less browning, line the sheet pan with parchment paper and roast at 400°F (200°C) for 15 minutes in step 1 and 20 to 25 minutes in step 3.

Replace the apples with 3 firm-ripe pears, each cut into quarters and cores removed.

An equal amount of rosemary or sage can be used in place of the thyme.

- Preheat oven to 475°F (240°C)
- 18- by 13-inch (45 by 33 cm) rimmed sheet pan, lined with foil and sprayed with nonstick cooking spray

| | | |
|---|---|---|
| 4 | bone-in center-cut pork loin chops (each about 8 oz/250 g and 1 inch/2.5 cm thick) | 4 |
| 3 tbsp | olive oil, divided | 45 mL |
| 2 tsp | minced fresh thyme leaves | 10 mL |
| | Salt and freshly ground black pepper | |
| 2 | large tart-sweet apples (such as Braeburn or Gala), each cut into 8 wedges and cores removed | 2 |
| 2 cups | frozen pearl onions, thawed | 500 mL |

1. Place pork chops on prepared pan. Drizzle with 2 tbsp (30 mL) oil, sprinkle with thyme and season generously with salt and pepper. Rub seasoning all over pork, turning to coat. Arrange evenly spaced on pan. Roast in preheated oven for 12 minutes.

2. Meanwhile, in a medium bowl, toss together apples, onions and the remaining oil. Season to taste with salt and pepper.

3. Remove pan from oven and turn pork chops over. Arrange apples and onions around chops. Roast for 12 to 15 minutes or until apples are tender and an instant-read thermometer inserted in the thickest part of the pork, without touching the bone, registers 145°F (63°C) for medium-rare.

# Streamlined Stuffed Peppers

Fully cooked roast beef from the deli section and frozen brown rice are perfect for breathing new life into this busy weeknight favorite.

## Tips

If packaged frozen rice is not available, use 2 cups (500 mL) cooled cooked brown or white rice.

Opt for a marinara sauce with a short list of ingredients that is free of preservatives, artificial flavors and added sweeteners.

## Variations

*Black Bean–Stuffed Peppers:* Replace the roast beef with 1 can (14 to 19 oz/398 to 540 mL) black beans, drained and rinsed. Replace the marinara sauce with an equal amount of salsa and use an equal amount of shredded pepper Jack or Cheddar cheese in place of the Italian cheese blend.

*Turkey-Stuffed Peppers:* Replace the roast beef with $1\frac{1}{2}$ cups (375 mL) diced cooked or sliced deli turkey (or chicken).

- Preheat oven to 375°F (190°C)
- 18- by 13-inch (45 by 33 cm) rimmed sheet pan, lined with parchment paper or foil

| | | |
|---|---|---|
| 4 | red or green bell peppers | 4 |
| 12 oz | sliced deli roast beef, chopped | 375 g |
| 1 | package (12 oz/375 g) frozen brown or white rice, thawed | 1 |
| 2 cups | shredded Italian cheese blend, divided | 500 g |
| $\frac{1}{2}$ cup | finely chopped green onions | 125 mL |
| 1 cup | marinara sauce | 250 mL |
| | Salt and freshly ground black pepper | |

1. Keeping stem intact, cut bell peppers in half lengthwise and discard seeds and membranes. Place bell pepper halves, cut side up, on prepared pan.

2. In a medium bowl, combine roast beef, rice, $\frac{1}{2}$ cup (125 mL) cheese, green onions and marinara sauce. Season to taste with salt and pepper.

3. Fill bell pepper halves with rice mixture. Sprinkle evenly with the remaining cheese.

4. Bake in preheated oven for 25 to 30 minutes or until peppers are tender and cheese is golden brown.

# Smoky BBQ Meatloaf with Sweet Potato Wedges

**Makes 4 servings**

Here you have the comfort of old-fashioned meatloaf with a kick of barbecue sauce and a lickety-split prep time. Extra-easy roasted sweet potato wedges are perfect partners.

## Variation

*Chipotle Meatloaf with Sweet Potato Wedges:* Replace the barbecue sauce with an equal amount of chipotle salsa, and add ¾ tsp (3 mL) ground cumin with the salt in step 1.

- Preheat oven to 375°F (190°C)
- 18- by 13-inch (45 by 33 cm) rimmed sheet pan, lined with parchment paper

| | | |
|---|---|---|
| 1 lb | lean ground beef | 500 g |
| ¼ cup | plain dry bread crumbs | 60 mL |
| ¾ tsp | salt, divided | 3 mL |
| ¼ tsp | freshly cracked black pepper | 1 mL |
| 1 | large egg | 1 |
| ½ cup | barbecue sauce | 125 mL |
| 3 | sweet potatoes (unpeeled), cut into thick wedges | 3 |
| 2 tbsp | vegetable oil | 30 mL |

1. In a large bowl, combine beef, bread crumbs, ¼ tsp (1 mL) salt, pepper, egg and barbecue sauce until just blended. Shape into a loaf (about 7 by 4 inches/18 by 10 cm) in center of prepared pan.

2. In a medium bowl, toss sweet potatoes with oil and the remaining salt. Arrange in a single layer around meatloaf.

3. Bake in preheated oven for 40 to 45 minutes or until sweet potatoes are browned and tender and an instant-read thermometer inserted in the thickest part of the meatloaf registers 160°F (71°C). Let meatloaf stand for 10 minutes before slicing.

# Blackberry Buckle

A buckle is a moist, fruit-filled, not-too-sweet cake that can pass as one of several other varieties of dessert. All that really matters, though, is that vanilla ice cream and blackberries become something new again in this incredibly easy, cakey buckle.

## Tips

No need to buy self-rising flour if you don't have it on hand; simply mix 3 cups (750 mL) all-purpose flour with 1½ tbsp (22 mL) baking powder and 1½ tsp (7 mL) salt.

For best results, use a good-quality ice cream with a high cream content and minimal additives.

## Variation

An equal amount of other berries (such as raspberries or blueberries) or diced fruit (such as peaches, nectarines or mangos) can be used in place of the blackberries.

- Preheat oven to 375°F (190°C)
- 18- by 13-inch (45 by 33 cm) rimmed sheet pan, lined with parchment paper and sprayed with nonstick cooking spray

| | | |
|---|---|---|
| 3 cups | self-rising flour (see tip, at left) | 750 mL |
| 4 cups | vanilla ice cream, melted | 1 L |
| ½ cup | unsalted butter, melted | 125 mL |
| 4 cups | blackberries | 1 L |

1. In a large bowl, whisk together flour, ice cream and butter until blended and smooth. Spread in prepared pan and sprinkle with blackberries.

2. Bake in preheated oven for 22 to 27 minutes or until golden brown and a tester inserted in the center comes out clean. Let cool in pan on a wire rack for 15 minutes. Serve warm or let cool completely and serve at room temperature.

# Nectarine Crostata with Cardamom Sugar

This rustic free-form tart is easy to make, even for a novice baker. A sprinkle of cardamom-scented sugar intensifies the flavor of the nectarines.

## Tips

An equal amount of ground ginger, allspice or cinnamon can be used in place of the cardamom.

Peeled peaches can be substituted for the nectarines.

## Variation

*Blueberry Crostata:* Replace the nectarines with 2 cups (500 mL) blueberries. Add 2 tsp (10 mL) cornstarch to the sugar mixture in step 1.

- Preheat oven to 375°F (190°C)
- 18- by 13-inch (45 by 33 cm) rimmed sheet pan, lined with parchment paper or foil

| | | |
|---|---|---|
| 3 tbsp | granulated sugar | 45 mL |
| ¾ tsp | ground cardamom | 3 mL |
| 1 | refrigerated rolled pie crust (half a 15-oz/435 g package) | 1 |
| 3 | medium-large nectarines, pitted and thinly sliced | 3 |
| 2 tbsp | unsalted butter, cut into small pieces | 30 mL |

1. In a small bowl or cup, combine sugar and cardamom.

2. Unroll pie crust on prepared pan. Arrange nectarines on top, leaving a 1½-inch (4 cm) border. Sprinkle fruit with butter and 2 tbsp (30 mL) cardamom sugar. Fold dough border toward the center to partially cover the filling.

3. Brush dough with 2 tsp (10 mL) water and sprinkle with the remaining cardamom sugar.

4. Bake in preheated oven for 35 to 40 minutes or until nectarine juices are bubbling and crust is golden, tenting with foil if the crust browns too quickly. Let cool on pan on a wire rack for at least 15 minutes before serving or let cool to room temperature.

# Coconut Macaroons

Don't say I didn't warn you! These crisp-chewy macaroons will be gobbled up as fast as you can make them. But don't worry, because the recipe is easily doubled. Or tripled. You're welcome.

## Storage Tip

Store the cooled cookies in an airtight container at room temperature for up to 2 days or in the refrigerator for up to 1 week.

## Variations

*Chocolate Chip Macaroons:* Add 1 cup (250 mL) miniature semisweet chocolate chips with the coconut.

*Citrus Macaroons:* Replace the almond extract with 1 tbsp (15 mL) finely grated lemon, lime or orange zest.

*Chocolate-Kissed Macaroons:* Press an unwrapped milk chocolate kiss candy into each cookie while still warm.

- Preheat oven to 350°F (180°C)
- 18- by 13-inch (45 by 33 cm) rimmed sheet pan, lined with parchment paper

| | | |
|---|---|---|
| 1 | can (14 oz or 300 mL) sweetened condensed milk | 1 |
| 1/2 tsp | salt | 2 mL |
| 1 1/2 tsp | almond extract | 7 mL |
| 4 cups | sweetened flaked coconut | 1 L |

1. In a large bowl, whisk together milk, salt and almond extract until blended. Stir in coconut until blended.

2. Drop dough by tablespoonfuls (15 mL) into mounds on prepared baking pan, spacing them 2 inches (5 cm) apart.

3. Bake in preheated oven for 10 to 13 minutes or until golden brown on top and at edges. Immediately transfer parchment paper with cookies to a wire rack to cool completely.

4. Reline pan with parchment paper and repeat steps 2 and 3 with the remaining dough.

# Chocolate-Dipped Frozen Bananas

You don't have to tell your inner child to wait for dessert! These frozen bananas have the rich, creamy texture of ice cream, but are healthy enough for you to indulge your sweet tooth (almost) any time it strikes.

## Storage Tip

After the chocolate coating has set, wrap the bananas individually in foil and store in the freezer for up to 3 days.

## Variation

Toast the coconut first. Preheat the oven to 300°F (150°C). Spread coconut in a thin, even layer on an 18- by 13-inch (45 by 33 cm) rimmed sheet pan lined with parchment paper or foil. Bake for 15 to 20 minutes, stirring every 5 minutes, until golden brown and fragrant. Transfer to a plate and let cool completely before using.

- 6 wooden ice-pop sticks
- 18- by 13-inch (45 by 33 cm) rimmed sheet pan, lined with parchment paper

| | | |
|---|---|---|
| 3 | large firm-ripe bananas, halved crosswise | 3 |
| 1 cup | semisweet chocolate chips | 250 mL |
| 1/3 cup | unsweetened shredded coconut | 75 mL |

1. Carefully push an ice-pop stick into the cut end of each banana half, leaving about 2 inches (5 cm) of the stick poking out. Place bananas on prepared pan. Freeze for 30 to 45 minutes or until just solid.

2. Place chocolate chips in a medium microwave-safe bowl and microwave on High, stopping to stir every 20 to 30 seconds, until completely melted and smooth.

3. Place coconut in a wide, shallow bowl.

4. Dip frozen bananas in chocolate, turning to coat evenly, then sprinkle with coconut, allowing excess coconut to fall back into the bowl. Return dipped bananas to pan. Freeze for 15 to 20 minutes or until chocolate is set.

# Breakfast and Brunch

# Maple Pecan Granola

Homemade granola is a great anytime treat, but it's most satisfying at the breakfast table. This simple recipe is layered with favorite flavors – cinnamon, maple, brown sugar and toasted pecans – and makes enough to carry you through many mornings.

## Tip

An equal amount of virgin coconut oil, warmed, vegetable oil or olive oil can be used in place of the butter.

## Storage Tip

Store the cooled granola in an airtight container at room temperature for up to 3 weeks or in the freezer for up to 3 months.

## Variations

Use any variety of chopped nuts (such as hazelnuts, walnuts, almonds or cashews) or seeds (such as sunflower, green pumpkin or hemp) in place of the pecans.

Add up to 1½ cups (375 mL) dried fruit (such as raisins, cranberries or chopped apricots) to the cooled granola.

- Preheat oven to 300°F (150°C)
- 18- by 13-inch (45 by 33 cm) rimmed sheet pan, lined with parchment paper

| | | |
|---|---|---|
| 5 cups | large-flake (old-fashioned) rolled oats | 1.25 L |
| 1½ cups | chopped pecans | 375 mL |
| 1 cup | wheat germ | 250 mL |
| 1½ tsp | ground cinnamon | 7 mL |
| 1¼ tsp | salt | 6 mL |
| ¾ cup | packed light brown sugar | 175 mL |
| ½ cup | pure maple syrup | 125 mL |
| ½ cup | unsalted butter, melted | 125 mL |
| 2 tsp | vanilla extract | 10 mL |

1. In a large bowl, whisk together oats, pecans, wheat germ, cinnamon and salt.

2. In a medium bowl, whisk together brown sugar, maple syrup, butter and vanilla until well blended.

3. Add the maple mixture to the oats mixture, stirring until well coated. Spread mixture in a single layer on prepared pan.

4. Bake in preheated oven for 30 to 35 minutes, stirring twice, until oats are golden brown. Let cool completely on pan.

# Toasted Almond Muesli with Coconut and Chocolate

Life is uncertain, so treat yourself to some chocolate for breakfast. Don't worry, despite the decadent taste, this muesli also packs a healthy dose of protein and whole-grain goodness. Enjoy it with sliced bananas and milk (dairy or non-dairy), or plain or vanilla-flavored yogurt (regular or Greek).

## Tip

An equal amount of vegetable oil, olive oil or unsalted butter, melted, can be used in place of the coconut oil.

## Storage Tip

Store the cooled muesli in an airtight container at room temperature for up to 3 weeks or in the freezer for up to 3 months.

- Preheat oven to 350°F (180°C)
- 18- by 13-inch (45 by 33 cm) rimmed sheet pan, lined with parchment paper

| | | |
|---|---|---|
| 4 cups | large-flake (old-fashioned) rolled oats | 1 L |
| 1¹/₂ cups | sliced almonds | 375 mL |
| 1¹/₂ cups | unsweetened flaked coconut | 375 mL |
| ³/₄ tsp | salt | 3 mL |
| 3 tbsp | liquid honey | 45 mL |
| 3 tbsp | virgin coconut oil, warmed | 45 mL |
| 1 tsp | almond extract | 5 mL |
| ²/₃ cup | miniature semisweet chocolate chips | 150 mL |

1. In a large bowl, whisk together oats, almonds, coconut and salt.

2. In a medium bowl, whisk together honey, coconut oil and almond extract until well blended.

3. Add the honey mixture to the oats mixture, stirring until well coated. Spread mixture in a single layer on prepared pan.

4. Bake in preheated oven for 15 to 20 minutes, stirring halfway through, until oats are light golden and almonds are toasted and fragrant. Let cool completely on pan.

5. Add the chocolate chips to the cooled muesli.

# Brown Sugar and Vanilla Baked Oatmeal

**Makes 8 servings**

Few breakfast treats can match the comfort of warm oatmeal with brown sugar. Added bonus: this version can be made ahead, cut into squares and rewarmed for a week of instant breakfasts on the go!

## Tip
For the dried fruit, try raisins, chopped apricots or cranberries, or a combination.

## Storage Tip
Store the cooled baked oatmeal by cutting it into squares and then individually wrapping squares in plastic wrap or parchment paper. Enjoy cold or at room temperature, or warm in the microwave at 70% for 60 to 75 seconds.

- Preheat oven to 375°F (190°C)
- 18- by 13-inch (45 by 33 cm) rimmed sheet pan, sprayed with nonstick cooking spray

| | | |
|---|---|---|
| 4½ cups | large-flake (old-fashioned) rolled oats | 1.125 L |
| 1 cup | dried fruit | 250 mL |
| 2½ tsp | baking powder | 12 mL |
| ¾ tsp | salt | 3 mL |
| 2 | large eggs | 2 |
| ⅔ cup | packed light brown sugar | 150 mL |
| ¼ cup | unsalted butter, melted | 60 mL |
| 1 tbsp | vanilla extract | 15 mL |
| 4 cups | milk (dairy or non-dairy) | 1 L |
| 1 cup | chopped walnuts (optional) | 250 mL |

1. In a medium bowl, stir together oats, dried fruit, baking powder and salt.

2. In a large bowl, whisk eggs. Whisk in brown sugar, butter and vanilla until blended. Whisk in milk.

3. Add the oats mixture to the egg mixture, stirring until combined. Pour into prepared pan, spreading evenly. Sprinkle with walnuts, if using.

4. Bake in preheated oven for 15 to 20 minutes or until golden brown at the edges and just set at the center. Serve warm.

### Variations
*Pumpkin Cranberry Baked Oatmeal:* Replace 1 cup (250 mL) of the milk with pumpkin purée (not pie filling). Add 2 tsp (10 mL) pumpkin pie spice or ground cinnamon in step 1 and use dried cranberries for the dried fruit.

*Apple Pie Baked Oatmeal:* Add 2 cups (500 mL) diced apples and 2 tsp (10 mL) ground cinnamon after stirring in the oats mixture in step 3.

*Berry Baked Oatmeal:* Replace the brown sugar with granulated sugar and omit the dried fruit. Add 2 cups (500 mL) raspberries, blueberries, blackberries or diced strawberries, or a mixture of two or more types of berries, after stirring in the oats mixture in step 3.

# Peach Crumbles with Greek Yogurt

Try these buttery, pecan-stuffed peaches for a simple but impressive morning meal. A generous dollop of Greek yogurt adds creamy, protein-powered flair.

## Tips

Large firm-ripe nectarines can be used in place of the peaches.

The nuts, spice, sweetener and fat in this recipe are all variable, so use what you have on hand or create your own favorite combinations. For example, for the nuts, try walnuts, almonds or pistachios. Use ground allspice, ginger or cardamom in place of the cinnamon. Try pure maple syrup, agave nectar or packed brown sugar for the sweetener, and consider olive oil or virgin coconut oil, melted, in place of the butter.

## Storage Tip

Store leftover peach crumbles in an airtight container in the refrigerator for up to 2 days.

- Preheat oven to 400°F (200°C)
- 18- by 13-inch (45 by 33 cm) rimmed sheet pan, lined with parchment paper or foil

| | | |
|---|---|---|
| 4 | large firm-ripe peaches | 4 |
| 1 cup | large-flake (old-fashioned) or quick-cooking rolled oats | 250 mL |
| $\frac{1}{3}$ cup | chopped pecans | 75 mL |
| $\frac{1}{2}$ tsp | ground cinnamon | 2 mL |
| $\frac{1}{8}$ tsp | salt | 0.5 mL |
| 5 tbsp | liquid honey, divided | 75 mL |
| 3 tbsp | unsalted butter, melted | 45 mL |
| 8 tbsp | plain or vanilla-flavored Greek yogurt | 120 mL |

1. Slice peaches in half vertically and remove pits. Arrange peaches, cut side up, on prepared pan, spacing evenly.

2. In a small bowl, combine oats, pecans, cinnamon and salt. Add 3 tbsp (45 mL) honey and butter, stirring until coated. Pack each peach hollow with oat mixture, dividing evenly.

3. Bake in preheated oven for 15 to 20 minutes or until peaches are softened and filling is golden brown. Let cool on pan on a wire rack for 5 minutes.

4. Top each peach half with 1 tbsp (15 mL) yogurt and drizzle with the remaining honey.

# Sheet Pan Rolled Omelet

Satisfy your appetite – and that of several friends or family members – with a perfect rolled omelet that requires minimal prep, is easy to clean up after and features (almost) hands-free assembly. The trick? Bake the omelet on a parchment-lined sheet pan, then lift and roll the omelet using the paper lining once cooking is complete. It's a cinch to master, and the potential variations are as broad as your imagination.

### Tip

To save time, consider blending all of the ingredients (except the cheese) in a blender on low speed until smooth.

### Variations

*Spinach-Feta Omelet:* Reduce the flour to $1/3$ cup (75 mL) and the eggs to 9. Sprinkle two packages (each 12 oz/375 g) frozen chopped spinach, thawed and squeezed dry, over the omelet at the end of step 3. Replace the Cheddar cheese with 4 oz (125 g) crumbled feta cheese.

*Pepper Jack Omelet:* Reduce the flour to $1/3$ cup (75 mL) and the eggs to 9. Sprinkle 1 jar (12 oz/375 mL) roasted red bell peppers, drained, patted dry and chopped, over the omelet at the end of step 3. Replace the Cheddar cheese with an equal amount of shredded pepper Jack cheese.

- Preheat oven to 375°F (190°C)
- 18- by 13-inch (45 by 33 cm) rimmed sheet pan, lined with parchment paper, leaving a paper overhang at short ends

| | | |
|---|---|---:|
| 2 tbsp | olive oil | 30 mL |
| $1/2$ cup | all-purpose flour | 125 mL |
| 1 tsp | salt | 5 mL |
| $1/8$ tsp | freshly ground black pepper | 0.5 mL |
| 1 cup | milk | 250 mL |
| 12 | large eggs | 12 |
| $1 1/2$ cups | shredded Cheddar cheese (6 oz/175 g) | 375 mL |

1. Brush parchment paper with oil.

2. In a large bowl, whisk together flour, salt and pepper. Gradually whisk in milk.

3. In a medium bowl, whisk eggs until blended. Whisk eggs into flour mixture until blended and smooth. Pour into prepared pan.

4. Bake in preheated oven for 13 to 17 minutes or until edges of omelet are set. Sprinkle with cheese and bake for 4 to 6 minutes or until cheese is melted.

5. Using the paper overhang on one of the short sides, lift and roll up omelet tightly, peeling back parchment as you roll. Cut omelet crosswise into 12 slices.

# Spinach and Feta Sheet Pan Quiche

Behold: the easiest quiche ever! Forget rolling out dough and stick with this buttery crumb option instead. The spinach-feta filling is reminiscent of Greek spanakopita, but the possible variations are vast.

## Storage Tip

Store cooled quiche squares in an airtight container in the refrigerator for up to 3 days or in the freezer for up to 3 months.

## Variations

*Green Chile and Pepper Jack Quiche:* Replace the dillweed with 2 tsp (10 mL) ground cumin and replace the spinach with 2 cans (each 4$\frac{1}{2}$ oz/127 mL) green chiles. Use 1$\frac{1}{2}$ cups (375 mL) shredded pepper Jack or Monterey Jack cheese in place of the feta.

*Broccoli and Bacon Quiche:* Omit the dillweed and add $\frac{3}{4}$ cup (175 mL) crumbled cooked bacon (about 8 slices) with the green onions. Replace the spinach with an equal-size package of frozen chopped broccoli, thawed and squeezed dry. Replace the feta with 1$\frac{1}{2}$ cups (375 mL) shredded sharp (old) Cheddar cheese.

- Preheat oven to 375°F (190°C)
- 18- by 13-inch (45 by 33 cm) rimmed sheet pan, lined with parchment paper and sprayed with nonstick cooking spray
- Food processor

**Crust**

| | | |
|---|---|---|
| 3 cups | cracker crumbs (such as Saltines) | 750 mL |
| $\frac{1}{2}$ cup | unsalted butter, melted | 125 mL |

**Filling**

| | | |
|---|---|---|
| 10 | large eggs | 10 |
| 1 | container (16 oz/500 g) cottage cheese | 1 |
| 1$\frac{1}{2}$ cups | milk, divided | 375 mL |
| 1 tbsp | dried dillweed | 15 mL |
| 1 tsp | salt | 5 mL |
| 1 tsp | freshly cracked black pepper | 5 mL |
| 1 | package (16 oz/500 g) frozen chopped spinach, thawed and squeezed dry | 1 |
| 1 cup | finely chopped green onions | 250 mL |
| 6 oz | feta cheese, crumbled | 175 g |

1. *Crust:* In a medium bowl, combine cracker crumbs and butter. Press evenly onto bottom of prepared pan. Bake in preheated oven for 10 minutes.

2. *Filling:* Meanwhile, in food processor, process eggs, cottage cheese and $\frac{1}{2}$ cup (125 mL) milk until smooth. Transfer to a large bowl and whisk in dill, salt, pepper and the remaining milk until blended. Stir in spinach, green onions and feta. Slowly and evenly pour into prepared crust.

3. Bake for 35 to 40 minutes or until custard is just set. Let cool in pan on a wire rack for at least 30 minutes before cutting into squares. Serve warm, at room temperature or chilled.

# Three-Cheese Potato Frittata

This hearty potato and cheese frittata supplies all of the energy you need for a weekend full of adventure (including reading about one while lounging in your favorite chair). Try it with sweet potatoes, too, or a combination of vegetables.

## Tips

For the best texture and flavor, choose regular or lower-fat ricotta cheese instead of nonfat.

Other varieties of shredded cheese, such as sharp (old) white Cheddar, Monterey Jack or fontina, can be used in place of the Gruyère.

## Storage Tip

Store cooled frittata squares in an airtight container in the refrigerator for up to 3 days or in the freezer for up to 3 months.

- Preheat oven to 425°F (220°C)
- 18- by 13-inch (45 by 33 cm) rimmed sheet pan, lined with foil and sprayed with nonstick cooking spray

| | | |
|---|---|---|
| 5 cups | diced peeled white or red round waxy potatoes | 1.25 L |
| 2 tbsp | olive oil | 30 mL |
| ¾ tsp | salt, divided | 3 mL |
| ¾ tsp | freshly ground black pepper, divided | 3 mL |
| 12 | large eggs | 12 |
| 1 tsp | baking powder | 5 mL |
| 1 | container (16 oz/500 g) ricotta cheese | 1 |
| ½ cup | milk | 125 mL |
| ⅓ cup | all-purpose flour | 75 mL |
| 8 oz | Gruyère or Swiss cheese, shredded | 250 g |
| 1 cup | grated Parmesan cheese | 250 mL |
| ½ cup | chopped fresh chives | 125 mL |

1. On prepared pan, toss potatoes with oil, ¼ tsp (1 mL) salt and ¼ tsp (1 mL) pepper. Spread in a single layer. Roast in preheated oven for 20 to 25 minutes or until potatoes are tender. Remove pan from oven and reduce heat to 350°F (180°C).

2. Meanwhile, in a large bowl, whisk together eggs, baking powder, and the remaining salt and pepper until blended. Whisk in ricotta and milk until blended and smooth. Stir in Gruyère, Parmesan and chives. Pour evenly over potatoes, smoothing top.

3. Bake for 30 to 35 minutes or until frittata is browned and puffed and a tester inserted near the center comes out clean. Let cool in pan on a wire rack for at least 20 minutes before cutting into squares. Serve warm or at room temperature.

California Fish Tacos with
Cucumber and Pineapple (page 23)

Pork Chops with Roasted Apples,
Pearl Onions and Thyme (page 34)

Nectarine Crostata with
Cardamom Sugar (page 38)

Ham and Cheese Egg Puffs
(page 52)

Huevos Rancheros Tortilla Tarts (page 54)

Raspberry Drop Scones (page 62)

Farmers' Market Salad with
Goat Cheese Toasts (page 77)

Persian Rice–Stuffed
Butternut Squash (page 92)

# Sheet Pan British Breakfast

This recipe is based on the classic British full breakfast, or fry-up, without the frying (and subsequent dishes and splatters). Only so much can fit on one sheet pan, but don't sweat, purists – I haven't forgotten the suggestion of warmed baked beans and malt vinegar on the side.

## Tip

Choose a variety of sliced white bread that is made with all-natural ingredients (without additives) and that is both sturdy and soft.

- Preheat oven to 425°F (220°C)
- 18- by 13-inch (45 by 33 cm) rimmed sheet pan, lined with foil

| | | |
|---|---|---|
| 8 | breakfast sausage links | 8 |
| 4 | thick-cut slices bacon, cut in half crosswise | 4 |
| 1½ cups | cherry or grape tomatoes | 375 mL |
| 1½ tbsp | unsalted butter | 22 mL |
| 4 | slices white bread | 4 |
| 4 | large eggs | 4 |
| | Salt and freshly ground black pepper | |

### Suggested Accompaniments
Warmed baked beans
Malt vinegar

1. Place sausages and bacon on prepared pan, spacing evenly. Roast in preheated oven for 10 minutes. Open oven door, turn sausages over and scatter tomatoes around pan. Close door and roast for 5 to 7 minutes or until sausages and bacon are just cooked through.

2. Meanwhile, butter one side of each bread slice.

3. Remove pan from oven and make 4 spaces on pan for the eggs. Lay bread slices, buttered side up, over bacon and sausage. Carefully crack eggs into empty spots and season with salt and pepper. Bake for 5 to 10 minutes or until egg whites are set. Serve eggs with bacon, sausages, tomatoes, bread and the suggested accompaniments, as desired.

# French Country Breakfast Bake

An all-American breakfast casserole takes on mouth-watering French flavors in this crowd-pleasing casserole. Hungry teenagers, VIP guests and everyone in between will be impressed.

## Variation

*Italian Breakfast Bake:* Replace the ham with 1 lb (500 g) Italian sausage, cooked and drained. Omit the mustard and replace the thyme with dried oregano. Replace the Gruyère with an equal amount of shredded fontina or Italian cheese blend.

- 18- by 13-inch (45 by 33 cm) rimmed sheet pan, lined with parchment paper and buttered

| | | |
|---|---|---|
| 1 | loaf (about 1¼ lbs/625 g) soft French- or Italian-style bakery bread, cubed | 1 |
| 2 cups | chopped cooked ham | 500 mL |
| 2 cups | shredded Gruyère or Swiss cheese, divided | 500 mL |
| 6 | large eggs | 6 |
| ¼ cup | Dijon mustard | 60 mL |
| 1 tsp | dried thyme | 5 mL |
| ½ tsp | freshly cracked black pepper | 2 mL |
| ¼ tsp | salt | 1 mL |
| 3 cups | milk | 750 mL |

1. Spread bread and ham in an even layer on prepared pan. Sprinkle with half the cheese.

2. In a large bowl, whisk together eggs, mustard, thyme, pepper and salt until blended. Whisk in milk until blended. Pour evenly over bread in pan. Sprinkle with the remaining cheese. Place a large piece of parchment paper over pan and press down to help bread absorb liquid. Let stand for 20 minutes.

3. Meanwhile, preheat oven to 375°F (190°C).

4. With the top piece of parchment still in place, bake for 25 to 30 minutes or until casserole is bubbling and browned around the edges. Remove top piece of parchment and turn broiler to high. Broil for 2 to 4 minutes or until top is golden and bubbling. Transfer to a wire rack and let cool for 10 minutes before cutting into squares.

# Smoked Sausage Hash Brown Casserole

**Makes 8 servings**

Potatoes, sausage and cheese are a favorite combination of flavors, especially on chilly mornings. This casserole combines the trio with significantly fewer calories than classic recipes.

## Tips

An equal amount of sour cream can be used in place of the yogurt.

Regular smoked sausage can be used in place of the reduced-fat sausage.

- Preheat oven to 400°F (200°C)
- 18- by 13-inch (45 by 33 cm) rimmed sheet pan, lined with foil and sprayed with nonstick cooking spray

| | | |
|---|---|---|
| 4 cups | frozen diced hash brown potatoes with peppers and onions, thawed | 1 L |
| 12 oz | reduced-fat smoked sausage, diced | 375 g |
| 10 | large eggs | 10 |
| 1/2 tsp | salt | 2 mL |
| 1/4 tsp | freshly cracked black pepper | 1 mL |
| 2/3 cup | plain Greek yogurt | 150 mL |
| 1 1/2 cups | shredded sharp (old) Cheddar cheese | 375 mL |

1. Spread hash browns and sausage in a single layer in prepared pan. Bake in preheated oven for 15 minutes.

2. Meanwhile, in a large bowl, whisk eggs until blended. Whisk in salt, pepper and yogurt until blended.

3. Remove pan from oven and pour egg mixture evenly over hash browns and sausages. Sprinkle with cheese. Bake for 15 to 20 minutes or until eggs are just set (the eggs will continue to cook from the heat of the hot pan). Let cool on a wire rack for at least 10 minutes before cutting into squares. Serve hot or warm.

# Ham and Cheese Egg Puffs

Don't be deceived by the short list of everyday ingredients – these egg puffs are something special.

## Tip

It is easier to separate the whites from the yolks while eggs are cold. However, the whites will whip to greater volume if they are not super-cold, so consider letting the egg whites warm for 5 minutes at room temperature before beating.

## Variation

Replace the ham with an equal amount of crumbled cooked bacon.

- Preheat oven to 450°F (230°C)
- 18- by 13-inch (45 by 33 cm) rimmed sheet pan, lined with foil and sprayed with nonstick cooking spray

| | | |
|---|---|---|
| 6 | large eggs | 6 |
| ¼ tsp | freshly ground black pepper | 1 mL |
| ½ cup | grated Parmesan cheese | 125 mL |
| ⅓ cup | finely chopped cooked ham | 75 mL |
| ¼ cup | chopped fresh chives | 60 mL |

1. Separate the eggs, placing the whites in a large bowl and the yolks in 6 separate small cups or bowls.

2. Using an electric mixer on high speed, beat egg whites and pepper until stiff peaks form. Using a rubber spatula, gently fold in cheese, ham and chives.

3. Spoon egg white mixture into 6 equal mounds on prepared pan, spacing them 3 inches (7.5 cm) apart. Using the back of the spoon, make a deep cavity in the center of each.

4. Bake in preheated oven for 3 minutes. Remove pan from oven and carefully add 1 yolk to the center of each mound. Bake for 2 to 4 minutes or until yolks are just set. Serve immediately.

# Egg, Ham and Portobello Brunch

**Makes 4 servings**

This all-in-one dish will have everyone asking for seconds, so you might want to buy twice the ingredients for a backup batch. As the name implies, it's perfect for weekend brunches – impressive, but a breeze for the host to prepare.

## Tip

It is important to use ham slices that are thin enough to be shaped into cups to hold the eggs.

## Variation

*Egg, Ham and Tomato Brunch:* In place of the mushrooms, use 4 medium-large tomatoes, with their tops cut off about $\frac{1}{4}$ inch (0.5 cm) from the top. Brush with oil (cut side up) and season as directed for mushrooms. Increase the roasting time in step 1 to 20 minutes.

- Preheat oven to 400°F (200°C)
- 18- by 13-inch (45 by 33 cm) rimmed sheet pan, lined with parchment paper or foil

| | | |
|---|---|---|
| 4 | large portobello mushrooms, stems removed and dark gills scraped out | 4 |
| 2 tbsp | olive oil | 30 mL |
| | Salt and freshly ground black pepper | |
| 4 | medium-thin slices deli ham | 4 |
| 4 | large eggs | 4 |
| | Chopped fresh chives (optional) | |

1. Place mushrooms, cut side up, close together (but not touching) on prepared pan. Brush with oil and season with salt and pepper. Roast in preheated oven for 15 minutes.

2. Remove pan from oven and tuck ham slices between the mushrooms to create small cups. Crack 1 egg into each ham cup. Season with salt and pepper. Bake for 10 to 12 minutes or until egg whites are set. Sprinkle with chives, if desired.

# Huevos Rancheros Tortilla Tarts

Give your breakfast or brunch a kick-start with this so-simple, irresistible recipe for huevos rancheros. It makes a satisfying (and frugal!) dinner entrée, too.

## Tips

An equal-size can of black beans or pinto beans, drained, rinsed and mashed with a fork, can be used in place of the refried beans.

Flour tortillas can be used in place of the corn tortillas.

- Preheat oven to 375°F (190°C)
- 18- by 13-inch (45 by 33 cm) rimmed sheet pan, lined with parchment paper or foil

| | | |
|---|---|---|
| 1 | can (15 oz/425 mL) refried beans | 1 |
| 1/4 cup | chipotle salsa, divided | 60 mL |
| 4 | 6-inch (15 cm) soft corn tortillas | 4 |
| 1 tbsp | olive oil or vegetable oil | 15 mL |
| 4 | large eggs | 4 |
| 2 | Hass avocados, sliced | 2 |
| 1/2 cup | crumbled queso fresco or mild feta cheese | 125 mL |

**Suggested Accompaniments**

Fresh cilantro leaves
Thinly sliced green onions
Thinly sliced jalapeño peppers
Additional chipotle salsa

1. In a small bowl, combine refried beans and salsa until blended.

2. Lightly brush both sides of tortillas with oil. Place on prepared pan, spacing evenly. Divide bean mixture evenly among tortillas, spreading to 1/2 inch (1 cm) from the edges and using the back of a spoon to create a slight well in the center of each. Break 1 egg into each well.

3. Bake in preheated oven for 14 to 18 minutes or until egg whites and yolks are firm, not runny. Serve topped with avocados, queso fresco and any of the suggested accompaniments, as desired.

# Sunny-Side-Up Pizza

One of my favorite rise-and-shine weekend recipes, this pizza comes together quickly when you start with ready-made dough. Cheese times two (Parmesan and ricotta) makes a perfect complement to the sunny-side-up eggs.

## Variations

Sprinkle the baked pizza with chopped fresh herbs (such as parsley, cilantro, dill, tarragon or chives) just before serving.

*Sunny-Side-Up Asparagus Pizza:* Sprinkle 8 oz (250 g) asparagus, trimmed and cut on the diagonal into 1/2-inch (1 cm) pieces, onto the ricotta layer before drizzling with oil.

- Preheat oven to 450°F (230°C)
- 18- by 13-inch (45 by 33 cm) rimmed sheet pan

| | All-purpose flour | |
|---|---|---|
| 1 lb | frozen pizza dough, thawed | 500 g |
| 1½ cups | ricotta cheese | 375 mL |
| 1 cup | grated Parmesan cheese, divided | 250 mL |
| 1 tbsp | olive oil | 15 mL |
| 4 | large eggs | 4 |
| ½ tsp | freshly cracked black pepper | 2 mL |

1. Lightly flour a large piece of foil. Place dough on top of foil and press out into a 14- by 10-inch (35 by 25 cm) oval. Transfer foil and dough to prepared pan.

2. In a small bowl, stir together ricotta and 1/2 cup (125 mL) Parmesan. Spread over dough, leaving a 1-inch (2.5 cm) border. Drizzle with oil.

3. Bake in preheated oven for 20 minutes. Remove pan from oven and, working quickly, crack eggs over top of pizza. Sprinkle with pepper and the remaining Parmesan. Bake for 5 to 10 minutes or until egg whites are set and crust is golden brown. Slide pizza onto a wire rack and let cool for 5 minutes before cutting into slices.

# Oven-Puffed Pancake

This simple recipe comes straight from my mother's kitchen. Also known as a Dutch baby or Dutch puff, it's the easiest way to make pancakes for a crowd without standing over the stove for an hour. A splash of vanilla and a sprinkle of confectioners' sugar add eye-opening flavor to this breakfast classic.

## Tips

An equal amount of virgin coconut oil can be used in place of the butter.

For the non-dairy milk, try hemp, almond, soy or rice milk.

## Variations

*Mixed Berry Puffed Pancake:* Add 4 cups (1 L) fresh berries (such as blueberries, raspberries, sliced strawberries or blackberries) after pouring the batter into the pan in step 3.

*Spiced Apple Puffed Pancake:* Add 2 tsp (10 mL) pumpkin pie spice or ground cinnamon to batter with the salt. Peel and thinly slice 2 large tart-sweet apples. Arrange in a single layer on top of melted butter in step 3. Pour batter over top and proceed as directed.

- 18- by 13-inch (45 by 33 cm) rimmed sheet pan

| | | |
|---|---|---|
| 6 | large eggs | 6 |
| 1²⁄₃ cups | all-purpose flour | 400 mL |
| ¹⁄₂ cup | confectioners' (icing) sugar, divided | 125 mL |
| ¹⁄₂ tsp | salt | 2 mL |
| 1²⁄₃ cups | milk or plain non-dairy milk, at room temperature | 400 mL |
| 1 tsp | vanilla extract | 5 mL |
| 6 tbsp | unsalted butter, cut into pieces | 90 mL |

**Suggested Accompaniments**

Berries or diced fruit

Pure maple syrup, liquid honey or agave nectar

Jam, preserves or marmalade

1. Place pan in oven. Preheat oven to 425°F (220°C).

2. In a large bowl, using an electric mixer on high speed, beat eggs for 1 to 2 minutes or until frothy. Add flour, ¹⁄₄ cup (60 mL) sugar, salt, milk and vanilla; beat on low speed for 30 seconds to incorporate flour. Stop to scrape down bottom and sides of bowl with a spatula. Beat on medium-high speed for 30 to 45 seconds or until smooth (batter will be thin).

3. Remove pan from oven. Add butter and melt, swirling to coat. Pour batter into pan and immediately return pan to oven. Bake for 19 to 24 minutes or until puffed and golden brown. Cut into pieces and serve immediately, sprinkled with the remaining sugar and with any of the suggested accompaniments, as desired.

# French Toast with Strawberries and Maple Syrup

This easy-to-make French toast is a delicious addition to any breakfast or brunch menu. A pinch of cardamom in the egg mixture adds subtle sophistication without any additional effort.

## Variations

Other berries or diced fruits can be used in place of the strawberries.

An equal amount of ground ginger or cinnamon can be used in place of the cardamom.

- 13- by 9-inch (33 by 23 cm) glass or ceramic baking dish
- 18- by 13-inch (45 by 33 cm) rimmed sheet pan, lined with parchment paper or foil and sprayed with nonstick cooking spray

| | | |
|---|---|---|
| 3 | large eggs | 3 |
| 5 tbsp | confectioners' (icing) sugar, divided | 75 mL |
| $\frac{1}{2}$ tsp | ground cardamom | 2 mL |
| $\frac{1}{4}$ tsp | salt | 1 mL |
| 2 tsp | vanilla extract | 10 mL |
| $1\frac{1}{4}$ cups | milk | 300 mL |
| 8 | slices (each 1 inch/2.5 cm thick) challah, brioche or other sturdy white bread | 8 |
| 3 cups | sliced hulled strawberries | 750 mL |
| $\frac{1}{2}$ cup | pure maple syrup, warmed | 125 mL |

1. In baking dish, whisk together eggs, 2 tbsp (30 mL) sugar, cardamom, salt and vanilla until blended. Whisk in milk until blended.

2. Arrange bread slices in a single layer in egg mixture, gently pressing down on bread to help it absorb liquid. Turn bread slices over and gently press down again. Let stand for 15 minutes.

3. Meanwhile, preheat oven to 400°F (200°C).

4. Remove bread from egg mixture and place in single layer on prepared pan, spacing evenly.

5. Bake for 10 minutes. Open oven door and, using a spatula, turn bread over. Close door and bake for 8 to 13 minutes or until browned and puffed. Sprinkle with the remaining sugar and serve with strawberries and syrup.

# PB&J Baked French Toast

Usually reserved for kids' lunches, peanut butter and jelly (PB&J, for short) also makes a wonderful variation on French toast.

## Tip
Choose a variety of sliced white bread that is made with all-natural ingredients (without additives) and that is both sturdy and soft.

## Variations
Use any flavor of jam, jelly or preserves in place of the raspberry jam.

An equal amount of any other creamy nut butter (such as cashew or almond) or seed butter (such as sunflower seed or tahini) can be used in place of the peanut butter.

- 13- by 9-inch (33 by 23 cm) glass or ceramic baking dish
- 18- by 13-inch (45 by 33 cm) rimmed sheet pan, lined with parchment paper or foil and sprayed with nonstick cooking spray

| | | |
|---|---|---:|
| 2 cups | mixed berries (fresh or frozen) | 500 mL |
| 1/2 cup | raspberry jam or preserves, divided | 125 mL |
| 1/3 cup | water | 75 mL |
| 3 | large eggs | 3 |
| 1/4 tsp | salt | 1 mL |
| 1 tsp | vanilla extract | 5 mL |
| 1 1/3 cups | milk | 325 mL |
| 8 | slices white sandwich bread | 8 |
| 1/2 cup | creamy peanut butter | 125 mL |
| 2 tbsp | confectioners' (icing) sugar | 30 mL |

1. In a medium saucepan, combine berries, 1/4 cup (60 mL) jam and water. Bring to a boil over medium-high heat. Reduce heat and simmer, stirring occasionally and crushing berries with a fork, for 8 to 10 minutes or until sauce is slightly thickened. Remove from heat and let cool until ready to serve.

2. Meanwhile, in baking dish, whisk together eggs, salt and vanilla until blended. Whisk in milk until blended.

3. Place bread slices in a single layer on work surface. Spread half the slices with peanut butter. Spread the remaining slices with the remaining jam and place on top of peanut butter slices to form sandwiches. Cut each sandwich in half diagonally.

4. Arrange sandwiches in a single layer in egg mixture, gently pressing down on bread to help it absorb liquid. Turn sandwiches over and gently press down again. Let stand for 15 minutes.

5. Meanwhile, preheat oven to 400°F (200°C).

6. Remove sandwiches from egg mixture and place in single layer on prepared pan, spacing evenly.

7. Bake for 10 minutes. Open oven door and, using a spatula, turn sandwiches over. Close door and bake for 8 to 13 minutes or until browned and puffed. Sprinkle with sugar and serve with berry sauce.

# Brown Sugar–Glazed Bacon

Popular throughout the American South, this salty-sweet preparation is known as "pig candy." Best of luck limiting yourself to one piece.

## Tip

For a fancy but still easy variation, twist each strip of bacon into a spiral before sprinkling with brown sugar.

## Variations

*Oven-Baked Bacon:* Prepare as directed, but omit the sugar.

*Spicy Glazed Bacon:* Sprinkle bacon with $\frac{1}{4}$ tsp (1 mL) cayenne pepper after the brown sugar.

- Preheat oven to 400°F (200°C), with oven rack placed in highest position
- 18- by 13-inch (45 by 33 cm) rimmed sheet pan, lined with foil
- Large ovenproof wire cooling rack

| | | |
|---|---|---|
| 1 lb | thick-cut bacon | 500 g |
| $\frac{1}{4}$ cup | packed light brown sugar | 60 mL |

1. Place cooling rack in sheet pan, on top of foil.

2. Arrange bacon in a single layer on rack, making sure the slices are lying flat. Sprinkle evenly with brown sugar.

3. Bake in preheated oven for 15 to 20 minutes or until bacon is crisp and glazed. Let cool for 5 minutes on rack.

# Roasted Breakfast Sausages

The gang's all here – so feed them sausages! This oven method is so simple (and there's minimal cleanup, too!), you'll soon wonder why you ever cooked sausages any other way.

## Tip

You can easily fit up to 2 lbs (1 kg) of breakfast sausage onto the pan if you are serving a large crowd.

## Variation

*Maple Cinnamon Sausages:* In a small cup, combine 3 tbsp (45 mL) pure maple syrup, 1 tbsp (15 mL) packed brown sugar and $\frac{1}{4}$ tsp (1 mL) ground cinnamon. In step 2, liberally brush sausages with syrup mixture before broiling them as directed.

- Preheat oven to 400°F (200°C)
- 18- by 13-inch (45 by 33 cm) rimmed sheet pan, lined with foil

| | | |
|---|---|---|
| 1 lb | breakfast sausage links | 500 g |

1. Place sausages in a single layer on prepared pan, spacing evenly. Roast in preheated oven for 10 minutes. Open oven door and turn sausages over. Close door and roast for 4 to 7 minutes or until sausages are cooked through.

2. Remove pan from oven and move oven rack to the highest position. Preheat broiler. Broil sausages for 1 to 3 minutes or until browned. Serve immediately.

# Scottish Oat Drop Scones

This simplified oat scone recipe makes eating a tasty and nutritious breakfast easy. "Dropping" the batter, instead of rolling and cutting a stiff dough into pieces, is a traditional method for oat scones in Scotland, so this rendition is tradition-approved.

## Tip

Due to differences in humidity, you may need to add an extra 1 to 2 tbsp (15 to 30 mL) milk to the dough make it "dropping" consistency.

## Storage Tip

Store the cooled scones in an airtight container at room temperature for up to 2 days or in the freezer for up to 3 months. Let thaw at room temperature for 1 to 2 hours before serving.

## Variations

Replace 1 cup (250 mL) of the all-purpose flour with whole wheat pastry flour.

Add 1 cup (250 mL) dried fruit (such as raisins, cranberries, cherries, chopped apricots or chopped figs) or diced dates with the oats in step 1.

Add 1 cup (250 mL) chopped toasted pecans or walnuts with the oats in step 1.

- Preheat oven to 400°F (200°C)
- Food processor
- 18- by 13-inch (45 by 33 cm) rimmed sheet pan, lined with parchment paper

| | | |
|---|---|---|
| 2¼ cups | all-purpose flour | 550 mL |
| ⅓ cup | packed light brown sugar | 75 mL |
| 1 tbsp | baking powder | 15 mL |
| ½ tsp | baking soda | 2 mL |
| ½ tsp | salt | 2 mL |
| ½ cup | cold unsalted butter, cut into small pieces | 125 mL |
| 1 cup | large-flake (old-fashioned) rolled oats | 250 mL |
| 1 | large egg | 1 |
| ¾ cup | milk | 175 mL |
| 1 tbsp | vanilla extract | 15 mL |

1. In food processor, pulse together flour, brown sugar, baking powder, baking soda and salt. Add butter and pulse until mixture resembles fresh bread crumbs. Transfer to a large bowl and stir in oats.

2. In a 2-cup (500 mL) glass measuring cup, whisk together egg, milk and vanilla until blended.

3. Add the egg mixture to the flour mixture, stirring gently with a fork until just blended.

4. Drop dough by ⅓-cup (75 mL) measures onto prepared pan, spacing scones 2 inches (5 cm) apart.

5. Bake in preheated oven for 14 to 19 minutes or until tops are golden brown and a tester inserted in the center comes out clean. Let cool on pan on a wire rack for 5 minutes, then transfer to the rack to cool for 5 minutes. Serve warm or let cool completely.

# Raspberry Drop Scones

Treat yourself – or a good friend – to these raspberry-stuffed scones for an idyllic handheld breakfast. Butter and buttermilk blend with a hint of vanilla for a rich flavor and tender texture.

## Tip

Due to differences in humidity, you may need to add an extra 1 to 2 tbsp (15 to 30 mL) buttermilk to the dough to make it "dropping" consistency.

## Storage Tip

Store the cooled scones in an airtight container at room temperature for up to 2 days or in the freezer for up to 3 months. Let thaw at room temperature for 1 to 2 hours before serving.

## Variations

Replace 1 cup (250 mL) of the all-purpose flour with whole wheat pastry flour.

Replace the raspberries with an equal amount of blueberries, blackberries, diced peaches or sliced strawberries.

- Preheat oven to 400°F (200°C)
- Food processor
- 18- by 13-inch (45 by 33 cm) rimmed sheet pan, lined with parchment paper

| | | |
|---|---|---|
| 2½ cups | all-purpose flour | 625 mL |
| 6 tbsp | granulated sugar, divided | 90 mL |
| 1 tbsp | baking powder | 15 mL |
| ½ tsp | salt | 2 mL |
| ½ cup | cold unsalted butter, cut into small pieces | 125 mL |
| 1 | large egg | 1 |
| ¾ cup | buttermilk | 175 mL |
| 1½ tsp | vanilla extract | 7 mL |
| 1½ cups | raspberries | 375 mL |

1. In food processor, pulse together flour, 4 tbsp (60 mL) sugar, baking powder and salt. Add butter and pulse until mixture resembles fresh bread crumbs. Transfer to a large bowl.

2. In a 2-cup (500 mL) glass measuring cup, whisk together egg, buttermilk and vanilla until blended.

3. Add the egg mixture to the flour mixture, stirring gently with a fork until just blended. Gently fold in raspberries.

4. Drop dough by ⅓-cup (75 mL) measures onto prepared pan, spacing scones 2 inches (5 cm) apart. Sprinkle with the remaining sugar.

5. Bake in preheated oven for 14 to 19 minutes or until tops are golden brown and a tester inserted in the center comes out clean. Let cool on pan on a wire rack for 5 minutes, then transfer to the rack to cool for 5 minutes. Serve warm or let cool completely.

# Big Easy Butter Biscuits

These flaky biscuits are easy to make and big in size. They are inspired by biscuits I swooned over at Dante's Kitchen, a great spot for breakfast in the Big Easy (New Orleans). Crispy on the edges, pillowy and buttery on the inside, they are best served with everything.

## Storage Tip
Store the cooled biscuits in an airtight container at room temperature for up to 2 days or in the freezer for up to 3 months. Let thaw at room temperature for 1 to 2 hours before serving.

## Variation
Replace 1 cup (250 mL) of the all-purpose flour with whole wheat pastry flour.`

- Preheat oven to 400°F (200°C)
- Food processor
- 18- by 13-inch (45 by 33 cm) rimmed sheet pan, lined with parchment paper

| | | |
|---|---|---|
| 2 cups | all-purpose flour | 500 mL |
| 1 tbsp | baking powder | 15 mL |
| ¾ tsp | salt | 3 mL |
| ½ cup | cold unsalted butter, cut into small pieces | 125 mL |
| 1 cup | milk or light (5%) cream | 250 mL |

**Suggested Accompaniments**
Softened butter
Fruit jam, preserves, jelly, lemon curd or marmalade
Chocolate hazelnut spread
Liquid honey or light (fancy) molasses

1. In food processor, pulse together flour, baking powder and salt. Add butter and pulse until mixture resembles fresh bread crumbs. Add milk and pulse 3 to 4 times until dough is just moistened. Scrape down bottom and sides of bowl with a rubber spatula; pulse one more time.

2. Drop dough by ½-cup (125 mL) measures onto prepared pan, spacing biscuits 2 inches (5 cm) apart.

3. Bake in preheated oven for 18 to 23 minutes or until tops are golden brown and a tester inserted in the center comes out clean. Let cool on pan on a wire rack for 5 minutes, then transfer to the rack to cool for 5 minutes. Serve warm or let cool completely. Serve with any of the suggested accompaniments, as desired.

## Variations
*Easy Cheesy Breakfast Biscuits:* Add 1½ cups (375 mL) shredded sharp (old) Cheddar cheese and ¼ cup (60 mL) grated Parmesan cheese to the dough in step 1 after scraping down bottom and sides of bowl.

*Buttermilk Big Easy Biscuits:* Reduce baking powder to 2 tsp (10 mL) and add ½ tsp (2 mL) baking soda. Replace the milk with an equal amount of buttermilk.

*Herbed Big Easy Biscuits:* Add ½ cup (125 mL) minced fresh chives or chopped fresh parsley, dill, cilantro or basil, or a combination, to the dough along with the milk.

# Raspberry Almond Brunch Kuchen

**Makes 20 servings**

This raspberry and sour cream custard-topped coffee cake is an irresistible family breakfast you'll want to make again and again. You can vary the fruit according to what is in season.

## Tip

Do not use frozen raspberries in place of fresh for this recipe. Their high water content will make the cake soggy.

## Storage Tip

Store the cooled cake, loosely wrapped in foil or waxed paper, in the refrigerator for up to 5 days. Alternatively, wrap it in plastic wrap, then foil, completely enclosing it, and freeze for up to 6 months. Let thaw at room temperature for 4 to 6 hours before serving.

- Preheat oven to 350°F (180°C)
- 18- by 13-inch (45 by 33 cm) rimmed sheet pan, lined with parchment paper and sprayed with nonstick cooking spray

**Cake**

| | | |
|---|---|---|
| 3 cups | all-purpose flour | 750 mL |
| 1 tbsp | baking powder | 15 mL |
| 1 tsp | salt | 5 mL |
| 1⅓ cups | granulated sugar, divided | 325 mL |
| 1 cup | unsalted butter, softened | 250 mL |
| 2 tsp | almond extract | 10 mL |
| 2 | large eggs, at room temperature | 2 |
| 1 cup | milk | 250 mL |
| 3 cups | raspberries | 750 mL |

**Topping**

| | | |
|---|---|---|
| 3 tbsp | granulated sugar | 45 mL |
| 2 | large eggs, at room temperature | 2 |
| 1½ cups | sour cream | 375 mL |
| ½ cup | sliced almonds | 125 mL |

1. *Cake:* In a medium bowl, whisk together flour, baking powder and salt.

2. In a large bowl, using an electric mixer on medium speed, beat 1 cup (250 mL) sugar, butter and almond extract until light and fluffy. Beat in eggs, one at a time, until just blended. With the mixer on low speed, beat in flour mixture alternately with milk until just blended.

3. Spread batter evenly in prepared pan. Top with raspberries and sprinkle evenly with the remaining sugar.

4. Bake in preheated oven for 25 to 30 minutes or until top is golden.

5. *Topping:* Meanwhile, in the same bowl used to beat cake batter (no need to clean it), whisk together sugar, eggs and sour cream until blended. Remove pan from oven and spoon topping over berries and cake and sprinkle with almonds. Bake for 15 to 20 minutes or until topping is barely set. Let cool in pan on a wire rack for 20 minutes and serve warm, or let cool completely and serve at room temperature.

# Cinnamon Crumb Coffee Cake

Ubiquitous in New York bakeries and coffee shops (and featured in a classic episode of *Seinfeld*), cinnamon crumb coffee cake is a simple and scrumptious way to start the day. Bonus: this batch will last all week.

## Storage Tip

Store the cooled cake, loosely wrapped in foil or waxed paper, at room temperature for up to 3 days. Alternatively, wrap it in plastic wrap, then foil, completely enclosing it, and freeze for up to 6 months. Let thaw at room temperature for 4 to 6 hours before serving.

## Variation

*Blueberry Crumb Coffee Cake:* Stir 1 1/2 cups (375 mL) fresh or frozen (not thawed) blueberries into batter before spreading in pan.

- Preheat oven to 350°F (180°C)
- 18- by 13-inch (45 by 33 cm) rimmed sheet pan, lined with parchment paper and sprayed with nonstick cooking spray

**Cake**

| | | |
|---|---|---|
| 3 cups | all-purpose flour | 750 mL |
| 1 tbsp | baking powder | 15 mL |
| 1 tsp | salt | 5 mL |
| 1 1/2 cups | granulated sugar | 375 mL |
| 3 | large eggs, at room temperature | 3 |
| 1 1/3 cups | buttermilk | 325 mL |
| 1/2 cup | unsalted butter, melted and cooled slightly | 125 mL |
| 1 tbsp | vanilla extract | 15 mL |

**Topping**

| | | |
|---|---|---|
| 2 cups | all-purpose flour | 500 mL |
| 1 cup | packed light or dark brown sugar | 250 mL |
| 1 tbsp | ground cinnamon | 15 mL |
| 1/4 tsp | salt | 1 mL |
| 3/4 cup | unsalted butter, melted and cooled slightly | 175 mL |

1. *Cake:* In a large bowl, whisk together flour, baking powder and salt.

2. In another large bowl, whisk together sugar, eggs, buttermilk, butter and vanilla until well blended.

3. Add the egg mixture to the flour mixture, stirring until just blended (do not overmix). Spread evenly in prepared pan.

4. *Topping:* In the same bowl used to mix the batter (no need to clean it), combine flour, brown sugar, cinnamon and salt. Using a wooden spoon, stir in butter until coarse crumbs form. Sprinkle evenly over batter.

5. Bake in preheated oven for 25 to 30 minutes or until a tester inserted in the center comes out with a few moist crumbs attached. Let cool completely in pan on a wire rack.

# Simplified Cinnamon Rolls

Flaky, buttery pastry layered with a cinnamon–brown sugar filling makes a memorable breakfast or brunch. And if my 9-year-old son can make these (granted, with a wee bit of help from yours truly), so can you!

## Storage Tip

Store the cooled, unfrosted rolls in an airtight container at room temperature for up to 2 days or in the freezer for up to 3 months. Let thaw at room temperature for 1 to 2 hours before serving.

## Variation

Replace 1 cup (250 mL) of the all-purpose flour with whole wheat pastry flour.

- Preheat oven to 375°F (190°C)
- Food processor
- 18- by 13-inch (45 by 33 cm) rimmed sheet pan, lined with parchment paper

| | | |
|---|---|---|
| $\frac{1}{2}$ cup | packed light brown sugar | 125 mL |
| $2\frac{1}{2}$ tsp | ground cinnamon | 12 mL |
| $2\frac{1}{2}$ cups | all-purpose flour | 625 mL |
| $\frac{1}{4}$ cup | granulated sugar | 60 mL |
| 1 tbsp | baking powder | 15 mL |
| $\frac{3}{4}$ tsp | salt | 3 mL |
| $\frac{1}{2}$ cup | cold unsalted butter, cut into small pieces | 125 mL |
| 2 | large eggs | 2 |
| 8 tbsp | milk, divided | 120 mL |
| 2 tsp | vanilla extract | 10 mL |
| $\frac{2}{3}$ cup | confectioners' (icing) sugar | 150 mL |

1. In a small bowl, stir together brown sugar and cinnamon.

2. In food processor, pulse together flour, granulated sugar, baking powder and salt. Add butter and pulse until mixture resembles fresh bread crumbs. Transfer to a large bowl.

3. In a 2-cup (500 mL) glass measuring cup, whisk together eggs, 6 tbsp (90 mL) milk and vanilla until blended.

4. Add the egg mixture to the flour mixture, gently stirring with a fork until just blended.

5. On a lightly floured surface, knead dough for 30 seconds or until less sticky. Pat into a 12- by 10-inch (30 by 25 cm) rectangle. Brush with 1 tbsp (15 mL) milk and sprinkle evenly with cinnamon sugar. Beginning with a long side, roll up jelly-roll-style to form a 12-inch (30 cm) log. Cut crosswise into 8 rolls. Place rolls on prepared pan, with seams touching.

6. Bake in preheated oven for 17 to 21 minutes or until tops are golden brown and a tester inserted in the center comes out clean. Let cool on pan on a wire rack for 5 minutes, then transfer to the rack to cool for 15 minutes.

7. In a small bowl, stir together confectioners' sugar and the remaining milk until smooth; drizzle over rolls. Serve warm or let cool completely.

# Apricot Cream Cheese Danishes

## Makes 4 Danishes

It's surprisingly easy to make these pretty and so-pleasing Danishes. They are best eaten right away, so either invite some friends or prepare to indulge.

## Tips

Any other flavor of jam, preserves or lemon curd can be used in place of the apricot jam.

The Danishes can be assembled ahead of time through step 5. Loosely cover with plastic wrap and refrigerate for up to 12 hours before baking.

For optimal crispness, serve the Danishes soon after baking.

- Preheat oven to 375°F (190°C)
- 18- by 13-inch (45 by 33 cm) rimmed sheet pan, lined with parchment paper

| | | |
|---|---|---|
| 8 oz | cream cheese, softened | 250 g |
| 3 tbsp | granulated sugar, divided | 45 mL |
| 1 | large egg | 1 |
| 2 tsp | water | 10 mL |
| | All-purpose flour | |
| 1 | sheet frozen puff pastry (half a 17.3-oz/490 g package), thawed | 1 |
| 4 tbsp | apricot jam or preserves | 60 mL |

1. In a small bowl, vigorously stir together cream cheese and 2 tbsp (30 mL) sugar until blended and smooth.

2. In another small bowl or cup, whisk together egg and water until blended.

3. On a lightly floured surface, roll out puff pastry into a 12-inch (30 cm) square. Cut into four 6-inch (15 cm) squares. Transfer to prepared pan, spacing evenly.

4. Gently spread about $1/4$ cup (60 mL) cream cheese mixture in a 5-inch (12.5 cm) diagonal strip across each square. Spoon and spread 1 tbsp (5 mL) jam over cheese.

5. For each Danish, pull a corner over the filling almost to the other corner. Brush top of dough with egg wash. Fold opposite corner over the first one and press to seal. Leave the remaining corners flat. Brush dough all over with the remaining egg wash. Sprinkle with the remaining sugar.

6. Bake in preheated oven for 25 to 30 minutes or until pastry is puffed, golden brown and appears crisp. Let cool on pan on a wire rack for 5 minutes, then transfer to the rack to cool completely.

# Croissant Jelly Donuts

## Makes 9 donuts

Fresh puff pastry donuts, filled with jam and dusted with sugar — is there a better way to start the day? Better still, you won't need to leave your house to get them.

## Tip

Commercial puff pastry loses it crispness quickly, so it is best to eat the donuts shortly after baking. However, they can be assembled ahead of time through step 3. Cover loosely with plastic wrap and refrigerate for up to 12 hours before baking.

## Variation

*Chocolate Raspberry Donuts:* Decrease the amount of jam in each donut to 1 tsp (5 mL). Top the jam with 5 to 6 semisweet, milk or white chocolate chips in each donut. Proceed as directed.

- Preheat oven to 400°F (200°C)
- 3-inch (7.5 cm) round biscuit or cookie cutter
- 18- by 13-inch (45 by 33 cm) rimmed sheet pan, lined with parchment paper

| | | |
|---|---|---|
| 1 | large egg | 1 |
| 1 tbsp | water | 15 mL |
| | All-purpose flour | |
| 1 | package (17.3 oz/490 g) frozen puff pastry sheets, thawed | 1 |
| ¼ cup | raspberry jam or preserves | 60 mL |
| ¼ cup | confectioners' (icing) sugar | 60 mL |

1. In a small bowl or cup, whisk together egg and water until blended.

2. On a lightly floured surface, unfold one pastry sheet. Using the biscuit cutter, cut out 9 circles. Repeat with the remaining pastry sheet. (Discard pastry scraps.)

3. Place half the circles on prepared pan, spacing evenly. Spoon $1\frac{1}{2}$ tsp (7 mL) jam into the center of each circle. Brush edges of circles with egg wash. Place the remaining circles on top and press out the air while pressing the edges firmly to seal. Using a sharp knife, cut a $\frac{1}{2}$-inch (1 cm) slit in the top of each pastry.

4. Bake in preheated oven for 12 to 17 minutes or until donuts are puffed and golden brown. Let cool on pan on a wire rack for 15 minutes. Transfer donuts to the rack and sprinkle with sugar. Serve slightly warm or let cool completely.

# Cinnamon Donut Breakfast Cookies

Frying homemade donuts can be time-consuming and messy, but you can capture the flavor of homemade cake donuts with these dainty cookies. Need I mention that coffee is a perfect accompaniment?

## Tips

An equal amount of sour cream can be used in place of the yogurt.

Whole wheat pastry flour can be used in place of the all-purpose flour.

Be sure to use Greek-style plain yogurt as opposed to regular plain yogurt. The latter has a higher water content, which will make the batter runny.

## Storage Tip

Store cooled cookies in an airtight container in the refrigerator for up to 5 days.

## Variation

*Chocolate Chip Donut Cookies:* Stir ⅔ cup (150 mL) miniature semisweet chocolate chips into the batter at the end of step 2.

- Preheat oven to 375°F (190°C)
- 18- by 13-inch (45 by 33 cm) rimmed sheet pan, lined with parchment paper

| | | |
|---|---|---|
| 1½ cups | all-purpose flour | 375 mL |
| 1¾ tsp | ground cinnamon, divided | 8 mL |
| ¾ tsp | baking powder | 3 mL |
| ½ tsp | salt | 2 mL |
| ¼ tsp | baking soda | 1 mL |
| 9 tbsp | granulated sugar, divided | 135 mL |
| ⅓ cup | packed light brown sugar | 75 mL |
| ½ cup | plain Greek yogurt | 125 mL |
| ⅓ cup | unsalted butter, softened | 75 mL |
| 1 | large egg | 1 |
| 1½ tsp | vanilla extract | 7 mL |

1. In a medium bowl, whisk together flour, ¾ tsp (3 mL) cinnamon, baking powder, salt and baking soda.

2. In a large bowl, using an electric mixer on medium speed, beat 6 tbsp (90 mL) granulated sugar, brown sugar, yogurt and butter until smooth. Beat in egg and vanilla until completely blended. With the mixer on low speed, beat in flour mixture until just combined.

3. Drop batter by 2-tbsp (30 mL) measures onto prepared pan, spacing cookies 2 inches (5 cm) apart.

4. In a small cup, combine the remaining granulated sugar and cinnamon. Sprinkle over tops of cookies.

5. Bake in preheated oven for 10 to 13 minutes or until edges are golden brown and cookies are just set at the center. Let cool on pan on a wire rack for 5 minutes, then transfer to the rack to cool.

# Carrot Cake Breakfast Cookies

Try these multigrain carrot
cookies for a tasty breakfast
on the go. They're delightful
with a small smear of cream
cheese, too.

## Tip
An equal amount of vegetable
oil, olive oil or unsalted butter,
melted, can be used in place
of the coconut oil.

## Storage Tip
Store cooled cookies in
an airtight container in the
refrigerator for up to 5 days.

## Variations
*Zucchini Breakfast Cookies:*
Use an equal amount of finely
shredded zucchini in place of
the carrots.

Fold in $\frac{1}{2}$ cup (125 mL) raisins
and $\frac{1}{2}$ cup (125 mL) chopped
toasted pecans or walnuts
along with the carrots. This will
yield about 3 additional cookies
(for a total of 15 cookies).

- Preheat oven to 350°F (180°C)
- 18- by 13-inch (45 by 33 cm) rimmed sheet pan, lined with parchment paper

| | | |
|---|---|---|
| 1 cup | whole wheat flour | 250 mL |
| $\frac{3}{4}$ cup | large-flake (old-fashioned) rolled oats | 175 mL |
| $\frac{1}{2}$ cup | ground flax seeds (flaxseed meal) | 125 mL |
| 2 tsp | ground cinnamon | 10 mL |
| 1 tsp | baking powder | 5 mL |
| $\frac{1}{4}$ tsp | salt | 1 mL |
| 1 | large egg, lightly beaten | 1 |
| $\frac{1}{2}$ cup | pure maple syrup | 125 mL |
| $\frac{1}{4}$ cup | virgin coconut oil, warmed | 60 mL |
| $1\frac{1}{4}$ cups | finely shredded carrots | 300 mL |

1. In a large bowl, whisk together flour, oats, flax seeds, cinnamon, baking powder and salt. Stir in egg, maple syrup and coconut oil until just blended. Gently fold in carrots.

2. Drop batter by $\frac{1}{3}$-cup (75 mL) measures onto prepared pan, spacing cookies 2 inches (5 cm) apart.

3. Bake in preheated oven for 12 to 16 minutes or until just set at the center. Let cool completely on pan on a wire rack.

# Blueberry Mini Muffin Tops

Here's a recipe for making perfect miniature muffin tops. They look like pillowy cookies, but you can eat several for breakfast, no questions asked. Once you've mastered the basics – mix the wet and dry ingredients separately, don't overmix, fold in the fruit – a range of possibilities opens.

### Tip

If using thawed frozen blueberries, gently pat them dry with a paper towel before adding them to the batter.

### Storage Tip

Store cooled muffin tops in an airtight container in the refrigerator for up to 5 days.

### Variation

*Cranberry Orange Mini Muffin Tops:* Replace the vanilla with 2 tsp (10 mL) finely grated orange zest, and replace the blueberries with 1 1/2 cups (375 mL) fresh or thawed frozen cranberries, coarsely chopped.

- Preheat oven to 350°F (180°C)
- 18- by 13-inch (45 by 33 cm) rimmed sheet pan, lined with parchment paper

| | | |
|---|---|---:|
| 1 1/2 cups | all-purpose flour | 375 mL |
| 1 1/2 tsp | baking powder | 7 mL |
| 3/4 tsp | salt | 3 mL |
| 2/3 cup | granulated sugar | 150 mL |
| 1 | large egg | 1 |
| 6 tbsp | unsalted butter, melted | 90 mL |
| 1/4 cup | milk | 60 mL |
| 1 tsp | vanilla extract | 5 mL |
| 2 cups | fresh or thawed frozen blueberries | 500 mL |
| 3 tbsp | turbinado sugar | 45 mL |

1. In a large bowl, whisk together flour, baking powder and salt.

2. In a medium bowl, whisk together granulated sugar, egg, butter, milk and vanilla until blended.

3. Add the egg mixture to the flour mixture, stirring until just blended. Gently fold in blueberries.

4. Drop batter by 2-tbsp (30 mL) measures onto prepared pans, spacing muffin tops 2 inches (5 cm) apart. Sprinkle tops with turbinado sugar.

5. Bake in preheated oven for 10 to 13 minutes or until just set at the center. Let cool in pan on a wire rack for 2 minutes, then transfer to the rack to cool.

# Sheet Pan Granola Bars

Not every brunch is a sit-down affair; sometimes it's a springtime hike through the mountains or a picnic at the park with the kids. When it's one of the latter, pack a few of these make-ahead granola bars. Together with thermoses of orange juice and coffee, they're portable brunch bliss.

## Tip

It is much easier to cut the bars while they are still warm than when they are completely cooled.

## Storage Tip

Store cooled granola bars in an airtight container at room temperature for up to 1 week. Or wrap them in plastic wrap, then foil, completely enclosing them, and freeze for up to 6 months. Let thaw at room temperature for 1 hour before serving.

## Variations

Use any variety of chopped nuts (such as walnuts, almonds or peanuts) or seeds (such as sunflower or green pumpkin) in place of the pecans.

Add up to 1 1/2 cups (375 mL) chopped dried fruit (such as cranberries, raisins or apricots) with the pecans.

- Preheat oven to 325°F (160°C)
- 18- by 13-inch (45 by 33 cm) rimmed sheet pan, lined with foil and sprayed with nonstick cooking spray
- Large sheet of waxed paper

| | | |
|---|---|---|
| 6 cups | large-flake (old-fashioned) rolled oats | 1.5 L |
| 2 cups | crisp rice cereal | 500 mL |
| 1 cup | finely chopped pecans | 250 mL |
| 3/4 cup | ground flax seeds (flaxseed meal) | 175 mL |
| 1 1/4 cups | packed dark brown sugar | 300 mL |
| 1/2 cup | unsalted butter, cut into small pieces | 125 mL |
| 1/2 cup | liquid honey | 125 mL |
| 1/4 cup | unsweetened apple juice | 60 mL |
| 1 tsp | salt | 5 mL |
| 1 tbsp | vanilla extract | 15 mL |
| | Nonstick cooking spray | |

1. In a large bowl, combine oats, cereal, pecans and flax seeds.

2. In a medium saucepan, combine brown sugar, butter, honey and apple juice. Cook over medium heat, stirring, until butter is melted and mixture comes to a low boil. Reduce heat to low and cook, stirring occasionally, for 2 minutes. Remove from heat and stir in salt and vanilla.

3. Immediately pour butter mixture over oat mixture, stirring until well coated. Spread mixture in prepared pan. Spray a large sheet of waxed paper with cooking spray and firmly press oat mixture into pan.

4. Bake in preheated oven for 23 to 28 minutes or until golden brown. Let cool in pan on a wire rack for 5 minutes. Using foil liner, lift mixture from pan and transfer to a cutting board. Peel off foil and cut into 36 bars while still warm. Let cool completely.

# Meatless Meals

# Summer Roasted Corn, Potato and Fresh Mozzarella Salad

Sweet corn and tiny potatoes are the backbone for this fresh but filling main-dish salad. Fresh mozzarella adds creaminess as well as significant protein.

## Tips

An equal amount of yellow-fleshed or new potatoes, cut into 1-inch (2.5 cm) pieces, can be used in place of the baby potatoes.

You can replace the grainy mustard with Dijon mustard, if you prefer.

If making the salad more than 2 hours ahead, wait until serving time to add the arugula.

- Preheat oven to 450°F (230°C)
- 18- by 13-inch (45 by 33 cm) rimmed sheet pan, lined with foil and sprayed with nonstick cooking spray

| | | |
|---|---|---|
| 1 lb | baby red, white or gold potatoes, halved | 500 g |
| 5 tbsp | olive oil, divided | 75 mL |
| 2 | cloves garlic, minced | 2 |
| 1 tsp | dried oregano | 5 mL |
| | Salt and freshly cracked black pepper | |
| 2 cups | fresh or thawed frozen corn kernels | 500 mL |
| 1 tbsp | white wine vinegar | 15 mL |
| 2 tsp | grainy mustard | 10 mL |
| 1 | ball (about 6 oz/175 g) fresh mozzarella, drained and diced | 1 |
| 4 cups | baby arugula | 1 L |

1. On prepared pan, toss potatoes with 2 tbsp (30 mL) oil, garlic, oregano, $\frac{1}{2}$ tsp (2 mL) salt and $\frac{1}{8}$ tsp (0.5 mL) pepper. Spread in a single layer. Roast in preheated oven for 15 minutes.

2. Open oven door and stir corn into potatoes. Close door and roast for 10 to 15 minutes or until potatoes are fork-tender and corn is lightly browned. Transfer mixture to a large platter and let cool to room temperature.

3. In a small bowl or cup, whisk together the remaining oil, vinegar and mustard until blended. Season to taste with salt and pepper. Add to potato mixture, along with mozzarella and arugula, tossing to coat. Serve at room temperature or cover and refrigerate until cold, for up to 2 hours.

# Warm Kale, Tomato and Chickpea Salad

### Makes 4 servings

Creamy, nutty chickpeas are roasted alongside red onions and tomatoes for this satisfying main-dish salad. A lemony yogurt tahini dressing adds contrasting fresh, bold flavor.

## Tips
You can use 2 cups (500 mL) cherry or grape tomatoes in place of the plum tomatoes.

An equal amount of ground cumin can be used in place of the coriander.

It is best to use regular yogurt, not Greek yogurt, in the sauce; the latter will make the sauce too thick. If Greek yogurt is what you have on hand, use 2 tbsp (30 mL) Greek yogurt plus 2 tbsp (30 mL) water in place of the 1/4 cup (60 mL) yogurt.

- Preheat oven to 400°F (200°C)
- 18- by 13-inch (45 by 33 cm) rimmed sheet pan, lined with foil or parchment paper

**Salad**

| | | |
|---|---|---|
| 2 | cloves garlic, minced | 2 |
| 1 tsp | ground coriander | 5 mL |
| | Salt and freshly cracked black pepper | |
| 1/4 cup | olive oil | 60 mL |
| 4 | plum (Roma) tomatoes, quartered lengthwise | 4 |
| 1 | large red onion, halved lengthwise and cut crosswise into 1/4-inch (0.5 cm) slices | 1 |
| 2 | cans (each 14 to 19 oz/398 to 540 mL) chickpeas, drained and rinsed | 2 |
| 6 cups | packed chopped kale (tough stems and center ribs removed) | 1.5 L |

**Yogurt Tahini Dressing**

| | | |
|---|---|---|
| 1/4 cup | plain yogurt | 60 mL |
| 2 tbsp | well-stirred tahini | 30 mL |
| 1 1/2 tbsp | freshly squeezed lemon juice | 22 mL |
| 1 tsp | liquid honey or granulated sugar | 5 mL |

1. *Salad:* In a small bowl, combine garlic, coriander, 1/2 tsp (2 mL) salt, 1/4 tsp (1 mL) pepper and oil.

2. In a large bowl, toss together tomatoes, onion, chickpeas and half the oil mixture. Spread in a single layer on prepared pan. Roast in preheated oven for 20 to 25 minutes or until tomatoes are softened.

3. In the same large bowl, toss kale with the remaining oil mixture.

4. Open oven door and distribute kale over chickpeas and vegetables. Close door and roast for 8 to 12 minutes or until edges of kale are slightly browned and appear crispy. Let cool on pan for 10 minutes.

5. *Dressing:* Meanwhile, in a small bowl, whisk together yogurt, tahini, lemon juice and honey. Season to taste with salt and pepper. Drizzle salad with 2 tbsp (30 mL) of the dressing and toss to coat.

6. Divide salad among four dinner plates or shallow dinner bowls. Drizzle with the remaining dressing.

# Warm Edamame, Quinoa and Corn Salad

Protein-rich quinoa and edamame make this vibrant salad hearty enough for a main course. Every spoonful includes a medley of fresh, citrusy flavor.

## Tips

An equal amount of frozen baby lima beans, thawed, can be used in place of the edamame.

If corn is in season, swap out the frozen corn kernels with an equal amount of fresh.

- Preheat oven to 350°F (180°C)
- Two 18- by 13-inch (45 by 33 cm) rimmed sheet pans

| | | |
|---|---|---|
| 2½ cups | boiling water | 625 mL |
| | Salt and freshly cracked black pepper | |
| 1¼ cups | quinoa, rinsed | 300 mL |
| 1 | package (12 oz/375 g) frozen shelled edamame, thawed | 1 |
| 1½ cups | frozen corn kernels | 375 mL |
| 1½ cups | cherry or grape tomatoes, halved | 375 mL |
| 1 cup | chopped green onions | 250 mL |
| ¼ cup | freshly squeezed lime juice | 60 mL |
| 2 tbsp | olive oil | 30 mL |

1. In a 4-cup (1 L) measuring cup, combine boiling water, 1 tsp (5 mL) salt and ¼ tsp (1 mL) pepper.

2. Spread quinoa and edamame on one of the pans in an even layer. Place pan on oven rack. With oven door open, carefully pour water mixture over quinoa mixture, stirring to combine. Cover with inverted sheet pan. Bake in preheated oven for 20 minutes.

3. Remove pan from oven and carefully remove top pan (hot steam will release). Scrape quinoa mixture into a large bowl. Stir in corn and let stand for 10 minutes to allow corn to defrost and quinoa to cool slightly.

4. Stir in tomatoes, green onions, lime juice and oil. Season to taste with salt and pepper. Serve warm, let cool to room temperature, or cover and refrigerate and serve cold.

# Farmers' Market Salad with Goat Cheese Toasts

Goat cheese–topped toasts and farmers' market vegetables – radishes, mushrooms, green beans and baby kale – give this quick entrée salad sophisticated, yet still homey, flair.

## Tips

Other soft cheeses, such as creamy blue cheese or herbed garlic cheese spread, can be used in place of the goat cheese.

Baby arugula or baby spinach can be used in place of the baby kale.

- Preheat oven to 425°F (220°C)
- 18- by 13-inch (45 by 33 cm) rimmed sheet pan, lined with foil

| | | |
|---|---|---|
| 12 oz | green beans, trimmed and cut in half crosswise | 375 g |
| 12 oz | cremini or button mushrooms, trimmed | 375 g |
| 1 | small bunch radishes, trimmed and halved | 1 |
| 1 | red onion, halved lengthwise and each half cut into 6 wedges | 1 |
| 4 tbsp | olive oil, divided | 60 mL |
| | Salt and freshly cracked black pepper | |
| 4 | thick-cut slices country bread | 4 |
| 4 oz | soft goat cheese | 125 g |
| 1 tbsp | white wine vinegar | 15 mL |
| 1 tsp | liquid honey | 5 mL |
| 6 cups | baby kale | 1.5 L |

1. On prepared pan, toss together green beans, mushrooms, radishes, onion, half the oil, $\frac{1}{2}$ tsp (2 mL) salt and $\frac{1}{4}$ tsp (1 mL) pepper. Spread in a single layer. Roast in preheated oven for 15 minutes.

2. Meanwhile, spread one side of bread slices with goat cheese, dividing equally. Open oven door and place bread, cheese side up, on top of vegetables. Close door and bake for 5 to 8 minutes or until vegetables are tender-crisp and cheese is melted. Remove from oven and transfer bread to a plate.

3. In a small bowl, whisk together vinegar, honey and the remaining oil. Season to taste with salt and pepper.

4. Add kale to pan, drizzle with dressing and toss to coat. Serve salad immediately, with bread.

# Winter Salad with Acorn Squash, Mushrooms and Tempeh

Half-moons of acorn squash, dusted with smoked paprika and nestled among bell peppers, mushrooms and tempeh, make for a healthy, easy and inspired weeknight meal.

## Tips

You can use 2 cups (500 mL) cubed peeled butternut squash in place of the acorn squash.

A 12-oz (375 g) package of frozen pearl onions, thawed, can be used in place of the red onion.

- Preheat oven to 425°F (220°C)
- 18- by 13-inch (45 by 33 cm) rimmed sheet pan, lined with foil and sprayed with nonstick cooking spray

| | | |
|---|---|---|
| 1 | acorn squash, halved lengthwise and seeded | 1 |
| 1 | large red bell pepper, cut into 1-inch (2.5 cm) pieces | 1 |
| 1 | red onion, cut into 1-inch (2.5 cm) chunks | 1 |
| 6 tbsp | olive oil, divided | 90 mL |
| 1 tsp | smoked paprika (pimentón), divided | 5 mL |
| | Salt | |
| 8 oz | cremini or button mushrooms | 250 g |
| 8 oz | tempeh, cut crosswise into 12 strips | 250 g |
| 6 cups | arugula or baby spinach leaves | 1.5 L |
| 1 tbsp | sherry vinegar or white wine vinegar | 15 mL |
| | Freshly cracked black pepper | |

1. Thinly slice squash into half-moons. In a large bowl, toss together squash, red pepper, onion, 2 tbsp (30 mL) oil, 1/2 tsp (2 mL) paprika and 1/2 tsp (2 mL) salt. Spread in a single layer in prepared pan. Roast in preheated oven for 10 minutes.

2. Meanwhile, in the same bowl, toss together mushrooms, tempeh, 1 tbsp (15 mL) oil and the remaining paprika.

3. Remove pan from oven and gently stir vegetables. Distribute mushrooms and tempeh in between vegetables. Roast for 10 to 15 minutes or until mushrooms are browned and squash is tender. Let cool on pan for 15 minutes.

4. Add arugula to the pan and drizzle with vinegar and the remaining oil. Gently toss to coat. Season to taste with salt and pepper. Serve warm.

# Crispy Sweet Potato Cakes with Kale and Black Bean Salad

Sweet potatoes, kale and black beans make this main-dish salad hearty and colorful. Sriracha, ginger and lime lend an exotic twist.

**Tip**

An equal amount of Asian chili-garlic sauce or 1 tsp (5 mL) hot pepper sauce (such as Tabasco) can be used in place of the Sriracha.

- Preheat oven to 450°F (230°C)
- 18- by 13-inch (45 by 33 cm) rimmed sheet pan, lined with foil and sprayed with nonstick cooking spray

| | | |
|---|---|---|
| 1 | large egg | 1 |
| 1 tsp | ground ginger | 5 mL |
| | Salt | |
| 2 tsp | Sriracha, divided | 10 mL |
| 1½ lbs | sweet potatoes (about 3 medium), peeled and grated | 750 kg |
| ¾ cup | chopped green onions | 175 mL |
| | Nonstick cooking spray | |
| 1 | bunch curly kale, tough stems removed, leaves thinly sliced (about 5 cups/1.25 L) | 1 |
| 4 tbsp | olive oil, divided | 60 mL |
| 2 | cans (each 14 to 19 oz/398 to 540 mL) black beans, drained and rinsed | 2 |
| 2 tbsp | freshly squeezed lime juice | 30 mL |

1. In a large bowl, whisk together egg, ginger, ½ tsp (2 mL) salt and 1 tsp (5 mL) Sriracha until blended. Stir in sweet potatoes and green onions until combined.

2. Using your hands, shape sweet potato mixture into 12 compact patties (about ¼ cup/60 mL each). Place patties 2 inches (5 cm) apart on prepared pan and flatten slightly with your palm or a pancake turner. Spray tops of patties with cooking spray.

3. Bake in preheated oven for 10 minutes.

4. Meanwhile, in another large bowl, toss kale with 2 tbsp (30 mL) oil and season to taste with salt.

5. Remove pan from oven and arrange kale around the patties (avoid covering the patties). Bake for 15 to 18 minutes or until patties are browned at the edges. Transfer 3 sweet potato patties to each of four dinner plates.

6. In the bowl used for the kale, toss beans with lime juice, the remaining oil and the remaining Sriracha. Season to taste with salt.

7. Spoon beans over kale, gently tossing to combine. Serve salad with sweet potato patties.

# Crispy Baked Falafel

Vegetarians and carnivores alike will munch happily on these crispy-perfect falafel. The secret to their success is using soaked dried chickpeas for an ideal texture, and cumin, red onion and fresh herbs for great flavor.

## Tips

Do not substitute canned chickpeas for the soaked dried chickpeas; the texture will be very mushy and the mixture will be too loose to shape into patties.

The patties can be prepared through step 3, but place them on a sheet pan lined with parchment paper instead of an oiled pan. Freeze until firm, then transfer patties to an airtight container or sealable freezer bag and freeze for up to 3 months. Thaw at room temperature for 2 hours, then bake as directed.

- 18- by 13-inch (45 by 33 cm) rimmed sheet pan
- Food processor

| | | |
|---|---|---|
| 1¼ cups | dried chickpeas | 300 mL |
| 4 tbsp | olive oil, divided | 60 mL |
| 4 | cloves garlic | 4 |
| ¾ cup | packed fresh flat-leaf (Italian) parsley leaves | 175 mL |
| ¾ cup | packed fresh cilantro leaves | 175 mL |
| ⅔ cup | coarsely chopped red onion | 150 mL |
| 1½ tsp | ground cumin | 7 mL |
| 1 tsp | salt | 5 mL |
| ½ tsp | freshly ground black pepper | 2 mL |

### Suggested Accompaniments

Warm pita bread

Sliced cucumber

Sliced tomatoes

Fresh spinach, arugula or lettuce leaves

Plain Greek yogurt

Crumbled feta or goat cheese

1. Pick through chickpeas and remove any stones or discolored peas. Place peas in a medium bowl and add enough water to cover by about 2 inches (5 cm). Cover bowl and let soak at room temperature overnight. Drain well.

2. Preheat oven to 375°F (190°C). Pour half the oil onto pan and, using your fingers, spread oil to cover pan.

3. In food processor, combine chickpeas, garlic, parsley, cilantro, onion, cumin, salt, pepper and the remaining oil; process until smooth. Shape into patties that are ½ inch (1 cm) thick and 2 inches (5 cm) in diameter. Place on prepared pan, spacing evenly.

4. Bake in preheated oven for 15 minutes. Open oven door and, using a spatula, carefully turn patties over. Close door and bake for 12 to 15 minutes or until falafel are browned. Serve warm with any of the suggested accompaniments, as desired.

# Spinach Feta Phyllo Rolls

The filling for these rolls — green onions, spinach, feta and eggs — will transport you to sunny Greece on the grayest of days. Using purchased phyllo dough is a great timesaver for turning humble ingredients into a notable dinner.

**Tip**

You can use an equal amount of unseasoned dry bread crumbs in place of the panko.

- Preheat oven to 400°F (200°C)
- 18- by 13-inch (45 by 33 cm) rimmed sheet pan, lined with foil or parchment paper and sprayed with nonstick cooking spray

| | | |
|---|---|---|
| 2 tbsp | olive oil | 30 mL |
| 1 | bunch green onions (about 6 to 8), chopped (both green and white parts) | 1 |
| 2 | packages (each 10 oz/300 g) frozen chopped spinach, thawed | 2 |
| 3 | large eggs, lightly beaten | 3 |
| 4 oz | feta cheese, crumbled | 125 g |
| 1 tbsp | dried dillweed | 15 mL |
| | Salt and freshly ground black pepper | |
| 20 | sheets frozen phyllo dough, thawed | 20 |
| 1/2 cup | unsalted butter, melted and cooled slightly | 125 mL |
| 1 cup | panko (Japanese bread crumbs) | 250 mL |

1. In a large skillet, heat oil over medium-high heat. Add green onions and cook, stirring, for 4 to 5 minutes or until softened. Transfer to a large bowl.

2. Meanwhile, place spinach in center of a large, clean dish towel. Twist the ends and squeeze most of the water out of the spinach. Add spinach to the bowl with the green onions. Stir in eggs, feta, dill and 1/2 tsp (2 mL) each salt and pepper until blended.

3. Loosely cover phyllo sheets with a damp kitchen towel. Unfold 1 sheet on a flat surface. Lightly brush with butter and sprinkle with panko. Repeat, stacking 9 more phyllo sheets, brushing with butter and sprinkling panko between each layer, until 10 sheets have been used.

4. Spoon half the spinach mixture in a cylinder shape along one edge of the phyllo stack. Tuck in the ends, roll up and brush with butter.

5. Repeat steps 3 and 4 with the remaining phyllo, butter, panko and filling. Place rolls about 2 inches (5 cm) apart on pan.

6. Bake in preheated oven for 12 to 17 minutes or until pastry is light golden brown. Let cool on pan for 10 minutes, then slice each roll in half crosswise and serve warm.

# Asparagus and Gruyère Puff Pastry Tart

Try this elegant French-inspired tart for a simple dinner with family or friends. Don't skip the lemon zest – it adds bright zing that accentuates the nutty flavor of the Gruyère.

## Tip

If thick asparagus spears are the only available option, cut them in half lengthwise.

## Variation

*Artichoke and Gruyère Puff Pastry Tart:* Replace the asparagus with a 14-oz (398 mL) can of artichoke hearts, drained and quartered. Sprinkle the baked tart with 1 tbsp (15 mL) minced fresh chives in addition to the Parmesan and lemon zest.

- Preheat oven to 400°F (200°C)
- 18- by 13-inch (45 by 33 cm) rimmed sheet pan, lined with parchment paper

| | | |
|---|---|---|
| 1 | large egg | 1 |
| 1 tbsp | water | 15 mL |
| 1 | sheet puff pastry (half a 17.3-oz/490 g package), thawed | 1 |
| ¾ cup | shredded Gruyère cheese | 175 mL |
| 1 lb | thin asparagus spears, trimmed | 500 g |
| 1½ tbsp | olive oil | 22 mL |
| ¼ tsp | freshly cracked black pepper | 1 mL |
| ⅛ tsp | salt | 0.5 mL |
| ¼ cup | grated Parmesan cheese | 60 mL |
| 1 tbsp | finely grated lemon zest | 15 mL |

1. In a small bowl or cup, whisk together egg and water until blended.

2. Unfold pastry sheet on prepared pan and roll out to a 9-inch (23 cm) square if necessary. Using a sharp knife, score a line ½ inch (1 cm) inside the edges of the pastry sheet on all four sides, creating an interior square (be careful not to cut all the way through). Using a fork, prick pastry sheet all over inside the scored square. Brush pastry with egg wash. Place in freezer for 5 minutes.

3. Sprinkle Gruyère inside border on pastry.

4. In a large bowl, toss asparagus with oil, pepper and salt. Arrange on top of Gruyère (it is fine if the asparagus spears overlap slightly).

5. Bake in preheated oven for 18 to 23 minutes or until crust is golden brown and puffed. Sprinkle with Parmesan and lemon zest. Cut into pieces and serve immediately.

# Pepper Jack and Black Bean Oven Quesadillas

These flavorful quesadillas come together with just a handful of ingredients, but you can customize them with as many or as few of your favorite accompaniments, as you like.

### Tips

Pinto beans or red beans can be used in place of the black beans.

Cheddar or plain Monterey Jack cheese can be used in place of the pepper Jack cheese.

- Preheat oven to 400°F (200°C)
- 18- by 13-inch (45 by 33 cm) rimmed sheet pan, lined with parchment paper or foil

| | | |
|---|---|---:|
| 4 | 8-inch (20 cm) flour tortillas | 4 |
| 1½ tbsp | vegetable oil, divided | 22 mL |
| 2 cups | shredded pepper Jack cheese | 500 mL |
| 1 | can (14 to 19 oz/398 to 540 mL) black beans, drained and rinsed | 1 |
| 1 cup | drained roasted red peppers, chopped | 250 mL |
| 2 tbsp | chopped fresh cilantro | 30 mL |

**Suggested Accompaniments**

Sour cream or plain Greek yogurt

Prepared salsa

Guacamole

1. Brush one side of 2 tortillas with half the oil. Place tortillas, oiled side down, on prepared pan. Layer with half the cheese, then beans, roasted peppers, cilantro and the remaining cheese. Top with the remaining 2 tortillas. Brush with the remaining oil and lightly press to seal.

2. Bake in preheated oven for 9 to 12 minutes, turning once, until cheese has melted and tortillas are golden brown. Transfer to a cutting board and cut into quarters. Serve with any of the suggested accompaniments, as desired.

# Freestyle Eggplant Parmesan Melts

Typically a time-intensive dish, eggplant parmesan becomes a weeknight favorite with this "freestyle" variation. Another boon: cleanup happens to be a breeze.

## Tips

Opt for a marinara sauce with a short list of ingredients that is free of preservatives, artificial flavors and added sweeteners.

Do not worry about spreading the ricotta on the eggplant slices; it will melt and spread as it bakes.

- Preheat oven to 400°F (200°C)
- 18- by 13-inch (45 by 33 cm) rimmed sheet pan, sprayed with nonstick cooking spray

| | | |
|---|---|---|
| 1 | large eggplant (about 2 lbs/1 kg), trimmed and cut crosswise into $\frac{1}{2}$-inch (1 cm) thick slices | 1 |
| 3 tbsp | olive oil | 45 mL |
| | Salt and freshly cracked black pepper | |
| 1 cup | ricotta cheese | 250 mL |
| 2 tbsp | grated Parmesan cheese | 30 mL |
| 1 cup | marinara sauce | 250 mL |
| 1 cup | shredded mozzarella cheese | 250 mL |
| | Torn fresh basil leaves (optional) | |

1. Lightly brush both sides of eggplant slices with oil. Place on prepared pan, spacing evenly, and season with salt and pepper. Roast in preheated oven for 25 to 30 minutes or until softened.

2. Meanwhile, in a small bowl, stir together ricotta and Parmesan.

3. Remove pan from oven and spread marinara sauce evenly over eggplant slices. Top each slice with a dollop of ricotta mixture and sprinkle with mozzarella. Bake for 5 to 10 minutes or until cheese is melted. Top with basil, if desired.

# Potato, Goat Cheese and Arugula Pizza

The addictive competing elements of crispy potatoes, creamy goat cheese and plucky, peppery arugula guarantee a pizza worth savoring.

## Variation

*Cherry Tomato and Basil Pizza:* In place of the goat cheese, spread the pizza crust with 1 cup (250 mL) ricotta cheese. Replace the potatoes with 1 cup (250 mL) cherry tomatoes, and omit the thyme. Omit the arugula and remaining oil. Scatter with 1/2 cup (125 mL) grated Parmesan cheese and 1/2 cup (125 mL) torn basil leaves.

- Preheat oven to 450°F (230°C)
- 18- by 13-inch (45 by 33 cm) rimmed sheet pan, lined with foil and sprayed with nonstick cooking spray

| | All-purpose flour | |
|---|---|---|
| 1 lb | thawed frozen or refrigerated pizza dough | 500 g |
| 1 tbsp | yellow cornmeal | 15 mL |
| 4 oz | soft goat cheese, crumbled | 125 g |
| 2 | red-skinned potatoes, thinly sliced | 2 |
| 1 | small red onion, thinly sliced | 1 |
| 3 tbsp | olive oil, divided | 45 mL |
| 1 tsp | salt, divided | 5 mL |
| 3/4 tsp | freshly cracked black pepper, divided | 3 mL |
| 1/2 tsp | dried thyme | 2 mL |
| 4 cups | baby arugula or tender watercress sprigs | 1 L |

1. On a lightly floured surface, press and stretch dough into a 1/4-inch (0.5 cm) thick circle or rectangle.

2. Sprinkle prepared pan with cornmeal. Place dough on top and sprinkle with goat cheese.

3. In a large bowl, toss together potatoes, onion, 2 tbsp (30 mL) oil, 3/4 tsp (3 mL) salt, 1/2 tsp (2 mL) pepper and thyme. Arrange evenly over crust.

4. Bake in preheated oven for 20 to 25 minutes or until crust is golden and potatoes are tender.

5. Meanwhile, in the same large bowl, toss arugula with the remaining oil, salt and pepper.

6. Arrange arugula on top of pizza. Cut pizza into pieces and serve immediately.

# Spaghetti Squash with Roasted Tomatoes and Ricotta

*9/6/16* ✗

### Makes 4 servings

Golden squash "noodles" are the perfect foil for the simple (but winning) toppings of roasted tomatoes, ricotta cheese and Parmesan.

### Variation

Replace the tomatoes with an equal amount of button mushrooms (halved if large).

*Also added ½ large orange pepper + 3 cheddar sausages.*

- Preheat oven to 450°F (230°C)
- 18- by 13-inch (45 by 33 cm) rimmed sheet pan, lined with foil

| 2 | spaghetti squash (each about 1½ lbs/750 g) | 2 |
| 3 cups | cherry or grape tomatoes | 750 mL |
| 3 tbsp | olive oil, divided | 45 mL |
| | Salt and freshly cracked black pepper | |
| 1 cup | grated Parmesan cheese, divided | 250 mL |
| ½ cup | packed fresh flat-leaf (Italian) parsley leaves, chopped | 125 mL |
| ¾ cup | ricotta cheese | 175 mL |

1. Cut each squash in half lengthwise and remove seeds. Place squash, cut side down, on prepared pan, spacing evenly. Roast in preheated oven for 35 minutes.

2. Meanwhile, in a large bowl, toss tomatoes with 1 tbsp (15 mL) oil, ¼ tsp (1 mL) salt and ⅛ tsp (0.5 mL) pepper.

3. Open oven door and scatter tomatoes around squash. Close door and roast for 7 to 10 minutes or until tomatoes are bursting and a knife is easily inserted into squash.

4. Using a fork, rake squash into strands. Place strands in the bowl used for the tomatoes. Scrape tomatoes and any accumulated juices into bowl. Add half the Parmesan, parsley and the remaining oil, gently tossing to coat. Season to taste with salt and pepper.

5. Divide squash mixture among serving bowls. Serve with dollops of ricotta and sprinkle with the remaining Parmesan.

# Sheet Pan Ratatouille with Eggs

Oven-baked eggs turn this simplified Southern France favorite into a hearty entrée that's equally fitting for a fast weekday dinner or a casual weekend brunch.

**Tip**

Other squash, such as crookneck or pattypan, can be used in place of the zucchini; you'll need about 2 cups (500 mL) cubes.

- Preheat oven to 400°F (200°C)
- 18- by 13-inch (45 by 33 cm) rimmed sheet pan, lined with foil and sprayed with nonstick cooking spray

| | | |
|---|---|---|
| 2 | zucchini, cut into 1-inch (2.5 cm) cubes | 2 |
| 1 | eggplant (about 1½ lbs/750 g), trimmed and cut into 1-inch (2.5 cm) cubes | 1 |
| 1 | large red bell pepper, cut into 1-inch (2.5 cm) pieces | 1 |
| 1 | red onion, cut into 1-inch (2.5 cm) pieces | 1 |
| 3 tbsp | olive oil | 45 mL |
| 2 tsp | dried herbes de Provence or Italian seasoning | 10 mL |
| | Salt and freshly cracked black pepper | |
| 4 | cloves garlic, minced | 4 |
| 1 | can (14 to 15 oz/398 to 425 mL) diced tomatoes, with juice | 1 |
| 4 | large eggs | 4 |
| ¾ cup | packed fresh basil leaves, torn | 175 mL |

1. On prepared pan, toss together zucchini, eggplant, red pepper, onion, oil, herbes de Provence, ½ tsp (2 mL) salt and ¼ tsp (1 mL) pepper. Spread in a single layer. Roast in preheated oven for 40 minutes, stirring once.

2. Remove pan from oven and stir in garlic and tomatoes. Roast for 15 to 20 minutes or until vegetables are tender.

3. Remove pan from oven and make 4 holes for the eggs in the ratatouille. Crack an egg into each hole and season with salt and pepper. Bake for 2 to 5 minutes or until eggs are set as desired. Serve sprinkled with basil.

# Sheet Pan Stir-Fry with Napa Cabbage, Mushrooms and Cashews

No need to order Chinese takeout; this simplified oven-roasted "stir-fry" is ready in well under an hour – and far tastier, too!

## Tips

Black bean–garlic sauce is a savory condiment made from fermented black soybeans, garlic and rice wine. It is available in the Asian foods section of well-stocked supermarkets alongside soy sauce, or at Asian grocery stores.

Lightly salted roasted peanuts, coarsely chopped, can be used in place of the cashews.

- Preheat oven to 425°F (220°C)
- 18- by 13-inch (45 by 33 cm) rimmed sheet pan, sprayed with nonstick cooking spray

| | | |
|---|---|---|
| 1 | large red bell pepper, cut into 1/4-inch (0.5 cm) strips | 1 |
| 4 tbsp | black bean–garlic sauce, divided | 60 mL |
| 2 tbsp | vegetable oil, divided | 30 mL |
| 1 | head napa cabbage, cored and coarsely chopped | 1 |
| 1 | bunch green onions (about 6 to 8), cut into 1-inch (2.5 cm) pieces | 1 |
| 12 oz | button or cremini mushrooms, trimmed and halved | 375 g |
| 1 tbsp | dry sherry | 15 mL |
| 2 tsp | Sriracha | 10 mL |
| 3/4 cup | lightly salted roasted cashews, coarsely chopped | 175 mL |

1. On prepared pan, toss red pepper with 1 tbsp (45 mL) black bean sauce and half the oil. Spread in a single layer. Roast in preheated oven for 10 minutes.

2. Meanwhile, in a large bowl, toss together cabbage, green onions, mushrooms, sherry, Sriracha, the remaining black bean sauce and the remaining oil.

3. Remove pan from oven and stir red pepper. Add cabbage mixture, stirring to combine; spread out evenly on pan. Roast for 10 minutes.

4. Open oven door and stir gently. Close door and roast for 10 to 15 minutes or until vegetables are wilted and tender. Serve sprinkled with cashews.

# Portobellos Stuffed with Artichokes and Goat Cheese

Tender artichoke hearts and a crispy panko topping enliven this simple dish, while the goat cheese adds creamy goodness.

## Tips

You can use 8 medium portobello mushrooms in place of extra-large.

If you can't find herbed goat cheese, use plain goat cheese and add 1½ tsp (7 mL) dried herbes de Provence or Italian seasoning.

- Preheat oven to 500°F (260°C)
- 18- by 13-inch (45 by 33 cm) rimmed sheet pan, lined with foil and sprayed with nonstick cooking spray

| | | |
|---|---|---|
| 4 | extra-large portobello mushrooms | 4 |
| 3 tbsp | olive oil, divided | 45 mL |
| | Salt and freshly cracked black pepper | |
| 4 oz | herbed soft goat cheese, crumbled | 125 g |
| 1 | can (15 oz/425 mL) artichoke hearts, drained and chopped | 1 |
| ¾ cup | panko (Japanese bread crumbs) | 175 mL |

1. Remove stems from mushrooms. Chop stems and set aside. Using a spoon, gently scoop out black gills on underside of mushroom caps. Discard gills.

2. Place mushroom caps, hollow side down, on prepared pan, spacing evenly. Brush 2 tbsp (30 mL) oil over tops of mushrooms. Season with salt and pepper. Bake in preheated oven for 5 to 8 minutes or until tender.

3. Meanwhile, in a medium bowl, combine mushroom stems, goat cheese and artichokes.

4. In a small bowl, combine panko and the remaining oil.

5. Remove pan from oven. Turn mushrooms over and fill caps with cheese mixture. Divide panko mixture evenly among mushrooms. Bake for 7 to 10 minutes or until filling is melted and bread crumbs are golden brown.

# Poblano Peppers with Cheesy Rice and Bean Stuffing

Canned red beans, cooked brown rice and shredded pepper Jack (or any other shredded cheese you choose) make a hearty Tex-Mex meal.

## Tips

If packaged frozen rice is not available, substitute 2 cups (500 mL) cooled cooked brown or white rice.

Red beans are smaller and slightly softer than kidney beans. If they are not available, use black beans, pinto beans or light red kidney beans in their place.

- Preheat broiler, with rack set 4 to 6 inches (10 to 15 cm) from the heat source
- 18- by 13-inch (45 by 33 cm) rimmed sheet pan, lined with foil and sprayed with nonstick cooking spray

| | | |
|---|---|---|
| 8 | poblano peppers | 8 |
| 1 | can (14 to 19 oz/398 to 540 mL) red beans, drained and rinsed | 1 |
| 1 | package (12 oz/375 g) frozen brown or white rice, thawed | 1 |
| 1 cup | frozen corn kernels, thawed | 250 mL |
| 1/2 cup | chopped green onions | 125 mL |
| 1 tbsp | chili powder | 15 mL |
| 2 cups | shredded pepper Jack cheese, divided | 500 mL |
| | Salt and freshly cracked black pepper | |
| 1 | large egg, lightly beaten | 1 |

**Suggested Accompaniments**

Sour cream or plain Greek yogurt
Chopped fresh cilantro
Salsa

1. Place peppers on prepared pan, spacing evenly. Broil for 8 to 10 minutes or until skins blister and blacken in spots. Remove pan from oven and lift foil lining up and around peppers, completely enclosing peppers. Let stand for 10 minutes or until cool enough to handle. While warm, lift and peel off pepper skins (use a knife tip, if necessary).

2. Preheat oven to 375°F (190°C). Reline the same sheet pan with parchment paper or foil.

3. In a medium bowl, coarsely mash half the beans with a fork. Stir in the remaining beans, rice, corn, green onions, chili powder and half the cheese. Season to taste with salt and pepper. Stir in egg until combined.

4. Using a sharp knife, slit the roasted peppers lengthwise. Fill with stuffing. Place on prepared pan and sprinkle stuffing with the remaining cheese.

5. Bake in preheated oven for 15 to 20 minutes or until stuffing is heated through and cheese is melted. Serve with any of the suggested accompaniments, as desired.

# Sweet Potatoes Stuffed with Sun-Dried Tomatoes, Olives and Feta

The combination of oil-packed sun-dried tomatoes, tangy black olives and piquant feta cheese is a sensational stuffing for roasted sweet potatoes. Flat-leaf parsley contributes a fresh punch.

## Tips

For added flavor and frugality, use some of the oil from the jar of sun-dried tomatoes in place of the olive oil.

Crumbled goat cheese or blue cheese can be used in place of the feta cheese.

- Preheat oven to 425°F (220°C)
- 18- by 13-inch (45 by 33 cm) rimmed sheet pan, lined with foil

| | | |
|---|---|---|
| 4 | sweet potatoes (each about 12 oz/375 g) | 4 |
| ½ cup | drained oil-packed sun-dried tomatoes, thinly sliced | 125 mL |
| ⅓ cup | pitted oil- or brine-cured black olives, drained and coarsely chopped | 75 mL |
| ⅓ cup | packed fresh flat-leaf (Italian) parsley leaves, chopped | 75 mL |
| 1½ tbsp | olive oil | 22 mL |
| ½ tsp | dried oregano | 2 mL |
| | Salt and freshly cracked black pepper | |
| 1 cup | crumbled feta cheese | 250 mL |

1. Prick sweet potatoes all over with a fork and place on prepared pan, spacing evenly. Roast in preheated oven for about 1 hour or until tender.

2. Meanwhile, in a small bowl, combine sun-dried tomatoes, olives, parsley, oil and oregano. Season to taste with salt and pepper.

3. Transfer sweet potatoes to dinner plates and let cool for 5 minutes. Slit each lengthwise, press to open and spoon tomato mixture into the center. Top each with feta.

# Persian Rice–Stuffed Butternut Squash

**Makes 4 servings**

Dried cherries, pistachios and ready-cooked rice make an easy, flavorful stuffing. Roasted butternut squash is the perfect cooking vessel, with extra-easy cleanup!

## Tips

If packaged frozen rice is not available, substitute 2 cups (500 mL) cooled cooked brown rice.

Other dried fruits, such as cranberries, raisins or chopped apricots, can be used in place of the cherries.

- Preheat oven to 400°F (200°C)
- 18- by 13-inch (45 by 33 cm) rimmed sheet pan, lined with foil or parchment paper

| | | |
|---|---|---|
| 2 | butternut squash, halved lengthwise | 2 |
| 4 tbsp | olive oil, divided | 60 mL |
| | Salt and freshly ground black pepper | |
| 1 | red bell pepper, chopped | 1 |
| 1 | package (12 oz/375 g) frozen brown rice, thawed | 1 |
| ¾ cup | roasted pistachios or almonds, coarsely chopped | 175 mL |
| ½ cup | finely chopped green onions | 125 mL |
| ⅓ cup | chopped dried cherries | 75 mL |
| 1 tsp | ground cinnamon | 5 mL |
| ¾ tsp | ground cumin | 3 mL |

1. Using a metal spoon, scrape out seeds and membranes from squash halves. Using a sharp knife, score the flesh. Place squash, cut side up, on prepared pan, spacing evenly. Brush cut sides with 2 tbsp (30 mL) oil and season with salt and pepper. Roast in preheated oven for 35 minutes.

2. Remove pan from oven and add red pepper alongside squash. Drizzle pepper with 1 tbsp (15 mL) oil. Roast for 10 minutes.

3. Meanwhile, in a medium bowl, combine rice, pistachios, green onions, cherries, cinnamon, cumin and the remaining oil. Season to taste with salt and pepper.

4. Remove pan from oven and spoon rice mixture into squash cavities. Roast for 15 to 18 minutes or until squash is fork-tender and stuffing is warmed through.

# Butternut Squash Oven Risotto

You can make this streamlined oven risotto with fully cooked frozen rice or leftover cooked rice. Either way, you will have a wonderfully flavorful, wholesome and warming meal with very little effort.

## Tips

Look for bags of ready-to-use cubed butternut squash in the produce section of the supermarket.

If packaged frozen rice is not available, substitute 4 cups (1 L) cooled cooked brown or white rice.

- Preheat oven to 400°F (200°C)
- 18- by 13-inch (45 by 33 cm) rimmed sheet pan, oiled with olive oil

| | | |
|---|---|---|
| 4 cups | cubed butternut squash ($1/2$-inch/1 cm cubes) | 1 L |
| 2 tbsp | extra virgin olive oil | 30 mL |
| 2 | packages (each 12 oz/375 g) frozen brown or white rice, thawed | 2 |
| 8 oz | chive- or garlic-and-herb-flavored cream cheese | 250 g |
| $2/3$ cup | boiling water | 150 mL |
| 1 cup | grated Parmesan cheese, divided | 250 mL |
| | Salt and freshly cracked black pepper | |

**Suggested Toppings**

Chopped fresh parsley

Chopped toasted walnuts or pecans

Chopped dried cranberries

1. On prepared pan, toss squash with oil. Spread out in a single layer. Roast in preheated oven for 20 to 25 minutes, stirring once or twice, until golden brown and tender.

2. Remove pan from oven and scatter rice evenly over and around squash. Dollop with cream cheese. Pour boiling water over top and gently stir to combine. Bake for 10 to 15 minutes or until rice is hot.

3. Sprinkle risotto with half the Parmesan, gently stirring to combine. Season to taste with salt and pepper. Serve topped with the remaining Parmesan and any of the suggested toppings, as desired.

# Vegetable Paella

The traditional Spanish rice dish varies throughout the country, but it almost always gets its distinctive flavor from saffron. Nestle tomatoes, artichokes, peas and roasted peppers into the seasoned rice for an intensely satisfying vegetarian meal.

**Tip**

If you do not have a second sheet pan, cover the pan (in step 2) with a large sheet of foil, tightly sealing the edges.

- Preheat oven to 350°F (180°C)
- 2 large rimmed sheet pans (see tip, at left)

| | | |
|---|---|---|
| 2⅔ cups | boiling water | 650 mL |
| 1 | bay leaf | 1 |
| 1½ tsp | smoked paprika (pimentón) | 7 mL |
| ⅛ tsp | saffron threads | 0.5 mL |
| | Salt and freshly cracked black pepper | |
| 1½ cups | short-grain white rice | 375 mL |
| 1 cup | chopped onion | 250 mL |
| 3 | cloves garlic, minced | 3 |
| 1 | can (15 oz/425 mL) diced tomatoes, drained | 1 |
| 1 | can (15 oz/425 mL) artichoke hearts, drained and cut in half lengthwise | 1 |
| 1 cup | frozen peas | 250 mL |
| 1 cup | drained roasted red peppers, coarsely chopped | 250 mL |
| 2 tbsp | olive oil | 30 mL |
| ½ cup | packed fresh flat-leaf (Italian) parsley leaves, chopped | 125 mL |

**Suggested Accompaniments**

Quartered pitted green olives or brine-cured olives

Lemon wedges

Prepared mayonnaise, thinned with olive oil (for drizzling)

1. In a 4-cup (1 L) measuring cup, combine boiling water, bay leaf, paprika, saffron, 1 tsp (5 mL) salt and ¼ tsp (1 mL) pepper.

2. Spread rice, onion and garlic in a single layer on one of the pans. Place pan on oven rack. With oven door open, carefully pour water mixture over rice, stirring to combine. Cover with inverted sheet pan.

3. Bake in preheated oven for 20 minutes. Remove pan from oven and carefully remove top pan (hot steam will release). Stir rice mixture and top with tomatoes, artichokes, peas and roasted peppers. Drizzle with oil and gently stir to combine.

4. Bake, uncovered, for 10 minutes or until warmed through and rice is tender. Gently stir to combine and season to taste with salt and pepper. Sprinkle with parsley and serve with any of the suggested accompaniments, as desired.

# Moroccan Vegetable Couscous

**Makes 4 servings**

This vegetable-based, oven-cooked version of a North African tagine gets a boost from fresh mint, raisins and lemon. Cumin and cinnamon evoke an exotic warmth.

## Tips

If you do not have a second sheet pan, cover the pan (in step 3) with a large sheet of foil, tightly sealing the edges.

Other colors of bell pepper, such as orange or yellow, can be used in place of the red pepper.

- Preheat oven to 450°F (230°C)
- 2 large rimmed sheet pans (see tip, at left)

| | | |
|---|---|---|
| 1 lb | carrots, peeled and cut into ¾-inch (2 cm) thick slices | 500 g |
| 4 cups | small cauliflower florets (about 1 medium head) | 1 L |
| 3 tbsp | olive oil | 45 mL |
| 1 tbsp | ground cumin | 15 mL |
| 2 tsp | ground cinnamon | 10 mL |
| | Salt and freshly ground black pepper | |
| 1 | large red bell pepper, cut into 1-inch (2.5 cm) pieces | 1 |
| 1 | can (14 to 19 oz/398 to 540 mL) chickpeas, drained and rinsed | 1 |
| 1⅓ cups | couscous | 325 mL |
| ½ cup | raisins | 125 mL |
| 1½ cups | boiling water | 375 mL |
| 1 cup | chopped green onions | 250 mL |
| 1 cup | packed fresh mint leaves, chopped (optional) | 250 mL |
| 1 tbsp | finely grated lemon zest | 15 mL |
| 2 tbsp | freshly squeezed lemon juice | 30 mL |

1. On one pan, toss together carrots, cauliflower, oil, cumin, cinnamon, ¾ tsp (3 mL) salt and ½ tsp (2 mL) pepper. Spread in a single layer. Roast in preheated oven for 15 minutes.

2. Open oven door, add red pepper to pan and stir vegetables. Close door and roast for 10 to 15 minutes or until vegetables are tender.

3. Remove pan from oven and sprinkle chickpeas, couscous and raisins over vegetables. Carefully pour boiling water over top. Cover with inverted sheet pan and let stand for 5 minutes.

4. Remove top pan and add green onions, mint (if using), lemon zest and lemon juice, fluffing with a fork to separate couscous. Season to taste with salt and pepper.

# Roasted Broccoli Rabe with Gorgonzola Polenta

Prepared polenta topped with creamy gorgonzola and partnered with broccoli rabe, garlic and a splash of olive oil creates a sophisticated yet weekday-friendly meal with only one pan to clean!

**Tip**

Other varieties of soft, creamy blue cheese, or soft goat cheese, can be used in place of the gorgonzola.

- Preheat oven to 425°F (220°C)
- 18- by 13-inch (45 by 33 cm) rimmed sheet pan, lined with foil and sprayed with nonstick cooking spray

| | | |
|---|---|---|
| 1 lb | broccoli rabe, tough, fibrous stems removed (keep tender stems) | 500 g |
| 2 | cloves garlic, minced | 2 |
| 3 tbsp | olive oil, divided | 45 mL |
| 1/4 tsp | salt | 1 mL |
| 1/8 tsp | hot pepper flakes | 0.5 mL |
| 1 | roll (17 oz/482 g) prepared plain polenta | 1 |
| 3 oz | gorgonzola cheese, crumbled | 90 g |

1. On prepared pan, toss together broccoli rabe, garlic, 2 tbsp (30 mL) oil, salt and hot pepper flakes. Spread in a single layer.

2. Cut polenta crosswise into 1/2-inch (1 cm) slices. Arrange on pan between broccoli rabe. Brush polenta with the remaining oil and sprinkle with cheese.

3. Roast in preheated oven for 10 to 12 minutes or until broccoli rabe stems are tender, leaves are crisp and cheese is melted.

Spicy Pinto Bean Burgers (page 99)

Halibut with Greek Stuffed
Roasted Tomatoes (page 112)

Roasted Salmon and Root Vegetables
with Horseradish Sauce (page 116)

Sheet Pan Clam Bake
(page 126)

Weeknight Chicken and Stuffing (page 138)

Roast Chicken Quarters with
Lemon-Dill Spring Vegetables (page 139)

Punjabi Chicken with Cauliflower,
Potatoes and Peas (page 152)

Thai Chicken Tenders with
Broiled Pineapple Slaw (page 168)

# Crispy Parmesan Cauliflower Steaks

Move over, meat: thick slices of cauliflower breaded with a crispy Parmesan coating make swoon-worthy "steaks." Create a quick meal by pairing them with your favorite Italian sauce and a crisp green salad alongside.

**Tip**

Although panko is the ideal choice for this recipe, an equal amount of dry or fresh bread crumbs can be used in its place.

- Preheat oven to 400°F (200°C)
- 18- by 13-inch (45 by 33 cm) rimmed sheet pan, lined with parchment paper or foil and sprayed with nonstick cooking spray

| | | |
|---|---|---|
| 1 | large head cauliflower, leaves trimmed off, core intact | 1 |
| 2 | large eggs | 2 |
| ¼ tsp | salt | 1 mL |
| ⅛ tsp | freshly cracked black pepper | 0.5 mL |
| ⅓ cup | all-purpose flour | 75 mL |
| ¾ cup | grated Parmesan cheese | 175 mL |
| ¾ cup | panko (Japanese bread crumbs) | 175 mL |
| | Olive oil mister or nonstick cooking spray | |

**Suggested Accompaniments**

> Chopped fresh parsley or chives
> Warmed marinara sauce
> Pesto
> Olive or sun-dried tomato tapenade

1. Position cauliflower on cutting board with core side down. Using a large knife, cut four to six ½-inch (1 cm) thick slices (depending on size of cauliflower). Reserve the remaining cauliflower for another use.

2. In a large, shallow dish, whisk together eggs, salt and pepper. Spread flour on one large plate. On another large plate, combine Parmesan and panko; spread out over plate.

3. Dredge a cauliflower steak in flour; shake off excess. Dip in egg mixture, then press into panko mixture, using your hands to help fully coat the steak. Place on prepared pan. Repeat with the remaining steaks, flour, egg and panko mixture, spacing steaks evenly on pan. Mist steaks generously with oil.

4. Roast in preheated oven for 15 minutes. Remove pan from oven and, using a spatula, carefully turn steaks over. Mist generously with oil. Roast for 15 to 20 minutes or until steaks are golden brown and fork-tender. Serve with any of the suggested accompaniments, as desired.

# Broiled Eggplant Steaks with Yogurt, Pistachios and Pomegranate

Velvety eggplant steaks take a Mediterranean turn with bold flavors – Greek yogurt, garlic, pomegranate and mint – in a stunning dish ready in under 30 minutes.

### Tips

To mash garlic, working with one clove at a time, place the side of a chef's knife flat against the clove. Place the heel of your hand on the side of the knife and apply pressure so that the clove flattens slightly (this will loosen the peel). Remove and discard the peel, then roughly chop the garlic. Sprinkle a pinch of salt over the garlic. Use the flat part of the knife as before to press the garlic against the cutting board. Repeat until the garlic turns into a fine paste. The mashed garlic is now ready for use in your favorite recipe.

If pomegranates are unavailable, use $1/3$ cup (75 mL) chopped dried cherries or dried cranberries.

- Preheat broiler, with rack set 4 to 6 inches (10 to 15 cm) from the heat source
- 18- by 13-inch (45 by 33 cm) rimmed sheet pan, lined with foil and sprayed with nonstick cooking spray

| | | |
|---|---|---:|
| 2 | eggplants (each about 1 lb/500 g), cut crosswise into $3/4$-inch (2 cm) slices | 2 |
| | Olive oil | |
| $3/4$ tsp | salt, divided | 3 mL |
| 2 | cloves garlic, mashed (see tip, at left) | 2 |
| 1 cup | plain Greek yogurt | 250 mL |
| $1/2$ cup | chopped salted roasted pistachios | 125 mL |
| $1/2$ cup | pomegranate seeds | 125 mL |
| $1/4$ cup | packed fresh mint leaves, chopped | 60 mL |

1. Place eggplants on prepared pan and generously brush with oil. Season with $1/2$ tsp (2 mL) salt. Broil for 15 to 20 minutes, turning once, until very soft.

2. Meanwhile, in a small bowl, combine garlic, the remaining salt and yogurt.

3. Serve eggplant topped with garlic yogurt and sprinkled with pistachios, pomegranate seeds and mint.

# Spicy Pinto Bean Burgers

## Makes 4 burgers

Crushed tortilla chips add flavor and texture to these meaty south-of-the-border pinto bean burgers. Showcase an array of toppings before adding the top bun, for a crave-worthy burger by any measure.

## Tips

Shaping the bean mixture into patties will be easier if your hands are moistened.

If you can only find 19-oz (540 mL) cans of beans, you will need about 1½ cans (3 cups/750 mL drained).

## Variation

For vegan burgers, use 3 tbsp (45 mL) vegan mayonnaise alternative in place of the egg.

- Preheat oven to 400°F (200°C)
- Food processor
- 18- by 13-inch (45 by 33 cm) rimmed sheet pan, lined with parchment paper

| | | |
|---|---|---|
| 1½ cups | coarsely crushed tortilla chips | 375 mL |
| 2 | cans (each 14 to 15 oz/398 to 425 mL) pinto beans, drained and rinsed, divided | 2 |
| 1 | large egg | 1 |
| ½ cup | medium or hot salsa | 125 mL |
| 2 tsp | ground cumin | 10 mL |
| | Olive oil mister or nonstick cooking spray | |
| 4 | whole wheat hamburger buns, split | 4 |

**Suggested Accompaniments**

Sliced avocado or guacamole

Plain Greek yogurt or sour cream

Salsa

Sliced tomatoes

Spinach leaves

1. In food processor, pulse tortilla chips into crumbs. Add half the beans, egg, salsa and cumin; pulse until a chunky purée forms.

2. Transfer purée to a medium bowl and stir in the remaining beans. Form into four ³⁄₄-inch (2 cm) thick patties. Place patties on prepared pan, spacing evenly, and mist generously with oil.

3. Bake in preheated oven for 4 minutes. Open oven door and, using a spatula, turn burgers over. Mist with oil. Position buns, cut side up, around edges of pan. Close door and bake for 4 to 5 minutes or until buns are toasted and patties are crispy on the outside and hot in the center.

4. Transfer patties to toasted buns. Top with any of the suggested accompaniments, as desired.

# Crispy Baked Tofu

Baked tofu requires hours of draining and pressing to remove as much excess liquid as possible before baking. That is, unless you use my microwave method: a mere 2 minutes on High draws out an equivalent amount of liquid. Perfect for procrastinators!

## Tips

It is imperative to use tofu labeled "extra-firm." Anything less than extra-firm (including tofu labeled "firm") contains too much water and will explode in the microwave.

If you prefer, you can drain tofu the traditional way. Wrap the block of tofu in four or five layers of paper towels. Place on a dinner plate. Cover with a second dinner plate. Place two or three heavy cans on top. Let drain for 30 minutes. Remove cans, plates and paper towels. Repeat process once more. Cut tofu into 1-inch (2.5 cm) cubes.

The tofu can be tossed with a small amount of almost any herb or spice after it is tossed with the oil and before baking.

## Storage Tip

Store cooled tofu cubes in an airtight container in the refrigerator for up to 5 days.

- Preheat oven to 400°F (200°C)
- 18- by 13-inch (45 by 33 cm) rimmed sheet pan, lined with parchment paper

| | | |
|---|---|---|
| 1 lb | extra-firm tofu, packing water poured off | 500 g |
| 1 tbsp | vegetable or olive oil | 15 mL |

1. Cut tofu into 1-inch (2.5 cm) cubes and place in a single layer on a plate. Microwave on High for 2 minutes. Stir tofu gently. Microwave on High for 1 to 2 minutes or until surface of tofu appears dry.

2. On prepared pan, gently toss tofu with oil. Spread in a single layer. Bake in preheated oven for 20 minutes.

3. Remove pan from oven and, using a spatula, turn cubes over. Bake for 18 to 22 minutes or until tofu is golden brown and crispy.

## Variation

*Baked Tofu and Broccoli with Thai Peanut Sauce:* In a large bowl, toss 4 cups (1 L) small broccoli florets (about 1 small head) and 1 cup (250 mL) baby carrots with 1 1/2 tbsp (22 mL) vegetable oil. After turning the tofu cubes in step 3, add broccoli and carrots around tofu. Continue roasting as directed. Serve drizzle with prepared Thai peanut sauce.

# Miso Roasted Vegetables and Tempeh

Zucchini, eggplant and bell pepper amp up the flavor in this Asian-inspired one-pan meal. Miso, lime juice and fresh basil add depth. Feel free to substitute extra-firm tofu for the tempeh.

## Tips

If Japanese eggplants are unavailable, substitute 1 regular (globe) eggplant (about 1 lb/500 g), cut into 1-inch (2.5 cm) cubes.

A 1-lb (500 g) package of extra-firm tofu, packing water poured off and tofu cut into 1-inch (2.5 cm) cubes, can be used in place of the tempeh.

- Preheat oven to 450°F (230°C)
- 18- by 13-inch (45 by 33 cm) rimmed sheet pan, lined with foil and sprayed with nonstick cooking spray

| | | |
|---|---|---|
| 3 tbsp | olive oil | 45 mL |
| 2 tbsp | yellow miso paste | 30 mL |
| 1 1/2 tbsp | freshly squeezed lime juice | 22 mL |
| 3 | zucchini, halved lengthwise, then cut into 1/2-inch (1 cm) thick half-circles | 3 |
| 2 | Japanese eggplants, halved lengthwise, then cut into 1/2-inch (1 cm) thick half-circles | 2 |
| 1 | orange or red bell pepper, cut into 6 pieces | 1 |
| 1 | small red onion, cut into 8 wedges | 1 |
| | Salt and freshly cracked black pepper | |
| 8 oz | tempeh, cut crosswise into 12 strips | 250 g |
| 2 tbsp | chopped fresh basil, mint or cilantro | 30 mL |
| | Lime wedges | |

1. In a large bowl, whisk together oil, miso and lime juice until blended. Reserve 1 1/2 tbsp (22 mL) dressing. Add zucchini, eggplants, bell pepper and onion to dressing remaining in bowl, gently tossing to combine.

2. Spread vegetables in a single layer on prepared pan. Season with salt and pepper. Roast in preheated oven for 12 minutes.

3. Meanwhile, in the same large bowl, gently toss tempeh with the reserved dressing.

4. Remove pan from oven and nestle tempeh in between vegetables. Roast for 5 to 8 minutes or until vegetables are tender and tempeh is browned. Sprinkle with basil and serve with lime wedges.

# Hoisin Tempeh with Roasted Baby Bok Choy

Tempeh and baby bok choy, both coated in savory-sweet hoisin sauce, emerge deliciously caramelized after just 10 minutes in an extra-hot oven.

## Tips

If baby bok choy are unavailable, substitute one regular bunch of bok choy, trimmed, cut crosswise into 2-inch (5 cm) lengths, and separated.

One 1-lb (500 g) package of extra-firm tofu, packing water poured off and tofu cut into 1-inch (2.5 cm) cubes, can be used in place of the tempeh.

- Preheat oven to 450°F (230°C)
- 18- by 13-inch (45 by 33 cm) rimmed sheet pan, lined with foil

| | | |
|---|---|---|
| ⅓ cup | hoisin sauce | 75 mL |
| 3 tbsp | vegetable oil, divided | 45 mL |
| 1 lb | tempeh, cut crosswise into 24 strips | 500 g |
| 4 | heads baby bok choy (about 1¼ lbs/625 g), trimmed and leaves separated | 4 |
| | Salt and freshly ground black pepper | |

1. In a medium bowl, whisk together hoisin sauce and half the oil. Add tempeh, gently tossing to coat. Arrange tempeh in a single layer on prepared pan.

2. In a large bowl, toss bok choy with the remaining oil. Season with salt and pepper. Arrange on pan, covering tempeh slightly.

3. Roast in preheated oven for 7 to 10 minutes or until bok choy is wilted and tender-crisp.

# Fish and Seafood Meals

# Oven Fish and Chips

Panko – light and crisp bread crumbs – as well as an oven-safe wire rack are the secrets to creating perfectly crispy oven-roasted fish. Soaking the potatoes in hot water before roasting removes some of their starch, ensuring extra-crisp fries without deep-frying.

- Preheat oven to 450°F (230°C)
- 18- by 13-inch (45 by 33 cm) rimmed sheet pan, lined with foil and sprayed with nonstick cooking spray
- Oven-safe wire rack, sprayed with nonstick cooking spray

**Chips**

| | | |
|---|---|---|
| 1½ lbs | russet potatoes, peeled and cut lengthwise into ¼-inch (0.5 cm) thick sticks | 750 g |
| | Hot (not boiling) water | |
| 3 tbsp | olive oil | 45 mL |
| ¾ tsp | salt | 3 mL |

**Fish**

| | | |
|---|---|---|
| 2 cups | panko (Japanese bread crumbs) | 500 mL |
| 2 tsp | Old Bay or other seafood seasoning | 10 mL |
| 2 | large eggs | 2 |
| ½ tsp | salt | 2 mL |
| ⅛ tsp | freshly cracked black pepper | 0.5 mL |
| 1½ lbs | skinless pollock or cod fillets, patted dry and cut into 4- by 2-inch (10 by 5 cm) strips | 750 g |

1. *Chips:* Place potatoes in a large bowl and add enough hot water to cover. Let stand for 10 minutes. Drain, pat dry and return to dry bowl. Add oil and salt, tossing to coat. Spread in a single layer on prepared pan.

2. Roast in preheated oven for 20 minutes or until golden on the bottom.

3. *Fish:* Meanwhile, in a shallow dish, combine panko and Old Bay seasoning. In another shallow dish, beat eggs with salt and pepper.

## Tips

Sea bass, halibut or any other firm white fish fillets may be used in place of the pollock.

The fish can be prepared through step 4 and frozen. Wrap the fish pieces in plastic wrap, then foil, completely enclosing them, and freeze for up to 3 months. When ready to roast, unwrap the frozen fish pieces (do not thaw), place on wire rack on sheet pan and roast at 450°F (230°C) for 10 to 14 minutes or until coating on the fish is golden brown and fish flakes easily when tested with a fork.

4. Dip fish strips in egg, shaking off excess, then in panko mixture, pressing to adhere and shaking off excess. Place on prepared wire rack, spacing evenly. Discard any excess panko and egg.

5. Remove pan from oven and turn potatoes over. Place wire rack on the pan (over the potatoes), moving potatoes aside as needed to fit the feet of the rack. Roast for 10 to 14 minutes or until potatoes are golden and crisp, coating on the fish is golden brown and fish flakes easily when tested with a fork.

# Crispy Oven-Fried Catfish with Hushpuppy Fries

Fishing for a fast and frugal dinner recipe? You've found it. This one-pan, family-friendly meal features crispy oven-fried catfish fillets paired with my riff on hushpuppies: prepared polenta cut and seasoned to create fast cornmeal "fries."

## Tip

Other fish fillets, such as tilapia or grouper, can be used in place of the catfish.

- Oven-safe wire rack, sprayed with nonstick cooking spray
- 18- by 13-inch (45 by 33 cm) rimmed sheet pan

| | | |
|---|---|---|
| 4 | skinless catfish fillets (each 6 oz/175 g), patted dry | 4 |
| 1 cup | buttermilk | 250 mL |
| 1 tsp | salt | 5 mL |
| 3 cups | corn flakes cereal, crushed | 750 mL |
| 1½ to 2 tsp | Cajun or Creole seasoning, divided | 7 to 10 mL |
| 1 | roll (17 oz/482 g) prepared plain polenta | 1 |
| | Nonstick cooking spray | |
| | Chopped fresh parsley (optional) | |

**Suggested Accompaniments**
Lemon wedges
Tartar sauce

1. In a large sealable plastic bag, combine fish, buttermilk and salt. Refrigerate for 20 minutes, turning bag once.

2. Meanwhile, preheat oven to 425°F (220°C).

3. Place corn flakes in a shallow dish. Remove fish from buttermilk, shaking off excess, and discard buttermilk. Sprinkle both sides of fish with 1 tsp (5 mL) Cajun seasoning. Dredge fish in corn flakes, pressing gently to adhere. Place fish on prepared wire rack set on sheet pan.

4. Cut polenta into ½-inch (2 cm) thick strips. Arrange on wire rack around fish and sprinkle with the remaining Cajun seasoning. Spray polenta and fish with cooking spray.

5. Roast in preheated oven for 20 to 25 minutes or until fish flakes easily when tested with a fork and polenta fries are golden. Sprinkle fries with parsley, if desired. Serve with the suggested accompaniments, as desired.

# Roasted Cod with Smoked Paprika Potatoes and Olives

Crisp potatoes, briny olives and smoky paprika provide a bold, earthy counterpoint to the clean ocean flavor of the cod fillets in this quick dish.

## Tips

Sea bass, halibut or any other firm white fish fillets may be used in place of the cod.

An equal weight of regular-size yellow-fleshed potatoes, cut into 1-inch (2.5 cm) cubes, can be used in place of the halved baby potatoes.

- Preheat oven to 400°F (200°C)
- 18- by 13-inch (45 by 33 cm) rimmed sheet pan, lined with parchment paper or foil and sprayed with nonstick cooking spray

| | | |
|---|---|---|
| 1½ lbs | baby yellow-fleshed or new potatoes, halved | 750 g |
| 2½ tbsp | olive oil, divided | 37 mL |
| 1 tsp | hot smoked paprika | 5 mL |
| ¾ tsp | salt, divided | 3 mL |
| ½ cup | pitted kalamata olives, quartered lengthwise | 125 mL |
| 4 | skinless cod fillets (each 6 oz/175 g), patted dry | 4 |
| 1 tsp | finely grated orange zest | 5 mL |
| | Chopped fresh parsley (optional) | |

1. On prepared pan, toss potatoes with 2 tbsp (30 mL) oil, paprika and ½ tsp (2 mL) salt. Spread in a single layer. Roast in preheated oven for 22 to 25 minutes or until potatoes begin to soften.

2. Remove pan from oven and add olives to the potatoes. Nestle fish among the potatoes, spacing evenly. Drizzle fish with the remaining oil and season with the remaining salt. Roast for 10 to 12 minutes or until potatoes are golden brown and crisp and fish is opaque and flakes easily when tested with a fork. Sprinkle fish with orange zest and parsley (if using).

# Cod with Roasted Tomatoes and Basil

This satisfying supper combines meaty cod fillets with juicy, oven-sweetened cherry tomatoes and fragrant fresh basil, all in under 20 minutes combined prep and cooking time.

## Tips

Sea bass, halibut or any other firm white fish fillets may be used in place of the cod.

Fresh flat-leaf (Italian) parsley leaves can be used in place of the basil.

An equal amount of chopped plum (Roma) tomatoes (1-inch/2.5 cm pieces) can be used in place of the cherry tomatoes.

- Preheat oven to 400°F (200°C)
- 18- by 13-inch (45 by 33 cm) rimmed sheet pan, lined with parchment paper or foil

| | | |
|---|---|---|
| 4 cups | cherry or grape tomatoes | 1 L |
| 2 tbsp | olive oil, divided | 30 mL |
| | Salt | |
| 4 | skinless cod fillets (each about 6 oz/175 g), patted dry | 4 |
| | Freshly cracked black pepper | |
| ½ cup | packed fresh basil leaves, thinly sliced | 125 mL |

1. Place tomatoes on prepared pan. Drizzle with half the oil and season with salt. Roast in preheated oven for 5 minutes or until skins begin to burst.

2. Brush both sides of fish with the remaining oil, then season with salt and pepper. Remove pan from oven and nestle fish among the tomatoes, spacing evenly. Roast for 7 to 10 minutes or until fish is opaque and flakes easily when tested with a fork. Sprinkle fish and tomatoes with basil. Serve fish with tomatoes and their juices.

# Creole Baked Cod

**Makes 4 servings**

Roast red pepper, green pepper, onion and tomatoes with garlic and Creole seasoning to make the zesty sauce and side for hearty cod fillets. Serve with crusty bread to soak up all the sauce.

**Tip**

Sea bass, halibut or any other firm white fish fillets may be used in place of the cod.

- Preheat oven to 400°F (200°C)
- 18- by 13-inch (45 by 33 cm) rimmed sheet pan, lined with foil and sprayed with nonstick cooking spray

| | | |
|---|---|---|
| 1 | red bell pepper, cut into strips | 1 |
| 1 | green bell pepper, cut into strips | 1 |
| 1 | large onion, halved lengthwise, then sliced crosswise, half-rings separated | 1 |
| 2 tbsp | olive oil | 30 mL |
| 1 tbsp | Creole or Cajun seasoning, divided | 15 mL |
| 1 | can (28 oz/796 mL) diced tomatoes, with juice | 1 |
| 3 | cloves garlic, minced | 3 |
| 4 | skinless cod fillets (each 6 oz/175 g), patted dry | 4 |

**Suggested Accompaniments**

Crusty bread
Hot pepper sauce
Chopped fresh flat-leaf (Italian) parsley
Lemon wedges

1. On prepared pan, toss together red pepper, green pepper, onion, oil and 1 tsp (5 mL) Creole seasoning. Spread in a single layer. Roast in preheated oven for 12 minutes.

2. Remove pan from oven and stir in tomatoes and garlic. Spread in a single layer. Roast for 5 minutes.

3. Sprinkle one side of fish evenly with the remaining Creole seasoning. Remove pan from oven and place fish, seasoned side up, on top of tomato mixture, spacing evenly. Roast for 10 to 12 minutes or until fish flakes easily when tested with a fork. Serve with any of the suggested accompaniments, as desired.

# Broiled Halibut and Pepper Skewers with Pesto Butter Toasts

Prepared basil pesto elevates simple preparations like these halibut and bell pepper skewers. It also creates an instant compound butter for rustic bread, which toasts alongside.

**Tip**

Sea bass, cod or any other firm white fish fillets may be used in place of the halibut.

- Preheat broiler
- Four 12-inch (30 cm) metal skewers
- 18- by 13-inch (45 by 33 cm) rimmed sheet pan, lined with foil and sprayed with nonstick cooking spray

| 1½ lbs | skinless halibut fillet, patted dry and cut into 1-inch (2.5 cm) pieces | 750 g |
|---|---|---|
| 2 | red bell peppers, cut into 1-inch (2.5 cm) pieces | 2 |
| 5 tbsp | basil pesto, divided | 75 mL |
| 2 tbsp | white wine vinegar | 30 mL |
| 2 tbsp | unsalted butter, softened | 30 mL |
| 4 | thick slices rustic-style bread | 4 |
| ½ tsp | salt | 2 mL |

1. Place fish and red pepper in a shallow dish. Drizzle with 3 tbsp (45 mL) pesto and vinegar, then toss to coat. Let stand for 5 minutes.

2. Meanwhile, in a small bowl, stir together butter and the remaining pesto until blended. Spread on one side of each bread slice.

3. Alternately thread fish and pepper pieces onto skewers, discarding any excess marinade. Place on one side of prepared pan and season with salt.

4. Broil for 6 minutes. Open oven door and turn skewers over. Place bread, buttered side up, on opposite side of pan. Close door and broil for 2 to 3 minutes or until bread is golden brown and fish is opaque and flakes easily when tested with a fork.

# Halibut with Herbed Bread Crumbs and Broccoli

As a time-, dish- and energy-saving measure, emerald broccoli florets roast right along with the herbed and panko-topped halibut in this easy supper.

**Tip**

Other firm white fish fillets, such as cod or snapper, can be used in place of the halibut.

- Preheat oven to 425°F (220°C)
- 18- by 13-inch (45 by 33 cm) rimmed sheet pan, lined with foil and sprayed with nonstick cooking spray

| | | |
|---|---|---|
| 1 | large head broccoli, trimmed and cut into medium florets | 1 |
| 4 tbsp | unsalted butter, melted, divided | 60 mL |
| | Salt and freshly ground black pepper | |
| ¾ cup | panko (Japanese bread crumbs) | 175 mL |
| 1 tsp | dried Italian seasoning | 5 mL |
| 4 | pieces (each 6 oz/175 g) halibut fillet, patted dry | 4 |
| | Lemon wedges | |

1. On prepared pan, toss broccoli with half the butter, ¾ tsp (3 mL) salt and ¼ tsp (1 mL) pepper. Spread in a single layer. Roast in preheated oven for 15 minutes.

2. Meanwhile, in a small bowl, combine panko, Italian seasoning and the remaining butter.

3. Season fish with salt and pepper.

4. Remove pan from oven and nestle fish among the vegetables, spacing evenly. Top each fillet with enough bread crumbs to coat, pressing firmly to adhere. Roast for 8 to 12 minutes or until vegetables are fork-tender, bread crumbs are golden brown and fish is opaque and flakes easily when tested with a fork. Serve with lemon wedges.

# Halibut with Greek Stuffed Roasted Tomatoes

Create big, bold flavor with just a few ingredients in this fast, fresh and sophisticated dinner. The stuffed tomatoes are a spot-on match for the simply seasoned, meaty halibut fillets.

## Tips

Sea bass, cod or any other firm white fish fillets may be used in place of the halibut.

Substitute 1/2 cup (125 mL) grated Parmesan cheese for the feta.

Panko (Japanese bread crumbs) can be used in place of the fresh bread crumbs.

- Preheat oven to 425°F (220°C)
- 18- by 13-inch (45 by 33 cm) rimmed sheet pan, lined with foil and sprayed with nonstick cooking spray

| | | |
|---|---|---|
| 4 | medium-large tomatoes | 4 |
| 3 | cloves garlic, minced | 3 |
| 3/4 cup | packed fresh parsley leaves, chopped | 175 mL |
| 3/4 cup | fresh bread crumbs | 175 mL |
| 3/4 cup | crumbled feta cheese | 175 mL |
| 3 tbsp | olive oil, divided | 45 mL |
| | Salt and freshly cracked black pepper | |
| 4 | pieces (each 6 oz/175 g) halibut fillet, patted dry | 4 |
| | Lemon wedges | |

1. Cut tops off tomatoes. Scoop out pulp, roughly chop it and place it in a bowl. Stir in garlic, parsley, bread crumbs, feta, 2 tbsp (30 mL) oil, 1/2 tsp (2 mL) salt and 1/4 tsp (1 mL) pepper until blended.

2. Spoon bread crumb mixture into tomatoes and place on prepared pan, spacing evenly. Roast in preheated oven for 20 minutes.

3. Season fish with salt and pepper. Remove pan from oven and nestle fish in between tomatoes, spacing evenly. Drizzle fish with the remaining oil. Return pan to oven and roast for 8 to 12 minutes or until fish is opaque and flakes easily when tested with a fork.

# Buffalo Roasted Salmon with Broccolini

Here, roasted salmon gets the Buffalo wings treatment (melted butter and hot sauce) plus a buttery bread crumb topping. Lemony broccolini alongside clinches the meal.

**Tip**

An equal amount of broccoli florets, small cauliflower florets, trimmed asparagus or trimmed green beans can be used in place of the broccolini.

- Preheat oven to 425°F (220°C)
- 18- by 13-inch (45 by 33 cm) rimmed sheet pan, lined with foil and sprayed with nonstick cooking spray

| | | |
|---|---|---|
| $\frac{1}{3}$ cup | panko (Japanese bread crumbs) | 75 mL |
| 5 tbsp | unsalted butter, melted, divided | 75 mL |
| 3 tbsp | hot pepper sauce (such as Tabasco) | 45 mL |
| $\frac{1}{2}$ tsp | salt | 2 mL |
| 1 lb | broccolini, ends trimmed | 500 g |
| 1 tsp | finely grated lemon zest | 5 mL |
| 1 tbsp | freshly squeezed lemon juice | 15 mL |
| 4 | pieces (each 6 oz/175 g) skinless salmon fillet, patted dry | 4 |

1. In a small bowl, combine panko and 1 tbsp (15 mL) butter.

2. In a large bowl, combine the remaining butter, hot pepper sauce and salt. Remove and reserve $\frac{1}{4}$ cup (60 mL) sauce.

3. To the large bowl, add broccolini, lemon zest and lemon juice, tossing to coat. Arrange broccolini in a single layer on prepared pan.

4. Set half of the reserved butter sauce aside for serving. Nestle fish among broccolini on pan, spacing evenly. Brush fish generously with the remaining sauce and sprinkle with panko mixture.

5. Roast in preheated oven for 9 to 14 minutes or until broccolini is tender and fish is opaque and flakes easily when tested with a fork. Serve with the reserved sauce.

# Roasted Salmon and Beets with Tarragon Vinaigrette

Fresh baby greens and a tarragon-Dijon vinaigrette add brightness, while thinly sliced beets add complementary crispiness to roasted salmon fillets, all with minimal prep and cleanup.

**Tip**

An equal amount of sherry vinegar or red wine vinegar can be used in place of the white wine vinegar.

- Preheat oven to 450°F (230°C)
- 18- by 13-inch (45 by 33 cm) rimmed sheet pan, lined with foil and sprayed with nonstick cooking spray

| | | |
|---|---|---|
| 1½ lbs | medium beets, trimmed and thinly sliced crosswise | 750 g |
| 6 tbsp | olive oil, divided | 90 mL |
| | Salt and freshly ground black pepper | |
| 4 | pieces (each 6 oz/175 g) skinless salmon fillet, patted dry | 4 |
| 2 tsp | dried tarragon | 10 mL |
| 1 tbsp | white wine vinegar | 15 mL |
| 1 tsp | Dijon mustard | 5 mL |
| 4 cups | mixed baby salad greens (such as mesclun) | 1 L |

1. On prepared pan, toss beets with 2 tbsp (30 mL) oil, ½ tsp (2 mL) salt and ¼ tsp (1 mL) pepper. Arrange beets on pan in rows to cover pan, starting from the center outward, overlapping slightly. Roast in preheated oven for 18 to 22 minutes or until beets are tender-crisp.

2. Remove pan from oven and place fish on top of beets, spacing evenly. Brush fish with 1 tbsp (15 mL) oil and season with salt and pepper. Roast for 7 to 12 minutes or until fish is opaque and flakes easily when tested with a fork.

3. Meanwhile, in a large bowl, whisk together the remaining oil, vinegar and mustard until blended. Season to taste with salt and pepper. Remove and reserve 2 tbsp (30 mL) of the vinaigrette. Add salad greens to bowl, tossing to coat.

4. Divide greens among four plates. Arrange fish and beets on top and drizzle with the reserved vinaigrette.

# Garlic Salmon with Green Beans

Bring a dash of elegance to the table with white wine–infused salmon and vegetables. The addition of tarragon, Dijon mustard and garlic adds layers of French flavor with little fuss.

## Tips

An equal weight of trimmed asparagus can be used in place of the green beans.

You can substitute 1 tsp (5 mL) dried thyme for the tarragon.

- Preheat oven to 450°F (230°C)
- 18- by 13-inch (45 by 33 cm) rimmed sheet pan, lined with foil and sprayed with nonstick cooking spray

| | | |
|---|---|---|
| 1¼ tsp | dried tarragon | 6 mL |
| ¾ tsp | salt, divided | 3 mL |
| ½ tsp | freshly ground black pepper, divided | 2 mL |
| ¼ cup | olive oil | 60 mL |
| 2 tsp | Dijon mustard | 10 mL |
| 1 lb | green beans, trimmed | 500 g |
| 12 | large cloves garlic, cut in half lengthwise | 12 |
| ½ cup | dry white wine | 125 mL |
| 4 | pieces (each 6 oz/175 g) skinless salmon fillet, patted dry | 4 |
| 1 | large lemon, cut into wedges | 1 |

1. In a small bowl, whisk together tarragon, ½ tsp (2 mL) salt, ¼ tsp (1 mL) pepper, oil and mustard.

2. On prepared pan, toss green beans and garlic with 3 tbsp (45 mL) oil mixture. Spread in a single layer. Roast in preheated oven for 15 minutes.

3. Meanwhile, whisk wine into the remaining oil mixture.

4. Remove pan from oven and stir vegetables. Place fish on top, spacing evenly. Drizzle fish with wine mixture and season with the remaining salt and pepper. Roast for 7 to 12 minutes or until fish is opaque and flakes easily when tested with a fork.

# Roasted Salmon and Root Vegetables with Horseradish Sauce

Sour cream seasoned with horseradish and dill makes a quick and tasty sauce for roasted salmon and root vegetables in this Eastern European–inspired meal.

**Tip**

For a lighter dish, substitute an equal amount of nonfat plain Greek yogurt for the sour cream.

- Preheat oven to 425°F (220°C)
- 18- by 13-inch (45 by 33 cm) rimmed sheet pan, lined with foil

| | | |
|---|---|---|
| 6 | carrots, trimmed and cut into $\frac{1}{2}$-inch (1 cm) thick slices | 6 |
| 4 | parsnips, trimmed and cut into $\frac{1}{2}$-inch (1 cm) thick slices | 4 |
| 4 | beets, trimmed and cut into $\frac{1}{2}$-inch (1 cm) thick slices | 4 |
| 3 tbsp | olive oil, divided | 45 mL |
| | Salt and freshly cracked black pepper | |
| 1 tsp | dried dillweed | 5 mL |
| $\frac{1}{2}$ cup | sour cream | 125 mL |
| 3 tbsp | prepared horseradish | 45 mL |
| 2 tsp | cider vinegar | 10 mL |
| 4 | pieces (each 6 oz /175 g) skinless salmon fillet, patted dry | 4 |

1. On prepared pan, toss together carrots, parsnips, beets, 2 tbsp (30 mL) oil, $\frac{1}{2}$ tsp (2 mL) salt and $\frac{1}{4}$ tsp (1 mL) pepper. Spread in a single layer. Roast in preheated oven for 25 minutes.

2. Meanwhile, in a small cup, combine dill, sour cream, horseradish and vinegar until blended. Season to taste with salt and pepper.

3. Remove pan from oven and nestle fish among the vegetables, spacing evenly. Brush fish with the remaining oil and season with salt and pepper. Roast for 9 to 14 minutes or until vegetables are fork-tender and fish is opaque and flakes easily when tested with a fork. Serve with horseradish sauce.

# Broiled Salmon Gremolata with Zucchini

**Makes 4 servings**

A squeeze of lemon and a sprinkle of gremolata – an Italian topping of lemon zest, garlic and parsley – are the only enhancements you'll need for this fast and fresh salmon and zucchini dinner. The extra-brief cooking time makes it an especially welcome choice in the summertime.

**Tip**

The gremolata (parsley-lemon mixture) can be prepared up to 6 hours in advance. Cover and refrigerate until ready to use.

**Variation**

Replace the zucchini with 1 lb (500 g) asparagus spears or green beans, trimmed.

- Preheat broiler, with rack set 4 inches (10 cm) from the heat source
- 18- by 13-inch (45 by 33 cm) rimmed sheet pan, lined with foil and sprayed with nonstick cooking spray

| | | |
|---|---|---|
| $1\frac{1}{2}$ lbs | zucchini (about 3 medium), cut diagonally into 1-inch (2.5 cm) thick pieces | 750 g |
| 3 tbsp | olive oil, divided | 45 mL |
| | Salt and freshly ground black pepper | |
| 4 | pieces (each 6 oz/175 g) skinless salmon fillet, patted dry | 4 |
| 1 | lemon | 1 |
| 3 | cloves garlic, minced | 3 |
| $\frac{1}{4}$ cup | finely chopped fresh flat-leaf (Italian) parsley | 60 mL |

1. On prepared pan, toss zucchini with 2 tbsp (30 mL) oil and season with salt and pepper. Spread in a single layer. Nestle fish among zucchini, spacing evenly. Brush fish with the remaining oil and season with salt and pepper.

2. Broil for 5 to 8 minutes or until zucchini is tender and golden brown and fish is opaque and flakes easily when tested with a fork.

3. Meanwhile, using a vegetable peeler, remove yellow peel from lemon in long, thin strips. Finely chop zest and cut lemon into quarters. In a small bowl, combine lemon zest, garlic and parsley.

4. Squeeze some of the lemon juice from the lemon quarters over fish and zucchini. Sprinkle fish with gremolata.

# Chili-Glazed Salmon with Brussels Sprouts

Honey, chili powder and Dijon mustard create a luscious glaze for roasted salmon. Add oven-caramelized Brussels sprouts and dinner is done!

## Tip

An equal amount of agave nectar, pure maple syrup or packed light brown sugar can be used in place of the honey.

- Preheat oven to 425°F (220°C)
- 18- by 13-inch (45 by 33 cm) rimmed sheet pan, lined with foil and sprayed with nonstick cooking spray

| | | |
|---|---|---|
| 1 lb | Brussels sprouts, trimmed and halved lengthwise if large | 500 g |
| 3 tbsp | olive oil, divided | 45 mL |
| ¾ tsp | salt, divided | 3 mL |
| 1½ tsp | chili powder | 7 mL |
| 1 tbsp | liquid honey | 15 mL |
| 2 tsp | Dijon mustard | 10 mL |
| 4 | pieces (each 6 oz/175 g) skinless salmon fillet, patted dry | 4 |

1. On prepared pan, toss Brussels sprouts with 2 tbsp (30 mL) oil and ½ tsp (2 mL) salt. Spread in a single layer. Roast in preheated oven for 20 minutes.

2. Meanwhile, in a small cup, combine chili powder, the remaining salt, the remaining oil, honey and mustard.

3. Remove pan from oven and nestle fish among the Brussels sprouts, spacing evenly. Brush fish generously with mustard glaze. Roast for 9 to 14 minutes or until Brussels sprouts are browned and fish is opaque and flakes easily when tested with a fork.

# Harissa Salmon with Kale and Chickpeas

Brushing salmon fillets with harissa deepens their pinkish hue and adds a spicy kick. Roasted kale and chickpeas make a bed with a slight crunch and toasty flavor that complements the richness of the fish.

**Tip**

Harissa is a fiery North African and Middle Eastern hot sauce, most commonly found in Tunisia and Morocco, that is made of chiles, garlic, cumin, caraway, salt and a bit of olive oil. An equal amount of your favorite hot sauce (such as Tabasco or Asian chili-garlic sauce) can be used in its place.

- Preheat oven to 450°F (230°C)
- 18- by 13-inch (45 by 33 cm) rimmed sheet pan, lined with foil and sprayed with nonstick cooking spray

| | | |
|---|---|---|
| 1 | large bunch Tuscan kale, tough stems removed, leaves thinly sliced (about 6 cups/1.5 L) | 1 |
| 4 tbsp | vegetable oil, divided | 60 mL |
| | Salt | |
| 1 | can (14 to 19 oz/398 to 540 mL) chickpeas, drained and rinsed | 1 |
| 4 | pieces (each 6 oz/175 g) skinless salmon fillet, patted dry | 4 |
| 2 tbsp | harissa, divided | 30 mL |
| 1½ tbsp | freshly squeezed lemon juice | 22 mL |
| 2 tsp | liquid honey | 10 mL |

1. On prepared pan, toss kale with 2 tbsp (30 mL) oil. Spread in an even layer and season with salt. Roast in preheated oven for 6 minutes.

2. Remove pan from oven and stir in chickpeas. Brush top side of fish fillets with 1 tbsp (15 mL) harissa and season with salt. Nestle fish among the kale mixture, spacing evenly. Roast for 7 to 12 minutes or until fish is opaque and flakes easily when tested with a fork.

3. Meanwhile, in a small cup, whisk together the remaining oil, the remaining harissa, lemon juice and honey until blended. Season to taste with salt.

4. Divide salmon and vegetables among serving plates and drizzle with dressing.

# Miso Roasted Salmon with Sesame Snap Peas

Make a savory-sweet glaze for roasted salmon with miso paste, brown sugar, soy sauce and vinegar, and you will be bowled over by the results. Crisp-sweet sugar snap peas roast alongside, completing this winning meal in minutes.

## Tips

Cider vinegar or white vinegar can be used in place of the rice vinegar.

Yellow or red miso paste can be used in place of the white miso paste.

- Preheat oven to 450°F (230°C)
- 18- by 13-inch (45 by 33 cm) rimmed sheet pan, lined with foil and sprayed with nonstick cooking spray

| | | |
|---|---|---|
| 2 tbsp | packed brown sugar | 30 mL |
| ¼ cup | white miso paste | 60 mL |
| 2 tbsp | soy sauce | 30 mL |
| 1 tbsp | unseasoned rice vinegar | 15 mL |
| 4 | pieces (each 6 oz/175 g) skinless salmon fillet, patted dry | 4 |
| 1 lb | sugar snap peas, trimmed and strings removed | 500 g |
| 1 tbsp | toasted (dark) sesame oil | 15 mL |
| | Salt | |

**Suggested Garnishes**

Thinly sliced green onions
Toasted sesame seeds

1. In a small bowl, whisk together brown sugar, miso, soy sauce and vinegar until smooth.

2. Place fish on prepared pan, spacing evenly. Brush top side liberally with miso mixture. Roast in preheated oven for 4 minutes.

3. Meanwhile, in a medium bowl, toss peas with oil. Season to taste with salt.

4. Remove pan from oven and arrange peas around fish. Roast for 4 to 8 minutes or until fish is opaque and flakes easily when tested with a fork. Serve salmon and snap peas with suggested garnishes, as desired.

# Tilapia with Roasted Green Onions and Citrus Vinaigrette

Here, a vibrant citrus and ginger vinaigrette boosts the otherwise mild flavor of tilapia in one fell swoop. Minimally adorned green onions, roasted with the fish until they're caramelized, are a succulent contrast.

## Tips

An equal amount of lemon or lime zest can be used in place of the orange zest.

Sea bass, cod, halibut or any other firm white fish fillets may be used in place of the tilapia.

- Preheat oven to 400°F (200°C)
- 18- by 13-inch (45 by 33 cm) rimmed sheet pan, lined with parchment paper or foil and sprayed with nonstick cooking spray

| | | |
|---|---|---|
| 2 | large bunches green onions (about 12 to 16), trimmed | 2 |
| 4 tbsp | olive oil, divided | 60 mL |
| | Salt and freshly cracked black pepper | |
| 1 tsp | finely grated orange zest | 5 mL |
| 1/4 tsp | ground ginger | 1 mL |
| 1 tbsp | white wine vinegar | 15 mL |
| 1 1/2 tsp | liquid honey | 7 mL |
| 4 | skinless tilapia fillets (each 6 oz/175 g), patted dry | 4 |

1. On prepared pan, toss green onions with 1 tbsp (15 mL) oil. Spread in a single layer and season with salt and pepper. Roast in preheated oven for 5 minutes.

2. Meanwhile, in a large bowl, whisk together orange zest, ginger, the remaining oil, vinegar and honey until blended. Season to taste with salt and pepper.

3. Season fish with 1/4 tsp (1 mL) salt and 1/4 tsp (1 mL) pepper. Remove pan from oven and nestle fish among the onions, spacing evenly. Drizzle fish with half the vinaigrette. Roast for 10 to 12 minutes or until fish is opaque and flakes easily when tested with a fork. Serve fish and onions with the remaining vinaigrette.

# Red Curry Tilapia and Asparagus

Prepared Thai curry paste is a great shortcut for creating tasty Thai food in a flash. Here, it enlivens mild tilapia fillets with bold flavor. Roasted asparagus alongside completes this easy one-pan dinner.

## Tips

An equal weight of green beans, trimmed and cut into 1-inch (2.5 cm) pieces, can be used in place of the asparagus.

In place of the curry paste, you can use 2 tsp (10 mL) curry powder (any heat level) plus 1 tsp (5 mL) vegetable oil.

- Preheat oven to 450°F (230°C)
- 18- by 13-inch (45 by 33 cm) rimmed sheet pan, lined with foil and sprayed with nonstick cooking spray

| | | |
|---|---|---|
| 1 lb | thin asparagus spears, trimmed and cut into 1-inch (2.5 cm) pieces | 500 g |
| 4 tbsp | virgin coconut oil, melted, divided | 60 mL |
| ½ tsp | salt, divided | 2 mL |
| 4 | skinless tilapia fillets (each 6 oz/175 g), patted dry | 4 |
| 2 tsp | finely grated lime zest | 10 mL |
| 1 tbsp | freshly squeezed lime juice | 15 mL |
| 1 tbsp | Thai red curry paste | 15 mL |
| ⅛ tsp | freshly ground black pepper | 0.5 mL |

1. On prepared pan, toss asparagus with 2 tbsp (30 mL) coconut oil and ¼ tsp (1 mL) salt. Spread in a single layer over two-thirds of the pan. Place fish on remaining third of pan.

2. In a small bowl, combine the remaining coconut oil, lime zest, lime juice, curry paste, the remaining salt and pepper. Brush generously over fish.

3. Roast in preheated oven for 10 to 12 minutes or until asparagus is tender and fish is opaque and flakes easily when tested with a fork.

# Tuna Casserole Redux with Roasted Vegetables

**Makes 4 servings**

Forget the canned soup sauce and frozen vegetable cubes. To make this easy, fresh spin on tuna casserole, roast fresh, flavorful vegetables, arrange canned tuna throughout, then finish with a fragrant, crisp panko topping.

## Variation

An equal amount of canned salmon, flaked and bones removed, can be used in place of the tuna.

- Preheat oven to 450°F (230°C)
- 18- by 13-inch (45 by 33 cm) rimmed sheet pan, lined with foil and sprayed with nonstick cooking spray

| | | |
|---|---|---|
| 3 | zucchini (about 1¼ lbs/625 g total), cut into 1-inch (2.5 cm) pieces | 3 |
| 1 | red bell pepper, cut into 1-inch (2.5 cm) pieces | 1 |
| 1 lb | button or cremini mushrooms, trimmed and halved lengthwise | 500 g |
| 3 tbsp | olive oil, divided | 45 mL |
| 1 tsp | dried thyme, divided | 5 mL |
| ¾ tsp | salt, divided | 3 mL |
| ¼ tsp | freshly ground black pepper | 1 mL |
| 1½ cups | panko (Japanese bread crumbs) | 375 mL |
| 3 | cans (each 6 oz/170 g) water-packed tuna, drained and flaked with a fork | 3 |

1. On prepared pan, toss together zucchini, red pepper, mushrooms, 2 tbsp (30 mL) oil, ¾ tsp (3 mL) thyme, ½ tsp (2 mL) salt and pepper. Spread in a single layer. Roast in preheated oven for 20 minutes.

2. Meanwhile, in a large bowl, toss together panko and the remaining thyme, salt and oil.

3. Remove pan from oven and stir vegetables. Scatter tuna over vegetables. Sprinkle evenly with panko mixture. Roast for 4 to 7 minutes or until panko is golden.

# Italian Tuna Melts

Don't feel like making dinner? Say hello to the perfect solution: flavorful, satisfying and affordable tuna melts with an Italian twist.

## Tips

You can substitute 1½ tsp (7 mL) white or red wine vinegar for the lemon juice.

An equal amount of minced green olives or brine-cured black olives can be used in place of the capers.

- Preheat broiler to high
- 18- by 13-inch (45 by 33 cm) rimmed sheet pan, lined with foil and sprayed with nonstick cooking spray

| | | |
|---|---|---|
| ¼ cup | finely chopped red onion | 60 mL |
| 4 tsp | drained capers | 20 mL |
| ¼ tsp | dried oregano | 1 mL |
| ⅓ cup | mayonnaise | 75 mL |
| 1 tbsp | freshly squeezed lemon juice | 15 mL |
| 3 | cans (each 6 oz/170 g) water-packed tuna, drained and flaked with a fork | 3 |
| | Salt and freshly cracked black pepper | |
| 4 | thick-cut slices rustic-style bread | 4 |
| 1 | beefsteak tomato, cut into 8 slices | 1 |
| 8 | thin deli slices provolone cheese | 8 |

1. In a medium bowl, stir together onion, capers, oregano, mayonnaise and lemon juice until combined. Gently stir in tuna and season to taste with salt and pepper.

2. Place bread on prepared pan, spacing evenly. Divide tuna mixture evenly among slices, spreading to edges of bread. Top each bread slice with 2 slices tomato and 2 slices cheese.

3. Broil for 3 to 4 minutes or until cheese is golden brown and bubbling.

# Southeast Asian Tuna Burgers

Pantry-friendly canned tuna is enlivened with bold Asian flavors in these quick and easy burgers. Cooking them is a breeze on a sheet pan, and the fresh, crunchy slaw topping comes together in minutes.

**Tip**

Use any style of buns you like, but opt for ones that are both soft and sturdy.

- Preheat oven to 400°F (200°C)
- 18- by 13-inch (45 by 33 cm) rimmed sheet pan, lined with parchment paper or foil and sprayed with nonstick cooking spray

| | | |
|---|---|---|
| 3 tsp | packed light brown sugar, divided | 15 mL |
| | Salt and freshly ground black pepper | |
| 2 tsp | finely grated lime zest, divided | 10 mL |
| 3 tbsp | freshly squeezed lime juice, divided | 45 mL |
| 4 tsp | toasted (dark) sesame oil, divided | 20 mL |
| 2 cups | shredded coleslaw mix (shredded cabbage and carrots) | 500 mL |
| 1 | large egg | 1 |
| 2/3 cup | panko (Japanese bread crumbs) | 150 mL |
| 1/3 cup | finely chopped green onions | 75 mL |
| 4 | cans (each 6 oz/170 g) water-packed tuna, drained and flaked with a fork | 4 |
| | Nonstick cooking spray | |
| 4 | hamburger buns, split | 4 |
| 1/2 cup | packed fresh mint or cilantro leaves, or a mixture, roughly chopped | 125 mL |

1. In a medium bowl, whisk together 1 tsp (5 mL) brown sugar, 1/8 tsp (0.5 mL) salt, 1/8 tsp (0.5 mL) pepper, half the lime zest, 1 tbsp (15 mL) lime juice and half the oil. Add coleslaw mix and toss to combine. Let stand while you prepare the burgers.

2. In another medium bowl, whisk egg to blend. Stir in panko, green onions, 1/4 tsp (1 mL) salt, 1/4 tsp (1 mL) pepper and the remaining brown sugar, lime zest, lime juice and oil. Gently stir in tuna. Form into four 3/4-inch (2 cm) thick patties. Place on one side of prepared pan, spaced evenly, and lightly spray with cooking spray.

3. Bake in preheated oven for 10 minutes. Open oven door and place buns, cut side up, on other side of pan. Close door and bake for 5 to 7 minutes or until burgers and buns are golden.

4. Place tuna burgers on bun bottoms. Add mint to slaw and toss to coat. Divide among burgers and top with bun tops.

# Sheet Pan Clam Bake

No need to head to the beach: this sheet pan preparation delivers the New England flavors of a classic clam bake to your kitchen anytime.

## Tips

To make your own seafood seasoning, combine ¾ tsp (3 mL) celery salt, ½ tsp (2 mL) freshly ground black pepper, ½ tsp (2 mL) sweet paprika and a pinch of cayenne pepper.

It is best to discard any mussels or clams that do not open after cooking because that is a strong indicator that they are not safe to eat.

- Preheat oven to 450°F (230°C)
- 18- by 13-inch (45 by 33 cm) rimmed sheet pan, lined with foil

| | | |
|---|---|---|
| 1 lb | small yellow-fleshed or white new potatoes | 500 g |
| 1 tbsp | olive oil | 15 mL |
| ½ tsp | salt | 2 mL |
| ¼ tsp | freshly cracked black pepper | 1 mL |
| 1 lb | mussels, scrubbed | 500 g |
| 1 lb | littleneck clams, scrubbed | 500 g |
| 2 | corn cobs, cut crosswise into 2-inch (5 cm) pieces | 2 |
| 1 | package (12 oz/375 g) smoked sausage, cut into 2-inch (5 cm) pieces | 1 |
| ¼ cup | unsalted butter, cut into small pieces | 60 mL |
| 2 tsp | Old Bay or other seafood seasoning | 10 mL |
| 1 lb | jumbo shrimp, peeled and deveined | 500 g |

**Suggested Accompaniments**

Chopped fresh parsley

Lemon wedges

Crusty bread

1. On prepared pan, toss potatoes with oil, salt and pepper. Spread in a single layer. Roast in preheated oven for 20 to 25 minutes or until potatoes are slightly tender.

2. Remove pan from oven and scatter mussels, clams, corn and sausage evenly over pan. Sprinkle with butter and Old Bay seasoning. Roast for 8 minutes.

3. Remove pan from oven and scatter shrimp over pan; stir to combine, then spread evenly over pan. Roast for 3 to 6 minutes or until mussels and clams have opened, shrimp are pink and opaque and potatoes are tender. Discard any mussels or clams that do not open.

4. Scoop seafood mixture into bowls with any accumulated juices and serve with any of the suggested accompaniments, as desired.

# Crab Cakes with Roasted Corn and Arugula

**Makes 4 servings**

My father is a native of Maryland's Eastern Shore, which is renowned for its fresh seafood, including crab cakes. He insists on keeping crab simply seasoned, but when it comes to the sides, anything goes. Corn is a favorite accompaniment; it is loved all the more when roasted in butter and tossed with bitter arugula before serving.

## Tips

It will take about 4 to 5 large ears of corn to yield 3 cups (750 mL) corn kernels.

If fresh corn is out of season, use an equal amount of thawed frozen corn kernels. Thoroughly pat the kernels dry with paper towels before roasting.

For the best texture, use a dense (rather than light and fluffy) white sandwich bread, crusts removed, to make the bread crumbs.

- Preheat oven to 375°F (190°C)
- 18- by 13-inch (45 by 33 cm) rimmed sheet pan, lined with parchment paper or foil and sprayed with nonstick cooking spray

| | | |
|---|---|---|
| 1 | large egg | 1 |
| 1½ tsp | Old Bay or other seafood seasoning | 7 mL |
| 1 tsp | salt, divided | 5 mL |
| ¼ cup | mayonnaise | 60 mL |
| 4 tsp | freshly squeezed lemon juice, divided | 20 mL |
| 1½ tsp | Dijon mustard | 7 mL |
| 1 tsp | Worcestershire sauce | 5 mL |
| 1 lb | lump crabmeat, cooked fresh or canned, drained and picked over | 500 g |
| 1¼ cups | fresh bread crumbs | 300 mL |
| 3 tbsp | unsalted butter, melted, divided | 45 mL |
| 3 cups | fresh corn kernels (see tips, at left) | 750 mL |
| 4 cups | baby arugula | 1 L |

1. In a large bowl, whisk together egg, Old Bay seasoning, ¼ tsp (1 mL) salt, mayonnaise, 2 tsp (10 mL) lemon juice, mustard and Worcestershire sauce until well blended. Gently stir in crab until well combined, being careful not to overmix (maintain some of the lumps).

2. Sprinkle bread crumbs over crab mixture and mix in gently but thoroughly (do not mash). Shape into eight 1-inch (2.5 cm) thick cakes. Place on one side of prepared pan, spacing evenly, and brush with half the butter.

3. Roast in preheated oven for 10 minutes. Remove pan from oven and carefully turn crab cakes over. Pile corn on other side of pan. Drizzle corn with the remaining butter and season with ¼ tsp (1 mL) salt. Toss to combine, then spread corn evenly on its side of the pan. Roast for 15 to 20 minutes or until crab cakes are golden brown and corn is light golden brown.

4. Add arugula, the remaining salt and the remaining lemon juice to the corn, tossing gently to combine. Serve with crab cakes.

# Scallops with Roasted Zucchini and Garlicky Bread Crumbs

Zucchini, coated with bread crumbs seasoned with pungent garlic and umami-rich Parmesan, makes a great contrast for sweet, tender bay scallops. Parsley and lemon zest add finishing notes of freshness.

**Tip**

An equal amount of panko (Japanese bread crumbs) can be used in place of the fresh bread crumbs.

- Preheat oven to 425°F (220°C)
- 18- by 13-inch (45 by 33 cm) rimmed sheet pan, lined with foil and sprayed with nonstick cooking spray

| | | |
|---|---|---|
| 1 lb | bay scallops (fresh or thawed frozen), patted dry | 500 g |
| 4 tbsp | unsalted butter, melted, divided | 60 mL |
| ¾ tsp | salt, divided | 3 mL |
| ½ tsp | freshly cracked black pepper, divided | 2 mL |
| 3 | zucchini (about 1 lb/500 g total), cut into ½-inch (1 cm) cubes | 3 |
| 3 | cloves garlic, minced | 3 |
| 1¼ cups | fresh bread crumbs (from rustic-style bread) | 300 mL |
| ⅓ cup | grated Parmesan cheese | 75 mL |
| ¾ cup | packed fresh flat-leaf (Italian) parsley leaves, roughly chopped | 175 mL |
| 1 tbsp | finely grated lemon zest | 15 mL |

1. In a large bowl, gently toss scallops, 2 tbsp (30 mL) butter, ¼ tsp (1 mL) salt and ¼ tsp (1 mL) pepper. Distribute evenly on prepared pan.

2. In the same bowl, toss zucchini with the remaining butter, salt and pepper. Add garlic, bread crumbs and Parmesan, tossing to combine. Distribute around scallops.

3. Roast in preheated oven for 10 to 14 minutes or until zucchini and bread crumbs are golden brown and scallops are firm and just opaque. Toss in parsley and lemon zest just before serving.

# Southern BBQ Shrimp with Oven-Fried Okra

When it's cold outside, stay in and warm up with this soothing Southern supper. This version of "barbecue" shrimp – a classic combination of shrimp, butter, hot sauce and a dash of sweetness – plus oven-fried okra is comfort by the panful.

**Tip**

You can use 1 cup (250 mL) corn flakes cereal, crushed, in place of the panko.

- Preheat oven to 450°F (230°C)
- 18- by 13-inch (45 by 33 cm) rimmed sheet pan, lined with foil and sprayed with nonstick cooking spray

| | | |
|---|---|---|
| ¾ cup | yellow cornmeal | 175 mL |
| ⅔ cup | panko (Japanese bread crumbs) | 150 mL |
| 1 | large egg | 1 |
| ½ cup | buttermilk | 125 mL |
| 2 tbsp | hot pepper sauce (such as Tabasco), divided | 30 mL |
| 1 tsp | salt, divided | 5 mL |
| 1 lb | fresh okra pods, trimmed and cut crosswise into ¾-inch (2 cm) slices | 500 g |
| | Nonstick cooking spray | |
| 2 tsp | granulated sugar | 10 mL |
| 2 tbsp | unsalted butter, melted | 30 mL |
| 1 tbsp | freshly squeezed lemon juice | 15 mL |
| 1 lb | large shrimp, peeled and deveined | 500 g |

1. In a shallow dish, combine cornmeal and panko.

2. In another shallow dish, whisk egg until blended. Whisk in buttermilk, 1½ tsp (7 mL) hot pepper sauce and ½ tsp (2 mL) salt. Add okra, stirring to coat. Let stand for 5 minutes.

3. Remove okra from egg mixture, shaking off excess. Dredge in cornmeal mixture and arrange in a single layer on prepared pan, covering two-thirds of the pan. Discard any excess egg and cornmeal mixtures. Lightly spray okra with cooking spray. Roast in preheated oven for 25 minutes.

4. Meanwhile, in a medium bowl, combine sugar, the remaining salt, butter, the remaining hot pepper sauce and lemon juice. Add shrimp and toss to coat.

5. Remove pan from oven and stir okra. Place shrimp in a single layer on remaining third of pan. Roast for 5 to 9 minutes or until okra is golden brown and crispy and shrimp are pink, firm and opaque.

# Roasted Jerk Shrimp and Warm Black Bean Salad

**Makes 4 servings**

This interpretation of Caribbean jerk shrimp combines prepared jerk seasoning with fresh lime and brown sugar with exceptionally delicious results. A warm black bean and watercress salad completes the meal.

### Tips

Large shrimp typically have a count of 35 to 45 per pound (500 g).

Some jerk seasoning blends contain salt. Check the ingredients; if the blend contains salt, omit the $1/2$ tsp (2 mL) salt from the shrimp dressing.

- Preheat oven to 425°F (220°C)
- 18- by 13-inch (45 by 33 cm) rimmed sheet pan, lined with foil and sprayed with nonstick cooking spray

| | | |
|---|---|---:|
| 1 | red bell pepper, chopped | 1 |
| 1 | can (14 to 19 oz/398 to 540 mL) black beans, drained and rinsed | 1 |
| 3 tbsp | olive oil, divided | 45 mL |
| 2 tsp | finely grated lime zest, divided | 10 mL |
| 3 tbsp | freshly squeezed lime juice, divided | 45 mL |
| | Salt and freshly ground black pepper | |
| 1 tbsp | salt-free jerk seasoning | 15 mL |
| 1 tbsp | packed dark brown sugar | 15 mL |
| 1 lb | large shrimp, peeled and deveined | 500 g |
| 4 cups | tender watercress or baby arugula | 1 L |

1. In a large bowl, combine red pepper, beans, 2 tbsp (30 mL) oil, half the lime zest and 2 tbsp (30 mL) lime juice. Season to taste with salt and pepper. Spread over one-third of prepared pan.

2. In the same bowl, combine jerk seasoning, brown sugar, $1/2$ tsp (2 mL) salt and the remaining oil, lime zest and lime juice. Add shrimp and toss to coat. Place in a single layer on remaining two-thirds of pan.

3. Roast in preheated oven for 7 to 11 minutes or until shrimp are pink, firm and opaque. Add watercress to the pan, gently tossing to combine.

# Coconut Shrimp with Roasted Sweet Potato Rounds

Coconut oil, flaked coconut and lime zest ensure the incomparable tropical flavor of this shrimp and sweet potato dinner.

## Tips

Large shrimp typically have a count of 35 to 45 per pound (500 g).

An equal amount of vegetable oil or olive oil can be used in place of the coconut oil.

## Variation

*Coconut Chicken with Roasted Sweet Potato Rounds:* Substitute 1 $\frac{1}{2}$ lbs (750 g) chicken breast tenders for the shrimp. Reduce the sweet potato roasting time in step 1 to 10 minutes, and increase the roasting time in step 4 to 18 to 20 minutes.

- Preheat oven to 425°F (220°C)
- 18- by 13-inch (45 by 33 cm) rimmed sheet pan, lined with foil and sprayed with nonstick cooking spray
- Oven-safe wire rack, sprayed with nonstick cooking spray

| | | |
|---|---|---|
| 1 $\frac{1}{2}$ lbs | sweet potatoes (about 3 medium) | 750 kg |
| 2 tbsp | virgin coconut oil, melted | 30 mL |
| | Salt and freshly cracked black pepper | |
| 2 | large egg whites | 2 |
| $\frac{1}{4}$ cup | cornstarch | 60 mL |
| 1 cup | sweetened flaked coconut | 250 mL |
| 1 cup | panko (Japanese bread crumbs) | 250 mL |
| 2 tsp | finely grated lime zest | 10 mL |
| 1 $\frac{1}{2}$ lbs | large shrimp, peeled and deveined, tails on | 750 g |
| | Nonstick cooking spray | |

1. Peel sweet potatoes and cut crosswise into $\frac{1}{2}$-inch (2 cm) thick rounds. Arrange in a single layer on prepared pan. Drizzle with coconut oil and season with salt and pepper. Roast in preheated oven for 20 minutes.

2. Meanwhile, in a small bowl, whisk egg whites until foamy. In a shallow dish, combine cornstarch, $\frac{1}{2}$ tsp (2 mL) salt and $\frac{1}{8}$ tsp (0.5 mL) pepper. In another shallow dish, combine coconut, panko and lime zest.

3. Working with one shrimp at a time, dredge shrimp in cornstarch mixture, dip in egg whites, then dredge in coconut mixture, pressing gently to adhere. Lightly coat shrimp on each side with cooking spray. Place shrimp on prepared wire rack, spacing evenly. Discard any excess cornstarch mixture, egg whites and coconut mixture.

4. Remove pan from oven and place wire rack on the pan (over the sweet potatoes), moving sweet potatoes aside as needed to fit the feet of the rack. Roast for 7 to 11 minutes or until shrimp are pink, firm and opaque and sweet potatoes are tender and browned.

# Garlicky Shrimp with Roasted Tomatoes, Lemon and Feta

Fresh garlic and lemon, along with black pepper and feta, give a depth of flavor and rich fragrance to this incredibly easy sheet pan dinner.

## Tips

Large shrimp typically have a count of 35 to 45 per pound (500 g).

In place of the cut large tomatoes, you can use 3 cups (750 mL) cherry or grape tomatoes. Reduce the cooking time in step 1 to 10 minutes.

- Preheat oven to 450°F (230°C)
- 18- by 13-inch (45 by 33 cm) rimmed sheet pan, lined with foil and sprayed with nonstick cooking spray

| | | |
|---|---|---:|
| 2 tbsp | minced garlic | 30 mL |
| 2 tbsp | olive oil | 30 mL |
| 4 | large tomatoes, cut into eighths | 4 |
| ¾ tsp | salt | 3 mL |
| ½ tsp | freshly ground black pepper | 2 mL |
| 1 lb | large shrimp, peeled and deveined | 500 g |
| ½ cup | chopped fresh flat-leaf (Italian) parsley | 125 mL |
| 1 tsp | finely grated lemon zest | 5 mL |
| 1 tbsp | freshly squeezed lemon juice | 15 mL |
| 4 oz | feta cheese, crumbled | 125 g |

**Suggested Accompaniment**
Crusty bread

1. In a small bowl, combine garlic and oil. Place tomatoes on prepared pan, drizzle with garlic oil and season with salt and pepper. Spread in a single layer. Roast in preheated oven for 20 minutes.

2. Remove pan from oven and add shrimp, parsley, lemon zest and lemon juice, gently stirring to combine. Spread in a single layer and sprinkle with cheese. Roast for 5 to 9 minutes or until shrimp are pink, firm and opaque. Serve warm, with crusty bread, if desired.

# Spicy Sofrito Shrimp and Potatoes

The seductive flavors of Central America – garlic, cilantro and lime – permeate this spicy shrimp and potato preparation. Cherry tomatoes, bursting with sweetness, create an instant sauce.

## Tip

Large shrimp typically have a count of 35 to 45 per pound (500 g).

- Preheat oven to 425°F (220°C)
- 18- by 13-inch (45 by 33 cm) rimmed sheet pan, lined with foil and sprayed with nonstick cooking spray
- Food processor

| | | |
|---|---|---|
| 4 | red medium or new potatoes, cut into $\frac{1}{2}$-inch (1 cm) cubes | 4 |
| 2 tbsp | olive oil, divided | 30 mL |
| 1 tsp | salt, divided | 5 mL |
| 4 | cloves garlic | 4 |
| 1 | red bell pepper, coarsely chopped | 1 |
| 1 cup | coarsely chopped red onion | 250 mL |
| $\frac{2}{3}$ cup | packed fresh cilantro leaves | 150 mL |
| $\frac{1}{4}$ tsp | cayenne pepper | 1 mL |
| 1 tbsp | freshly squeezed lime juice | 15 mL |
| 2 cups | cherry tomatoes, halved | 500 mL |
| 1 lb | large shrimp, peeled and deveined | 500 g |

1. Pile potatoes in center of prepared pan. Drizzle with 1 tbsp (15 mL) oil and season with $\frac{1}{2}$ tsp (2 mL) salt. Toss to combine, then spread in a single layer. Roast in preheated oven for 25 minutes or until edges of potatoes are beginning to brown.

2. Meanwhile, in food processor, pulse together garlic, red pepper, onion, cilantro, cayenne, the remaining salt, lime juice and the remaining oil until finely chopped, but not puréed.

3. Remove pan from oven and spread half the tomatoes and half the pepper mixture over the potatoes. Place shrimp on top, spacing evenly. Top with the remaining tomatoes and pepper mixture. Roast for 7 to 11 minutes or until shrimp are pink, firm and opaque.

# Hoisin Shrimp Oven Stir-Fry

Hoisin sauce, sesame oil and a fiery (yet restrained) dose of cayenne create tremendous flavor for this mostly hands-off shrimp and vegetable "stir-fry."

## Tips

Large shrimp typically have a count of 35 to 45 per pound (500 g).

Cider vinegar or white vinegar can be used in place of the rice vinegar.

- Preheat oven to 450°F (230°C)
- 18- by 13-inch (45 by 33 cm) rimmed sheet pan, lined with foil and sprayed with nonstick cooking spray

| | | |
|---|---|---|
| ¼ tsp | cayenne pepper | 1 mL |
| ⅓ cup | hoisin sauce | 75 mL |
| 1 tbsp | unseasoned rice vinegar | 15 mL |
| 1 tbsp | toasted (dark) sesame oil | 15 mL |
| 2 | red bell peppers, cut into ½-inch (1 cm) strips | 2 |
| 1 | large head bok choy, trimmed and cut into 3-inch (7.5 cm) pieces | 1 |
| 1 lb | button or cremini mushrooms, trimmed and halved lengthwise | 500 g |
| 2 tbsp | vegetable oil | 30 mL |
| 1 lb | large shrimp, peeled and deveined | 500 g |

1. In a large bowl, whisk together cayenne, hoisin sauce, vinegar and sesame oil. Remove and reserve half the mixture.

2. Add red peppers, bok choy, mushrooms and vegetable oil to large bowl and toss to coat. Spread in a single layer on prepared pan. Roast in preheated oven for 12 minutes.

3. Meanwhile, in the same large bowl, toss together shrimp and the reserved hoisin mixture.

4. Remove pan from oven and stir vegetables, then spread out evenly on pan. Place shrimp on top, spacing evenly. Roast for 5 to 9 minutes or until shrimp are pink, firm and opaque.

# Chicken and Turkey Meals

# Spatchcocked Chicken with Roasted Red Onions

**Makes 6 servings**

Spatchcocking – cutting out the backbone and flattening the bird – makes roasting a whole chicken a quick and simple affair. You can add all sorts of good things to the pan to cook along with the bird (see the variations for examples), but don't miss out on this rustic favorite: roasted red onions, which caramelize and turn velvety as they cook.

**Tip**

In place of the oil in step 2, you can use 1 tbsp (15 mL) softened or melted unsalted butter.

- Preheat oven to 500°F (260°C)
- 18- by 13-inch (45 by 33 cm) rimmed sheet pan, lined with foil and sprayed with nonstick cooking spray

| | | |
|---|---|---|
| 1 | whole chicken (about 4 lbs/2 kg), rinsed and patted dry | 1 |
| 3 tbsp | olive oil, divided | 45 mL |
| 2 tsp | salt, divided | 10 mL |
| $\frac{3}{4}$ tsp | freshly ground black pepper, divided | 1 mL |
| 2 | large red onions, cut into $1\frac{1}{2}$-inch (4 cm) wedges | 2 |
| | Lemon wedges | |
| | Chopped fresh flat-leaf (Italian) parsley (optional) | |

1. Remove giblets and neck from cavity, if necessary, and reserve for stock or discard. Place chicken, breast side down, on a cutting board. Using poultry shears, cut along both sides of backbone and open chicken like a book. Reserve backbone for stock or discard. Turn chicken breast side up and, using the heel of your hand, press firmly against the breastbone until it cracks.

2. Rub chicken all over with 1 tbsp (15 mL) oil, $1\frac{1}{2}$ tsp (7 mL) salt and $\frac{1}{2}$ tsp (2 mL) pepper. Place skin side up on prepared pan. Roast in preheated oven for 15 minutes.

3. Meanwhile, in a large bowl, gently toss onions with the remaining oil, salt and pepper.

4. Remove pan from oven and arrange onions around chicken. Roast for 30 to 35 minutes or until onions are browned, chicken skin is crisp and golden, juices run clear when the chicken is pierced between breast and leg and an instant-read thermometer inserted in the thickest part of a thigh registers 165°F (74°C). Let rest for 5 minutes, then cut chicken into pieces.

5. Serve chicken with onions and lemon wedges on the side. Sprinkle with parsley (if using).

## Tip

The red onions can be replaced with an equal amount of yellow or white onions, or with 2 packages (each 12 oz/375 g) frozen pearl onions, thawed.

## Variations

*Spatchcocked Chicken with Cherry Tomatoes:* Roast chicken for 25 minutes in step 2. Replace the onions with 3 cups (750 mL) cherry or grape tomatoes. Roast for 20 to 25 minutes in step 4.

*Spatchcocked Chicken with Fennel and Olives:* Roast chicken for 25 minutes in step 2. Replace the onions with 2 large fennel bulbs, trimmed and sliced (fronds reserved). Roast for 20 to 25 minutes in step 4. Sprinkle the roasted fennel with $\frac{1}{2}$ cup (125 mL) thinly sliced brine-cured black olives and $\frac{1}{4}$ cup (60 mL) chopped fennel fronds.

*Spatchcocked Chicken with Tarragon Mushrooms:* Roast chicken for 30 minutes in step 2. Replace the onions with 3 cups (750 mL) button or cremini mushrooms and add $1\frac{1}{2}$ tsp (7 mL) dried tarragon with the salt and pepper in step 3. Roast for 15 to 20 minutes in step 4.

# Weeknight Chicken and Stuffing

Chicken and stuffing, made in minutes with pantry-friendly ingredients – what more could you want from a weeknight meal? How about easy cleanup, too.

## Tips

Look for packages (14 to 16 oz/398 to 500 g) of cornbread stuffing in the bread section of the supermarket.

An equal amount of torn crusty, rustic-style bread or dry crumbled cornbread can be used in place of the cornbread stuffing.

If the stuffing is browned before the chicken is done, loosely cover the entire sheet pan with foil.

- Preheat oven to 450°F (230°C)
- 18- by 13-inch (45 by 33 cm) rimmed sheet pan, lined with foil and sprayed with nonstick cooking spray

| | | |
|---|---|---|
| 1 | large tart-sweet apple (such as Gala, Braeburn or Golden Delicious), peeled and very coarsely chopped | 1 |
| 1 | onion, coarsely chopped | 1 |
| 1¼ cups | coarsely chopped celery | 300 mL |
| 5 tbsp | unsalted butter, melted, divided | 75 mL |
| 1¼ tsp | dried thyme | 6 mL |
| 6 cups | plain dry cornbread stuffing (see tips, at left) | 1.5 L |
| 1¼ cups | ready-to-use chicken broth | 300 mL |
| 1 | whole chicken (about 4 lbs/2 kg), rinsed, patted dry and cut into 10 pieces | 1 |
| | Salt and freshly cracked black pepper | |

**Suggested Stir-Ins**

| | | |
|---|---|---|
| ½ cup | dried cranberries, chopped | 125 mL |
| ½ cup | chopped fresh flat-leaf (Italian) parsley | 125 mL |

1. On prepared pan, toss together apple, onion, celery, 3 tbsp (45 mL) butter and thyme. Spread in a single layer. Roast in preheated oven for 10 minutes.

2. Remove pan from oven and stir apple mixture. Stir in cornbread stuffing. Pour broth over top, stirring until absorbed. Spread out evenly over pan.

3. Brush chicken with the remaining butter. Moving stuffing mixture aside to make room, add chicken to pan, spacing evenly. Season stuffing and chicken with salt and pepper.

4. Roast for 25 to 35 minutes or until stuffing is golden brown and an instant-read thermometer inserted in the center of the thickest chicken piece registers 165°F (74°C). If desired, stir cranberries and/or parsley into stuffing.

# Roast Chicken Quarters with Lemon-Dill Spring Vegetables

This combination of roasted chicken, fingerling potatoes and spring vegetables is fancy enough for a dinner party but quick and easy enough for a weeknight.

**Tip**

An equal amount of chopped fresh parsley or mint can be used in place of the dill.

- Preheat oven to 500°F (260°C)
- 18- by 13-inch (45 by 33 cm) rimmed sheet pan, lined with foil

| | | |
|---|---|---|
| 4 | chicken leg quarters (about 3 lbs/1.5 kg), patted dry | 4 |
| 3 tbsp | olive oil, divided | 45 mL |
| | Salt and freshly ground black pepper | |
| 1 | package (12 oz/375 g) frozen pearl onions, thawed | 1 |
| 1 | package (1 lb/500 g) peeled baby carrots | 1 |
| 1 lb | yellow-fleshed fingerling or baby potatoes, halved crosswise | 500 g |
| 2 cups | trimmed radishes, halved lengthwise | 500 mL |
| 1/4 cup | chopped fresh dill | 60 mL |
| 1 tbsp | finely grated lemon zest | 15 mL |
| 2 tbsp | freshly squeezed lemon juice | 30 mL |

1. Place chicken, skin side up, on prepared pan, spacing evenly. Brush with 1 tbsp (15 mL) oil and season generously with salt and pepper. Roast in preheated oven for 10 minutes.

2. Meanwhile, in a large bowl, gently toss together onions, carrots, potatoes, radishes, the remaining oil, 3/4 tsp (3 mL) salt and 1/2 tsp (2 mL) pepper.

3. Remove pan from oven and nestle vegetables around the chicken pieces. Roast for 20 to 25 minutes or until vegetables are tender, chicken skin is crispy and an instant-read thermometer inserted in the thickest part of a chicken thigh registers 165°F (74°C).

4. Transfer chicken to a serving platter or individual plates. Sprinkle vegetables with dill, lemon zest and lemon juice, then toss to coat. Serve with chicken.

# Crispy Oven-Fried Drumsticks with Cowboy Beans

In this lighter, simpler version of fried chicken, chicken drumsticks are coated in a Parmesan cheese and panko mixture, then roasted instead of fried. An easy side dish of "cowboy" beans makes it a complete meal that the whole family will love.

## Tips

You can use 3 cups (750 mL) corn flakes cereal, crushed, in place of the panko.

In place of the frozen onions and peppers, you can use $1/3$ cup (75 mL) chopped green bell peppers and $2/3$ cup (150 mL) chopped onion.

- 18- by 13-inch (45 by 33 cm) rimmed sheet pan, lined with foil and sprayed with nonstick cooking spray
- Large sheet of foil

**Drumsticks**

| | | |
|---|---|---|
| 8 | chicken drumsticks (about 2 lbs/1 kg), patted dry | 8 |
| 1 cup | buttermilk | 250 mL |
| | Salt and freshly ground black pepper | |
| 2 cups | panko (Japanese bread crumbs) | 500 mL |
| $1/2$ cup | grated Parmesan cheese | 125 mL |
| $1/4$ cup | unsalted butter, melted | 60 mL |

**Beans**

| | | |
|---|---|---|
| 1 | can (14 to 19 oz/398 to 540 mL) pinto beans, drained and rinsed | 1 |
| 1 cup | frozen chopped onions and green bell peppers, thawed | 250 mL |
| 2 tsp | chili powder | 10 mL |
| $1/4$ cup | barbecue sauce | 60 mL |
| 1 tbsp | water | 15 mL |

1. *Drumsticks:* In a large sealable plastic bag, combine chicken, buttermilk, $1/2$ tsp (2 mL) salt and $1/4$ tsp (1 mL) pepper. Press out most of the air, seal top and gently squeeze bag to combine. Refrigerate for at least 20 minutes or for up to 12 hours.

2. Preheat oven to 425°F (220°C).

3. In another large sealable plastic bag, combine panko and Parmesan. Remove 2 drumsticks from buttermilk, shaking off excess, and place in bag with panko mixture. Seal and shake well, coating completely. Place drumsticks on prepared pan, spacing evenly and leaving one end of pan clear for the beans. Repeat with the remaining drumsticks and panko mixture. Discard buttermilk marinade. Sprinkle the remaining panko mixture evenly over drumsticks on pan. Drizzle drumsticks with butter.

## Tips

Choose a barbecue sauce that is free of corn syrup and preservatives and has a short list of all-natural ingredients.

For a lighter preparation, omit the melted butter and lightly spray the coated drumsticks with nonstick cooking spray before roasting.

4. *Beans:* In the center of a large sheet of foil, gently stir together beans, onions and peppers, chili powder, barbecue sauce and water. Seal foil into a packet, completely enclosing the mixture. Place on unfilled end of pan.

5. Roast in preheated oven for 25 to 30 minutes or until drumsticks are golden brown and an instant-read thermometer inserted in the thickest part of a drumstick registers 165°F (74°C). Carefully open beans packet and stir before serving.

# Sticky Mango Drumsticks with Black Beans and Rice

Jerk seasoning, black beans and mango chutney make this island-inspired chicken and rice dish distinctly satisfying. Complete the dish with any number of fresh accompaniments, from diced fresh mango to green onions to lime wedges.

**Tip**

If the jerk seasoning contains salt, reduce the added salt to $\frac{1}{2}$ tsp (2 mL).

- Preheat oven to 375°F (190°C)
- Blender or food processor
- 18- by 13-inch (45 by 33 cm) rimmed sheet pan, sprayed with nonstick cooking spray

| | | |
|---|---|---|
| 1½ cups | packed fresh cilantro leaves and tender stems | 375 mL |
| 1 tbsp | salt-free jerk seasoning | 15 mL |
| 1 tsp | salt | 5 mL |
| 2 tbsp | vegetable oil | 30 mL |
| 2 tbsp | freshly squeezed lime juice | 30 mL |
| 8 | chicken drumsticks (about 2 lbs/1 kg), patted dry | 8 |
| 1½ cups | long-grain white rice | 375 mL |
| 1 | can (14 to 19 oz/398 to 540 mL) black beans, drained and rinsed | 1 |
| 2½ cups | ready-to-use chicken broth | 625 mL |
| 1 cup | prepared mango chutney | 250 mL |

**Suggested Accompaniments**

Thinly sliced green onions
Fresh cilantro leaves
Lime wedges
Additional mango chutney
Diced mango

1. In blender, combine cilantro, jerk seasoning, salt, oil and lime juice; process into a paste.

2. Transfer paste to a large bowl and add drumsticks, turning to coat. Let stand for at least 15 minutes or cover and refrigerate for up to 1 day.

3. Spread rice and beans in an even layer on prepared pan. Remove drumsticks from marinade (do not discard marinade) and place on top of beans and rice, spacing evenly.

Other varieties of chutney,
or orange marmalade, can
be used in place of the
mango chutney.

4. Whisk broth into reserved marinade and pour over
   chicken, rice and beans. Cover pan tightly with foil.

5. Roast in preheated oven for 25 minutes. Remove pan
   from oven, remove foil and increase temperature to 450°F
   (230°C). Spoon mango chutney over the drumsticks.
   Roast, uncovered, for 20 to 25 minutes or until chicken
   is browned, all of the liquid is absorbed into the rice and
   an instant-read thermometer inserted in the thickest part
   of a drumstick registers 165°F (74°C). Remove from oven
   and fluff rice with a fork. Serve with any of the suggested
   accompaniments, as desired.

# Roasted Chicken with Butternut Squash, Apples and Thyme

**Makes 4 servings**

Creamy bites of butternut squash, crisp tart-sweet apple and oven-caramelized red onion make this roast chicken dish irresistible. Hello, autumn.

**Tip**

An equal amount of dry rubbed sage or dried rosemary can be used in place of the thyme.

- Preheat oven to 400°F (200°C)
- 18- by 13-inch (45 by 33 cm) rimmed sheet pan, lined with foil and sprayed with nonstick cooking spray

| | | |
|---|---|---|
| 2 | large tart-sweet apples (such as Gala, Braeburn or Golden Delicious), peeled and cut into ¾-inch (2 cm) cubes | 2 |
| 1 | butternut squash (about 1½ lbs/750 g), peeled and cut into ¾-inch (2 cm) cubes | 1 |
| 1 | small red onion, cut into 1-inch (2.5 cm) pieces | 1 |
| 3 tbsp | olive oil, divided | 45 mL |
| 2 tsp | dried thyme | 10 mL |
| | Salt and freshly ground black pepper | |
| 4 | chicken leg quarters (about 3 lbs/1.5 kg), patted dry | 4 |

1. On prepared pan, toss together apples, squash, onion, 2 tbsp (30 mL) oil, thyme, 1 tsp (5 mL) salt and ¼ tsp (1 mL) pepper. Spread in a single layer. Place chicken on top of vegetables, spacing evenly. Brush chicken with the remaining oil and season generously with salt and pepper.

2. Roast in preheated oven for 35 to 45 minutes or until vegetables are tender, chicken skin is browned and an instant-read thermometer inserted in the thickest part of a chicken thigh registers 165°F (74°C).

Pork Tenderloin with
Charred Corn Salad (page 178)

Oven-Fried Pork Chops with
Lemony Broccoli and Cannellini (page 179)

Italian Sausage and
Pepper Supper (page 188)

Roast Beef with Potatoes, Green Beans
and Blue Cheese Mayo (page 194)

Lamb Meatballs with Zucchini, Tomatoes and Yogurt Tahini Sauce (page 206)

Roasted Plums with Honey,
Walnuts and Greek Yogurt (page 210)

Berries and Cream Pavlova (page 211)

Decadent Carrot Cake with
Cream Cheese Frosting (page 220)

# Oven-BBQ Chicken Thighs with Warm Dijon Potato Salad

Roasted rather than grilled, this rendition of BBQ chicken and potato salad will wow you with its combined ease and great flavor. To dial up the deliciousness, you can always add a bit of crumbled bacon to the warm potato salad.

**Tip**

Choose a barbecue sauce with a minimal number of all-natural ingredients that is free of preservatives and corn syrup.

- Preheat oven to 400°F (200°C)
- 18- by 13-inch (45 by 33 cm) rimmed sheet pan, lined with parchment paper or foil

| | | |
|---|---|---|
| 8 | bone-in skin-on chicken thighs (about 2 lbs/1 kg total), patted dry | 8 |
| 1½ lbs | red-skinned potatoes, cut into 1½-inch (4 cm) pieces | 750 g |
| 6 tbsp | olive oil, divided | 90 mL |
| | Salt and freshly cracked black pepper | |
| 1½ cups | barbecue sauce | 375 mL |
| 1 | bunch green onions (about 6 to 8), chopped, white and green parts separated | 1 |
| 1 tsp | granulated sugar | 5 mL |
| 1½ tbsp | red wine vinegar | 22 mL |
| 2 tsp | Dijon mustard | 10 mL |

1. Place chicken, skin side down, on prepared pan, spacing evenly.

2. In a large bowl, toss potatoes with 2 tbsp (30 mL) oil. Season with salt and pepper, tossing to coat. Arrange potatoes around chicken on pan.

3. Roast in preheated oven for 25 minutes. Remove pan from oven and brush chicken generously with some of the barbecue sauce. Turn chicken over and brush other side with sauce. Scatter white part of green onions evenly over potatoes. Roast for 5 minutes.

4. Open oven door and brush the top of the chicken with more sauce. Close door and roast for 5 minutes. Repeat, brushing chicken with more sauce. Roast for 5 to 10 minutes or until potatoes are golden brown and an instant-read thermometer inserted in the thickest part of a chicken thigh registers 165°F (74°C). Remove from oven and let stand for 10 minutes.

5. Meanwhile, in a small bowl, whisk together sugar, vinegar, mustard and the remaining oil. Season to taste with salt and pepper. Drizzle dressing over warm potatoes and sprinkle with green part of green onions, gently tossing to combine.

# Chicken Thighs with Roasted Onions and Fall Fruit

Fragrant sage seasons the crispy skin of bone-in chicken thighs, adding instant autumnal appeal. Onions and seasonal fruits, accentuated with maple syrup and Marsala wine, are roasted alongside the chicken for an easy, flavorful side dish.

## Tips

An equal amount of dried thyme can be used in place of the sage.

Other dried fruits, such as cherries, currants, golden raisins or snipped apricots or figs can be used in place of the cranberries.

- Preheat oven to 400°F (200°C)
- 18- by 13-inch (45 by 33 cm) rimmed sheet pan, lined with parchment paper or foil

| | | |
|---|---|---|
| 8 | bone-in skin-on chicken thighs (about 2 lbs/1 kg total), patted dry | 4 |
| 1½ tsp | dried rubbed sage | 7 mL |
| | Salt and freshly cracked black pepper | |
| 2 | Bosc or Anjou pears, peeled and coarsely chopped | 2 |
| 1 | large tart-sweet apple (such as Gala, Braeburn or Golden Delicious), peeled and coarsely chopped | 1 |
| 1 | large red onion, coarsely chopped | 1 |
| 2 tbsp | unsalted butter, cut into small pieces | 30 mL |
| 2 tbsp | pure maple syrup or liquid honey | 30 mL |
| ⅓ cup | dried cranberries | 75 mL |
| ¼ cup | Marsala, sherry or dry white wine | 60 mL |

1. Sprinkle chicken on all sides with sage, ½ tsp (2 mL) salt and ⅛ tsp (0.5 mL) pepper. Place chicken, skin side up, on prepared pan, spacing evenly. Rub seasonings into chicken skin.

2. Evenly distribute pears, apple and onion around chicken. Dot fruit and onions with butter, drizzle with maple syrup and sprinkle with salt and pepper. Roast in preheated oven for 30 minutes.

3. Meanwhile, in a small cup, combine cranberries and Marsala. Let stand for at least 10 minutes.

4. Open oven door and distribute cranberries and any remaining Marsala over fruit and onions. Close door and roast for 10 to 15 minutes or until onion is golden brown and an instant-read thermometer inserted in the thickest part of a chicken thigh registers 165°F (74°C).

# Apricot-Glazed Chicken Thighs with Swiss Chard

Mix apricot preserves with Dijon mustard and white wine vinegar to make an addictive sweet-savory glaze for roasted chicken thighs. Roasted garlic chard is a satisfying complement.

## Tips

You can substitute 1 tsp (5 mL) dried rosemary, crumbled, for the fresh rosemary.

Cider vinegar or white vinegar can be used in place of the white wine vinegar.

- Preheat oven to 400°F (200°C)
- 18- by 13-inch (45 by 33 cm) rimmed sheet pan, lined with parchment paper or foil

| | | |
|---|---|---|
| 2 tsp | minced fresh rosemary | 10 mL |
| 4 tbsp | olive oil, divided | 60 mL |
| 8 | bone-in skin-on chicken thighs (about 2 lbs/1 kg total), patted dry | 8 |
| | Salt and freshly cracked black pepper | |
| ½ cup | apricot jam or preserves | 125 mL |
| 1 tbsp | Dijon mustard | 15 mL |
| 2 tsp | white wine vinegar | 10 mL |
| 3 | cloves garlic, minced | 3 |
| 1 | large bunch Swiss chard, tough stems removed, coarsely chopped (about 6 cups/1.5 L) | 1 |

1. In a small bowl, combine rosemary and half the oil. Place chicken, skin side up, on prepared pan, spacing evenly. Brush skin side with rosemary oil and sprinkle with ½ tsp (2 mL) salt and ¼ tsp (1 mL) pepper. Roast in preheated oven for 30 minutes.

2. Meanwhile, in a small cup, combine jam, mustard and vinegar.

3. In another small cup, combine garlic and the remaining oil.

4. Remove pan from oven and generously brush chicken with jam mixture. Nestle chard around the chicken. Drizzle chard with garlic oil and season with salt and pepper. Roast for 10 to 15 minutes or until chard leaves are beginning to crisp, chicken skin is crispy and an instant-read thermometer inserted in the thickest part of a chicken thigh registers 165°F (74°C).

# Lemon-Honey Chicken and Broccolini

Two pantry staples, lemon and honey, create a quick, sophisticated flavor combination for roasted chicken thighs and broccolini. Roasted garlic – scrumptious as an instant condiment for the chicken or a spread for crusty bread – ups the ante.

**Tip**

The suggested slices of bread can be added to the pan (placed directly on top of the chicken) during the last 5 minutes of cooking if you prefer them toasted.

- Preheat oven to 425°F (220°C)
- 18- by 13-inch (45 by 33 cm) rimmed sheet pan, lined with parchment paper

| | | |
|---|---|---|
| 8 | bone-in skin-on chicken thighs (about 2 lbs/1 kg total), patted dry | 8 |
| | Salt and freshly cracked black pepper | |
| 2 | lemons, quartered | 2 |
| 1 | bulb garlic, broken into cloves, unpeeled | 1 |
| 1 tbsp | olive oil | 15 mL |
| 1 lb | broccolini, tough ends trimmed off | 500 g |
| 2 tbsp | liquid honey | 30 mL |

**Suggested Accompaniment**
Thick slices rustic bread

1. Sprinkle chicken on all sides with salt and pepper. Place, skin side up, on prepared pan, spacing evenly. Squeeze juice from lemon quarters over chicken. Tuck garlic cloves and squeezed lemon peels around chicken; drizzle all with oil. Roast in preheated oven for 30 minutes.

2. Remove pan from oven. Nestle broccolini among the chicken. Spoon accumulated juices from pan over chicken and broccolini. Season broccolini with salt and pepper. Drizzle honey over chicken. Roast for 10 to 15 minutes or until broccolini is tender-crisp and an instant-read thermometer inserted in the thickest part of a chicken thigh registers 165°F (74°C).

3. Serve bread spread with roasted garlic, if desired, or squeeze out the garlic to use as a condiment for the chicken.

# Garlicky Chicken Thighs with Balsamic Brussels Sprouts

**Makes 4 servings**

These garlicky chicken thighs are roasted to a crisp golden-brown. The fresh, nutty flavor of the Brussels sprouts, enhanced with a tangy balsamic glaze, provides the perfect balance for the rich taste of the chicken.

## Tip

Size matters with Brussels sprouts. Opt for sprouts that are about 1 inch (2.5 cm) in diameter (larger ones tend to have a strong cabbage flavor) and have firm, bright green, compact heads.

- Preheat oven to 400°F (200°C)
- 18- by 13-inch (45 by 33 cm) rimmed sheet pan, lined with parchment paper

| | | |
|---|---|---|
| 2 | cloves garlic, minced | 2 |
| 4 tbsp | olive oil, divided | 60 mL |
| 8 | bone-in skin-on chicken thighs (about 2 lbs/1 kg total), patted dry | 8 |
| | Salt and freshly ground black pepper | |
| 1½ lbs | Brussels sprouts, trimmed and halved | 750 g |
| 1 tbsp | balsamic vinegar | 15 mL |
| 1 tsp | liquid honey | 5 mL |

1. In a small cup, combine garlic and 2 tbsp (30 mL) oil. Place chicken, skin side up, on prepared pan, spacing evenly. Brush with garlic oil and season generously with salt and pepper. Roast in preheated oven for 20 minutes.

2. Meanwhile, in a medium bowl, toss Brussels sprouts with the remaining oil. Season with salt and pepper.

3. Remove pan from oven and nestle Brussels sprouts around the chicken. Roast for 20 to 25 minutes or until sprouts are fork-tender, chicken skin is crispy and an instant-read thermometer inserted in the thickest part of a chicken thigh registers 165°F (74°C).

4. In a small cup, combine vinegar and honey. Drizzle sprouts with vinegar mixture, tossing to combine.

# French Roasted Chicken Thighs with Artichokes and Thyme

Artichokes, garlic and thyme lend a French twist to roasted chicken thighs. Lots of lemon and fresh parsley amp up the Continental simplicity and flair.

## Tips

An equal weight of yellow-fleshed or red-skinned potatoes, cut into 1½-inch (4 cm) pieces, can be used in place of the baby potatoes.

A 14- to 15-oz (398 to 425 g) can of artichoke hearts, drained, can be used in place of the frozen artichoke hearts.

## Variation

Sprinkle the pan contents with ⅓ cup (75 mL) pitted brine-cured olives, quartered lengthwise, along with the parsley.

- Preheat oven to 400°F (200°C)
- 18- by 13-inch (45 by 33 cm) rimmed sheet pan, lined with foil and sprayed with nonstick cooking spray

| | | |
|---|---|---:|
| 8 | bone-in skin-on chicken thighs (about 2 lbs/1 kg total), patted dry | 8 |
| | Salt and freshly cracked black pepper | |
| 3 | lemons, divided | 3 |
| 1 lb | yellow-fleshed or red-skinned baby potatoes | 500 g |
| 1 | red onion, halved lengthwise, each half cut into 8 wedges | 1 |
| 4 tbsp | olive oil, divided | 60 mL |
| 1½ tsp | dried thyme, divided | 7 mL |
| 2 | cloves garlic, sliced | 2 |
| 1 | package (9 oz/270 g) frozen artichokes, thawed | 1 |
| ¾ cup | packed fresh parsley leaves, chopped | 175 mL |

**Suggested Accompaniment**

    Crusty bread

1. Place chicken, skin side up, on prepared pan, spacing evenly. Season generously with salt and pepper. Roast in preheated oven for 10 minutes.

2. Meanwhile, quarter 2 of the lemons. In a large bowl, toss together lemon quarters, potatoes, onion, half the oil, half the thyme, ½ tsp (2 mL) salt and ¼ tsp (1 mL) pepper.

3. Remove pan from oven and nestle potato mixture around the chicken. Roast for 25 minutes.

4. Meanwhile, grate zest and squeeze juice from the remaining lemon into a medium bowl. Whisk in garlic, the remaining thyme, ¼ tsp (1 mL) salt, ¼ tsp (1 mL) pepper and the remaining oil. Add artichokes, tossing to coat.

5. Open oven door and nestle artichoke mixture around the chicken and potatoes, being sure to scrape all the lemon-oil mixture from the bowl. Close door and roast for 15 to 20 minutes or until potatoes are fork-tender and an instant-read thermometer inserted in the thickest part of a chicken thigh registers 165°F (74°C). Sprinkle pan contents with parsley and serve with bread, if desired.

# Seville Chicken, Sausage and Onion Roast

Chicken and potatoes get a flavor kick from iconic ingredients of southern Spain: smoky paprika, oregano, orange and olive oil.

### Tips

Fully cooked chicken or pork sausage can be used in place of the turkey sausage.

An equal weight of yellow-fleshed or red-skinned potatoes, cut into 1½-inch (4 cm) pieces, can be used in place of the baby potatoes.

- Preheat oven to 450°F (230°C)
- 18- by 13-inch (45 by 33 cm) rimmed sheet pan, lined with foil and sprayed with nonstick cooking spray

| | | |
|---|---|---|
| 2 tsp | smoked paprika (pimentón) | 10 mL |
| 1 tsp | dried oregano | 5 mL |
| 1 tsp | salt | 5 mL |
| 3 tbsp | olive oil | 45 mL |
| 4 | bone-in skin-on chicken thighs (about 1 lb/500 g total), patted dry | 4 |
| 1 | large red onion, cut into 1-inch (2.5 cm) pieces | 1 |
| 1¼ lbs | yellow-fleshed or red-skinned baby potatoes | 625 g |
| 1 | package (12 to 14 oz/375 to 400 g) fully cooked smoked turkey sausage | 1 |
| | Grated zest and juice of 1 small to medium navel orange | |

1. In a large bowl, whisk together paprika, oregano, salt and oil. Add chicken, onion and potatoes, tossing to coat. Arrange in a single layer on prepared pan, placing chicken skin side up. Roast in preheated oven for 25 minutes.

2. Meanwhile, cut sausage crosswise into 8 equal pieces.

3. Open oven door and gently stir vegetables. Nestle sausage pieces among the chicken and vegetables. Close door and roast for 10 to 15 minutes or until potatoes are fork-tender and an instant-read thermometer inserted in the thickest part of a chicken thigh registers 165°F (74°C).

4. Sprinkle zest and juice from orange over pan contents. Gently toss to combine.

# Punjabi Chicken with Cauliflower, Potatoes and Peas

The combination of cauliflower, potatoes and peas appears in a number of northern Indian dishes, and once you try it, you'll understand the popularity. The amount of oil used here is less than in many classic Indian dishes, but you'll never know it's missing. A bevy of spices contributes rich flavor to the dish.

**Tip**

An equal amount of yellow-fleshed baby potatoes, left whole, can be used in place of the large potatoes.

- Preheat oven to 400°F (200°C)
- 18- by 13-inch (45 by 33 cm) rimmed sheet pan, lined with parchment paper or foil

**Spice Mixture**

| | | |
|---|---|---|
| 2 tsp | ground cumin | 10 mL |
| 2 tsp | ground coriander | 10 mL |
| 1½ tsp | ground ginger | 7 mL |
| 1¼ tsp | salt | 6 mL |
| ¼ tsp | freshly ground black pepper | 1 mL |

**Chicken and Vegetables**

| | | |
|---|---|---|
| 5 tbsp | vegetable oil, divided | 75 mL |
| 8 | bone-in skin-on chicken thighs (about 2 lbs/1 kg total), patted dry | 8 |
| 1 lb | yellow-fleshed potatoes, peeled and cut into 1½-inch (4 cm) pieces | 500 g |
| 1 | head cauliflower, trimmed and broken into florets | 1 |
| 1¼ cups | frozen peas, thawed | 300 mL |
| | Salt and freshly ground black pepper | |
| 1 cup | plain yogurt (not Greek-style) | 250 mL |

1. *Spice Mixture:* In a small bowl, stir together cumin, coriander, ginger, salt and pepper.

2. *Chicken and Vegetables:* In a large bowl, combine 2 tsp (10 mL) spice mixture and 1 tbsp (15 mL) oil. Add chicken, rubbing spice mixture into skin. Place chicken, skin side up, on prepared pan, spacing evenly.

3. In the same large bowl, combine half of the remaining spice mixture and 2 tbsp (30 mL) oil. Add potatoes, tossing to coat. Arrange potatoes around chicken. Roast in preheated oven for 15 minutes.

4. Meanwhile, in the same bowl, combine the remaining spice mixture and oil. Add cauliflower, tossing to coat.

5. Remove pan from oven, turn chicken pieces over and stir potatoes. Nestle cauliflower around the chicken and potatoes. Roast for 25 to 30 minutes or until cauliflower is beginning to brown and an instant-read thermometer inserted in the thickest part of a chicken thigh registers 165°F (74°C).

6. Remove pan from oven. Add peas to the pan, gently stirring to combine. Let stand for 10 minutes. Season to taste with salt and pepper. Serve with yogurt.

# Ginger-Garlic Chicken with Roasted Plums

**Makes 4 servings**

Caramelized ginger and garlic-dressed plums accompany sizzling chicken thighs in this lickety-split supper. It is far tastier than takeout, and healthier, too.

## Tips

Do not worry about the ripeness of the plums; roasting transforms even the hardest, least flavorful plums into a deeply delicious side.

Fresh ginger is preferable here, as it is a star flavor of the dish, but in a pinch, 2 tsp (10 mL) ground ginger can take its place.

- Preheat oven to 425°F (220°C)
- 18- by 13-inch (45 by 33 cm) rimmed sheet pan, lined with foil

| | | |
|---|---|---|
| 8 | bone-in skin-on chicken thighs (about 2 lbs/1 kg total), patted dry | 8 |
| 2 tbsp | vegetable oil | 30 mL |
| 3/4 tsp | salt | 3 mL |
| 1/2 tsp | freshly ground black pepper | 2 mL |
| 8 | plums, halved and pits removed | 8 |
| 4 | cloves garlic, chopped | 4 |
| 2 tbsp | minced gingerroot | 30 mL |
| 3 tbsp | soy sauce | 45 mL |

**Suggested Accompaniments**

Thinly sliced green onions
Hot cooked brown or white rice

1. Place chicken, skin side up, on prepared pan, spacing evenly. Brush with oil and sprinkle with salt and pepper. Roast in preheated oven for 20 minutes.

2. Meanwhile, in a medium bowl, gently toss together plums, garlic, ginger and soy sauce.

3. Remove pan from oven and nestle plums around the chicken. Scrape all of soy sauce mixture over chicken and plums. Roast for 20 to 25 minutes or until plums are softened, chicken skin is crispy and an instant-read thermometer inserted in the thickest part of a chicken thigh registers 165°F (74°C). Serve with the suggested accompaniments, as desired.

# Miso-Maple Chicken Thighs with Roasted Snap Peas

Miso paste, maple syrup and a splash of lime create layers of flavor in this quick and easy Asian-inspired supper. You'll never want to prepare snap peas any other way once you try them roasted!

**Tips**

Other varieties of miso paste, such as white or red, can be used in place of the yellow miso.

An equal amount of liquid honey or agave nectar can be used in place of the maple syrup.

- 18- by 13-inch (45 by 33 cm) rimmed sheet pan, lined with foil

| | | |
|---|---|---|
| 3 tbsp | yellow miso paste | 45 mL |
| 3 tbsp | pure maple syrup | 45 mL |
| 8 | bone-in skin-on chicken thighs (about 2 lbs/1 kg total), patted dry | 8 |
| 1 lb | sugar snap peas, trimmed | 500 g |
| 1 tbsp | vegetable oil | 15 mL |
| | Salt and freshly ground black pepper | |
| | Lime wedges | |

1. In a large bowl, whisk together miso and maple syrup. Add chicken and rub mixture into chicken. Let stand at room temperature for 20 minutes.

2. Meanwhile, preheat oven to 450°F (230°C).

3. Place chicken, skin side up, on prepared pan, spacing evenly. Roast in preheated oven for 25 minutes.

4. Meanwhile, in the same bowl, toss peas with oil. Season to taste with salt and pepper.

5. Remove pan from oven and nestle peas around the chicken. Roast for 9 to 12 minutes or until peas are just beginning to brown at the edges and an instant-read thermometer inserted in the thickest part of a chicken thigh registers 165°F (74°C). Serve with lime wedges.

# Sheet Pan Chicken Vesuvio

This all-in-one chicken dinner is a riff on chicken Vesuvio, an Italian-American dish made famous in the 1930s at Vesuvio Restaurant in Chicago. Recipes vary, but chicken, potatoes, peas and lemon are integral components of the dish.

## Tips

You can use 1 tsp (5 mL) dried rosemary in place of the fresh rosemary.

For added richness akin to the original recipe, scatter 2 tbsp (30 mL) unsalted butter (cut into small pieces) over the chicken and potatoes along with the peas.

- Preheat oven to 450°F (230°C)
- 18- by 13-inch (45 by 33 cm) rimmed sheet pan, lined with foil and sprayed with nonstick cooking spray

| | | |
|---|---|---|
| 6 | boneless skinless chicken thighs (about 1½ lbs/750 g total), patted dry and cut into 2-inch (5 cm) pieces | 6 |
| 1½ lbs | red-skinned potatoes, cut into 1-inch (2.5 cm) pieces | 750 g |
| 2 tbsp | olive oil | 30 mL |
| | Salt and freshly cracked black pepper | |
| 3 | cloves garlic, minced | 3 |
| 2 tsp | chopped fresh rosemary | 10 mL |
| ⅓ cup | dry white wine | 75 mL |
| 2 tsp | finely grated lemon zest | 10 mL |
| 3 tbsp | freshly squeezed lemon juice | 45 mL |
| 1¼ cups | frozen peas | 300 mL |

1. On prepared pan, toss together chicken, potatoes, oil, 1 tsp (5 mL) salt and ½ tsp (2 mL) pepper. Spread in a single layer. Roast in preheated oven for 20 minutes.

2. In small bowl or cup, whisk together garlic, rosemary, wine, lemon zest and lemon juice.

3. Open oven door and pour wine mixture evenly over chicken and potatoes. Close door and roast for 5 to 8 minutes or until potatoes are tender and juices run clear when chicken is pierced.

4. Remove pan from oven and scatter peas among chicken and potatoes. Let stand for 3 to 5 minutes or until peas are heated through, then stir gently. Season to taste with salt and pepper.

# Greek Chicken with Zucchini, Tomatoes and Mushrooms

Here's my pick for an impressive dish to serve guests that is also a breeze for the cook. You can even prep the chicken and vegetables hours ahead of time, then simply toss them on the sheet pan and roast. Now that's entertainment!

## Variation

Substitute 8 oz (250 g) asparagus or green beans, trimmed and cut into 1-inch (2.5 cm) pieces, for the zucchini.

- Preheat oven to 450°F (230°C)
- 18- by 13-inch (45 by 33 cm) rimmed sheet pan, lined with foil and sprayed with nonstick cooking spray

| | | |
|---|---|---:|
| 4 | cloves garlic, minced | 4 |
| 2 tsp | dried oregano | 10 mL |
| 1/2 tsp | ground cinnamon | 2 mL |
| | Salt and freshly cracked black pepper | |
| 1/4 cup | olive oil | 60 mL |
| 6 | boneless skinless chicken thighs (about 1 1/2 lbs/750 g total), patted dry and cut into 2-inch (5 cm) pieces | 6 |
| 2 | zucchini, cut into 1-inch (2.5 cm) pieces | 2 |
| 8 oz | button or cremini mushrooms, trimmed | 250 g |
| 2 cups | cherry or grape tomatoes | 500 mL |

**Suggested Accompaniments**

Lemon wedges

Crumbled feta cheese

1. In a large bowl, whisk together garlic, oregano, cinnamon, 1 tsp (5 mL) salt, 1/2 tsp (2 mL) pepper and oil. Add chicken, zucchini, mushrooms and tomatoes, tossing to coat. Spread in a single layer on prepared pan.

2. Roast in preheated oven for 25 to 28 minutes or until tomatoes are bursting, zucchini is tender and juices run clear when chicken is pierced. Season to taste with salt and pepper. Serve with the suggested accompaniments, as desired.

# Moroccan-Spiced Chicken and Chickpeas

Cumin, pepper and a mix of sweet spices add a North African accent to roasted chicken in this sheet pan riff on a tagine. Be sure to add at least some of the suggested toppings for a noteworthy dinner.

## Tips

An equal amount of ground cinnamon can be used in place of the pumpkin pie spice.

Fresh flat-leaf (Italian) parsley can be used in place of the cilantro.

- Preheat oven to 450°F (230°C)
- 18- by 13-inch (45 by 33 cm) rimmed sheet pan, lined with foil and sprayed with nonstick cooking spray

| | | |
|---|---|---|
| 1½ tsp | ground cumin | 7 mL |
| 1¼ tsp | pumpkin pie spice | 6 mL |
| | Salt and freshly cracked black pepper | |
| 2 tbsp | olive oil | 30 mL |
| 6 | boneless skinless chicken thighs (about 1½ lbs/750 g total), patted dry and cut into 2-inch (5 cm) pieces | 6 |
| 1 | onion, chopped | 1 |
| 1 | can (28 oz/796 mL) diced tomatoes, with juice | 1 |
| 1 | can (14 to 19 oz/398 to 540 mL) chickpeas, drained and rinsed | 1 |
| ½ cup | packed fresh cilantro leaves, chopped | 125 mL |

**Suggested Accompaniments**

Raisins, dried currants or chopped dried apricots

Plain yogurt

Lemon wedges

Hot cooked couscous

1. In a large bowl, whisk together cumin, pumpkin pie spice, ½ tsp (2 mL) salt, ½ tsp (2 mL) pepper and oil. Add chicken, onion, tomatoes and chickpeas, tossing to coat. Spread in a single layer on prepared pan.

2. Roast in preheated oven for 25 to 30 minutes or until juices run clear when chicken is pierced. Season to taste with salt and pepper, and sprinkle with cilantro. Serve with any of the suggested accompaniments, as desired.

# Chicken with Savoy Cabbage Wedge Salad

This sophisticated salad is packed with flavor and texture. The drippings from crispy bacon flavor the chicken and savoy cabbage wedges as they roast, while the bacon crumbles and a creamy blue cheese dressing top all.

**Tip**

An equal amount of buttermilk can be used in place of the yogurt.

- Preheat oven to 400°F (200°C)
- 18- by 13-inch (45 by 33 cm) rimmed sheet pan, lined with foil

| | | |
|---|---|---|
| 4 | small bone-in skin-on chicken breasts (about 2 lbs/1 kg total), patted dry | 4 |
| | Salt and freshly cracked black pepper | |
| 4 | thick-cut slices bacon | 4 |
| 1 | head savoy cabbage, tough outer leaves discarded, cut into 4 wedges | 1 |
| ⅔ cup | crumbled blue cheese | 150 mL |
| ½ cup | plain yogurt (not Greek-style) | 125 mL |
| 1 tbsp | white wine vinegar | 15 mL |

1. Season chicken on both sides with salt and pepper. Place chicken, skin side up, on one side of prepared pan, spacing evenly. Place bacon in a single layer on the other side of the pan. Roast in preheated oven for 15 to 20 minutes or until bacon is crisp.

2. Remove pan from oven and transfer bacon to a plate lined with paper towels. (Do not drain bacon fat from pan.)

3. Arrange cabbage wedges on pan, repositioning chicken as needed to make room. Spoon some of the bacon fat on pan over cabbage and chicken. Season cabbage with salt and pepper. Roast for 20 to 25 minutes or until cabbage is tender-crisp and browned at the edges and an instant-read thermometer inserted in the thickest part of a chicken breast registers 165°F (74°C).

4. Meanwhile, in a small bowl, combine blue cheese, yogurt and vinegar until blended and smooth. Season to taste with salt and pepper. Crumble bacon.

5. Transfer chicken breasts and cabbage wedges to plates. Spoon blue cheese dressing over cabbage and sprinkle with bacon.

# Provençal Chicken with Potatoes and Sun-Dried Tomatoes

Herbes de Provence, sun-dried tomatoes and lemon zest bring a riot of flavor to this Southern France dinner. The potatoes absorb some of the flavorful chicken fat as they roast, creating a sensational side dish with almost no effort.

## Tips

Dried Italian seasoning can be used in place of the herbes de Provence.

An equal weight of yellow-fleshed potatoes, cut into 1½-inch (4 cm) pieces, can be used in place of the fingerling potatoes.

- Preheat oven to 450°F (230°C)
- 18- by 13-inch (45 by 33 cm) rimmed sheet pan, lined with foil

| | | |
|---|---|---|
| 4 | small bone-in skin-on chicken breasts (about 2 lbs/1 kg total), patted dry | 4 |
| 4 tbsp | olive oil, divided | 60 mL |
| 3 tsp | dried herbes de Provence, divided | 15 mL |
| 1 tsp | salt, divided | 5 mL |
| ½ tsp | freshly cracked black pepper, divided | 2 mL |
| 1½ lbs | fingerling potatoes | 750 g |
| ½ cup | drained oil-packed sun-dried tomatoes, cut into slivers | 125 mL |
| ½ cup | packed fresh flat-leaf (Italian) parsley leaves, roughly chopped | 125 mL |
| 2 tsp | finely grated lemon zest | 10 mL |

1. In a large bowl, toss chicken with half each of the oil, herbes de Provence, salt and pepper, rubbing the oil and seasonings into the chicken. Place chicken, skin side up, on prepared pan, spacing evenly.

2. In the same bowl, toss potatoes with the remaining oil, herbes de Provence, salt and pepper. Arrange potato mixture in a single layer around the chicken.

3. Roast in preheated oven for 35 to 40 minutes or until potatoes are fork-tender and an instant-read thermometer inserted in the thickest part of a chicken breast registers 165°F (74°C). Spoon pan juices over chicken and potatoes. Sprinkle with sun-dried tomatoes, parsley and lemon zest.

# Parmesan Chicken Breasts with Roasted Zucchini Sticks

Crispy Parmesan-and-panko-coated chicken breasts are roasted, not fried, to make a main dish everyone in the family will love. The accompanying zucchini sticks are a fresh counterpoint, and could not be any easier to prepare.

**Tip**

You can use 1½ cups (375 mL) corn flakes cereal, crushed, in place of the panko.

- Preheat oven to 400°F (200°C)
- Oven-safe wire rack
- 18- by 13-inch (45 by 33 cm) rimmed sheet pan, lined with parchment paper or foil

| | | |
|---|---|---|
| | Nonstick cooking spray | |
| 2 | cloves garlic, minced | 2 |
| | Salt and freshly ground black pepper | |
| 4 tbsp | olive oil, divided | 60 mL |
| 1 cup | panko (Japanese bread crumbs) | 250 mL |
| ⅔ cup | grated Parmesan cheese | 150 mL |
| 4 | boneless skinless chicken breasts (about 1½ lbs/750 g total), patted dry | 4 |
| 2 | zucchini, ends trimmed, halved crosswise, then quartered lengthwise | 4 |

1. Place rack on prepared pan and spray rack with nonstick cooking spray.

2. In a shallow dish or pie plate, combine garlic, ¼ tsp (1 mL) salt, ¼ tsp (1 mL) pepper and 3 tbsp (45 mL) oil. In a separate shallow dish, combine panko and Parmesan.

3. Working with one breast at a time, place chicken in oil mixture, turning to coat. Transfer chicken to panko mixture, turning to coat and gently pressing crumbs onto chicken to adhere. Place chicken on rack, spacing evenly. Once all chicken is coated, sprinkle with any remaining panko mixture and drizzle with any remaining oil mixture. Roast in preheated oven for 10 minutes.

4. Remove pan from oven and place zucchini on rack, cut side up, spacing evenly around chicken. Brush zucchini with the remaining oil and season with salt and pepper. Roast for 20 to 25 minutes or until both chicken and zucchini are browned and an instant-read thermometer inserted in the thickest part of a chicken breast registers 165°F (74°C).

# Roasted Chicken Caesar Salad

A shortcut dressing of olive oil, lemon juice, minced garlic and Asian fish sauce (a convenient way to add an anchovy element) serves double duty as seasoning for the roasted romaine and as the flavor backbone for the crunchy chicken topping. Hail Caesar!

**Tip**

Look for Asian fish sauce in the international section of the supermarket where soy sauce is shelved.

- Preheat oven to 450°F (230°C)
- 18- by 13-inch (45 by 33 cm) rimmed sheet pan, lined with foil

| | | |
|---|---|---:|
| 2 | cloves garlic, minced | 2 |
| 5 tbsp | olive oil, divided | 75 mL |
| 1 tbsp | fish sauce (nam pla) | 15 mL |
| 1 tbsp | freshly squeezed lemon juice | 15 mL |
| 2/3 cup | panko (Japanese bread crumbs) | 150 mL |
| 3/4 cup | grated Romano or Parmesan cheese, divided | 175 mL |
| 4 | boneless skinless chicken breasts (about 1 1/2 lbs/750 g total), patted dry | 4 |
| | Salt and freshly cracked black pepper | |
| 2 | large hearts of romaine, halved lengthwise | 2 |

1. In a medium bowl, whisk together garlic, 4 tbsp (60 mL) oil, fish sauce and lemon juice until blended. Set half of the dressing aside. To the remaining dressing, add panko and half the cheese, tossing to combine.

2. Place chicken, smooth side up, on one side of prepared pan, spacing evenly. Lightly brush chicken with the remaining oil and season with salt and pepper. Divide panko mixture among breasts, spreading to cover. Roast in preheated oven for 10 minutes.

3. Remove pan from oven and place romaine, cut side up, on the other side of the pan. Brush romaine with the remaining dressing and season with salt and pepper. Roast for 4 to 8 minutes or until panko topping is golden brown, lettuce is browning at the edges and an instant-read thermometer inserted in the thickest part of a chicken breast registers 165°F (74°C).

4. Divide chicken and lettuce among plates and sprinkle lettuce with the remaining cheese.

# Ginger Chicken with Asparagus and Chili Vinaigrette

Moist, foil-cooked chicken breasts are permeated with the peppery-spicy flavor of fresh ginger as crisp-tender asparagus roasts alongside. A 1-minute sauce of sugar, soy sauce, vinegar and chili-garlic sauce adds great depth to this fresh, fragrant meal.

**Tip**

An equal amount of green beans, trimmed and cut into 2-inch (5 cm) pieces, or broccoli or cauliflower florets can be used in place of the asparagus.

- Preheat oven to 400°F (200°C)
- 18- by 13-inch (45 by 33 cm) rimmed sheet pan, lined with foil

| | | |
|---|---|---|
| 4 | boneless skinless chicken breasts (about 1½ lbs/750 g total), patted dry | 4 |
| 2 tbsp | minced gingerroot | 30 mL |
| ¾ tsp | salt, divided | 3 mL |
| 2 tbsp | vegetable oil, divided | 30 mL |
| 1 lb | asparagus, trimmed and cut into 2-inch (5 cm) pieces | 500 g |
| 2 tsp | granulated sugar | 10 mL |
| 1½ tbsp | soy sauce | 22 mL |
| 2 tsp | unseasoned rice vinegar | 10 mL |
| 2 tsp | Asian chili-garlic sauce | 10 mL |

1. Place chicken on prepared pan, sprinkle with ginger and ½ tsp (2 mL) salt, and drizzle with 1 tbsp (15 mL) oil. Lift edges of foil and crimp to completely enclose chicken. Position chicken packet on one side of pan. Roast in preheated oven for 15 minutes.

2. Remove pan from oven and add asparagus to the other side of the pan. Drizzle with the remaining oil and sprinkle with the remaining salt. Roast for 18 to 23 minutes or until asparagus is tender and an instant-read thermometer inserted in the thickest part of a chicken breast registers 165°F (74°C).

3. Meanwhile, in a small bowl or cup, whisk together sugar, soy sauce, vinegar and chili-garlic sauce.

4. Remove chicken from foil and cut crosswise into slices. Divide chicken and asparagus among plates and spoon vinaigrette over chicken.

# Dijon Chicken with Parsnip Fries

**Makes 4 servings**

Boneless chicken breasts, along with herbes de Provence, Dijon mustard and garlic, give this one-pan, bistro-inspired dish its characteristic flavor. Parsnips are a great swap-out for the usual potatoes: still golden and crispy, but with a subtle, earthy sweetness.

**Tip**

An equal amount of dried Italian seasoning can be used in place of the herbes de Provence.

- Preheat oven to 400°F (200°C)
- 18- by 13-inch (45 by 33 cm) rimmed sheet pan, lined with parchment paper or foil

| | | |
|---|---|---|
| 1 lb | parsnips, cut into sticks 3 inches (7.5 cm) long by ¼ inch (0.5 cm) thick | 500 g |
| 4 tbsp | olive oil, divided | 60 mL |
| ½ tsp | salt, divided | 2 mL |
| ¼ tsp | freshly cracked black pepper, divided | 1 mL |
| 3 | cloves garlic, minced | 3 |
| 2 tsp | dried herbes de Provence | 10 mL |
| 2 tbsp | Dijon mustard | 30 mL |
| 1 lb | boneless skinless chicken breasts, patted dry and cut into 3-inch (7.5 cm) pieces | 500 g |
| 2 tbsp | chopped fresh parsley | 30 mL |

1. On prepared pan, toss parsnips with half each of the oil, salt and pepper. Spread in a single layer. Roast in preheated oven for 15 minutes.

2. Meanwhile, in a large bowl, whisk together garlic, herbes de Provence, the remaining salt and pepper, mustard and the remaining oil. Add chicken and turn to coat. Let marinate at room temperature while the parsnips roast.

3. Remove pan from oven and gently turn parsnips over. Nestle chicken pieces among fries, spacing evenly. Roast for 15 to 18 minutes or until fries are crisp and chicken is no longer pink inside. Sprinkle fries with parsley. Serve immediately.

# Orange Chicken with Sesame and Green Onion Rice

Equal parts spicy, tangy, savory and sweet, the marinade is what makes this one-pan meal irresistible. The sesame and green onion rice alongside may be simple, but it's packed with flavor, too.

**Tip**

If packaged frozen rice is not available, use 4 cups (1 L) cooled cooked brown rice.

- Preheat oven to 400°F (200°C)
- 18- by 13-inch (45 by 33 cm) rimmed sheet pan, sprayed with nonstick cooking spray

| | | |
|---|---|---|
| 1 tsp | ground ginger | 5 mL |
| $\frac{1}{4}$ cup | orange marmalade | 60 mL |
| 3 tbsp | soy sauce, divided | 45 mL |
| 1 tbsp | hot Chinese mustard or Dijon mustard | 15 mL |
| 1 lb | boneless skinless chicken breasts, patted dry and cut into 1-$\frac{1}{2}$ inch (4 cm) pieces | 500 g |
| 2 | packages (each 12 oz/375 g) frozen brown rice, thawed | 2 |
| 2 tbsp | toasted (dark) sesame oil | 30 mL |
| 1$\frac{1}{2}$ cups | chopped green onions (about 1 large bunch) | 375 mL |

1. In a large bowl, combine ginger, marmalade, 2 tbsp (30 mL) soy sauce and mustard until blended. Add chicken, stirring to coat. Let marinate while baking the rice.

2. On prepared pan, toss rice with sesame oil and the remaining soy sauce. Spread evenly on pan. Roast in preheated oven for 5 minutes.

3. Remove pan from oven and stir green onions into rice, then push rice to one side of the pan. Place chicken pieces on the other side of the pan, spacing evenly. Spoon some of the marinade over chicken. Roast for 12 to 17 minutes or until rice is hot and chicken is no longer pink inside.

# Buttery Chicken and Rice Curry

Quick-roast chicken pieces and red onion with fragrant spices and butter, then add rice to the sheet pan for this one-pan weeknight curry. Set the table with bowls of yogurt, almonds, raisins and more so diners can assemble their own final dish.

## Tips

An equal amount of melted virgin coconut oil, vegetable oil or olive oil can be used in place of the butter.

Fresh mint, basil or parsley leaves, or a combination, can be used in place of the cilantro.

An equal amount of medium-grain white rice can be used in place of the long-grain rice.

- Preheat oven to 400°F (200°C)
- 18- by 13-inch (45 by 33 cm) rimmed sheet pan, lined with foil and sprayed with nonstick cooking spray

| | | |
|---|---|---|
| 5 tsp | curry powder, divided | 25 mL |
| 1½ tsp | ground cinnamon, divided | 7 mL |
| 1½ tsp | salt, divided | 7 mL |
| ½ tsp | freshly ground black pepper, divided | 2 mL |
| ¼ cup | unsalted butter, melted | 60 mL |
| 1 lb | boneless skinless chicken breasts, patted dry and cut into 1½-inch (4 cm) pieces | 500 g |
| 1 | small red onion, trimmed, halved horizontally and thinly sliced into half-rings | 1 |
| 1¾ cups | boiling water | 425 mL |
| 1⅓ cups | long-grain white rice | 325 mL |
| 1 cup | packed fresh cilantro leaves, roughly chopped | 250 mL |

### Suggested Toppings

Lightly salted roasted almonds, chopped

Plain yogurt

Golden or dark raisins

Flaked unsweetened coconut (plain or toasted)

Prepared chutney

1. In a medium bowl, whisk together 3 tsp (15 mL) curry powder, ½ tsp (2 mL) cinnamon, ¾ tsp (3 mL) salt, ¼ tsp (1 mL) pepper and butter. Add chicken and onion, tossing to coat. Spread in a single layer on prepared pan. Roast in preheated oven for 15 minutes, stirring halfway through.

2. Meanwhile, in a 2-cup (500 mL) glass measuring cup, combine boiling water and the remaining curry powder, cinnamon, salt and pepper.

3. Remove pan from oven and scatter rice over chicken and onions. Slowly pour boiling water mixture over top. Using oven mitts (pan is very hot), tightly cover pan with foil, sealing the edges. Bake for 25 minutes.

4. Remove pan from oven and let stand for 10 minutes. Carefully remove foil and fluff rice with a fork. Sprinkle pan contents with cilantro and gently toss to combine. Serve with any of the suggested toppings, as desired.

# Bacon-Roasted Chicken and Brussels Sprouts

Juicy, meaty and versatile chicken breasts go from good to utterly awesome when they, along with nutty Brussels sprouts, are roasted in bacon fat and seasoned with thyme and hot pepper. An easy wow of a dinner!

## Tips

An equal amount of chicken tenders can be used in place of the chicken breast pieces.

If using regular bacon (instead of thick-cut), reduce the roasting time in step 1 to 5 to 10 minutes.

- Preheat oven to 400°F (200°C)
- 18- by 13-inch (45 by 33 cm) rimmed sheet pan, lined with parchment paper

| | | |
|---|---|---|
| 3 | slices thick-cut bacon | 3 |
| 2 lbs | Brussels sprouts, trimmed and halved lengthwise if large | 1 kg |
| ³⁄₄ tsp | salt, divided | 3 mL |
| ³⁄₄ tsp | dried thyme | 3 mL |
| ¹⁄₄ tsp | hot pepper flakes | 1 mL |
| 1 lb | boneless skinless chicken breasts, patted dry and cut into 1¹⁄₂-inch (4 cm) pieces | 500 g |

1. Place bacon in a single layer on prepared pan, spacing evenly. Roast in preheated oven for 15 to 20 minutes or until crisp.

2. Remove pan from oven and transfer bacon to a plate lined with paper towels. (Do not drain bacon fat from pan.)

3. Add Brussels sprouts to pan and sprinkle with ¹⁄₂ tsp (2 mL) salt, thyme and hot pepper flakes. Gently toss to coat with bacon fat and seasonings. Roast for 20 minutes.

4. Season chicken with the remaining salt. Remove pan from oven and stir Brussels sprouts. Nestle chicken among the vegetables, spacing evenly, and spoon some of the bacon fat over top. Roast for 20 to 25 minutes or until Brussels sprouts are browned and tender and chicken is no longer pink inside.

5. Crumble bacon and sprinkle over sprouts.

# Warm Chicken Salad with Beets, Rustic Croutons and Goat Cheese

Start with canned baby beets to create an easy, exceptional component of this rustic, wine country–inspired salad. Tossing in creamy, piquant goat cheese at the end ups both the flavor and sophistication in seconds.

**Tip**

Feta or blue cheese can be used in place of the goat cheese.

- Preheat oven to 400°F (200°C)
- 18- by 13-inch (45 by 33 cm) rimmed sheet pan, lined with parchment paper

| | | |
|---|---|---|
| 1 lb | boneless skinless chicken breasts, patted dry and cut into 1-inch (2.5 cm) pieces | 500 g |
| 1 | baguette, torn or cut into bite-size chunks | 1 |
| 1 | can (14 to 15 oz/398 to 425 mL) baby beets, drained, beets halved lengthwise | 1 |
| 6 tbsp | olive oil, divided | 90 mL |
| | Salt and freshly cracked black pepper | |
| 1 tbsp | balsamic vinegar | 15 mL |
| 6 cups | mesclun or other mixed baby lettuces | 1.5 L |
| 4 oz | goat cheese, crumbled | 125 g |

1. Place chicken and bread in a single layer on prepared pan. Arrange beets in the spaces between the chicken and bread. Drizzle everything with half the oil and season with salt and pepper.

2. Roast in preheated oven for 12 to 15 minutes or until chicken is no longer pink inside and bread is golden and crisp. Let cool on pan for 10 minutes.

3. Meanwhile, in a small bowl, whisk together vinegar and the remaining oil until blended. Season to taste with salt and pepper.

4. Add mesclun to pan. Drizzle with dressing and toss to coat. Serve salad warm, sprinkled with cheese.

# Thai Chicken Tenders with Broiled Pineapple Slaw

This Thai-inspired chicken dish features peanut sauce–marinated chicken breasts seasoned with ginger and Sriracha. Tropical pineapple caramelizes alongside the chicken and is then tossed into a fresh, crunchy coleslaw with lime and basil.

## Tips

Thawed frozen pineapple can be used in place of the fresh pineapple.

In place of the chicken tenders, you can use 1 lb (500 g) boneless skinless chicken breasts, patted dry and cut into 3-inch (7.5 cm) pieces.

- 18- by 13-inch (45 by 33 cm) rimmed sheet pan, lined with foil and sprayed with nonstick cooking spray

| | | |
|---|---|---|
| 4 tbsp | packed light brown sugar, divided | 60 mL |
| 1 tsp | ground ginger | 5 mL |
| 3 tbsp | vegetable oil, divided | 45 mL |
| 2 tbsp | soy sauce, divided | 30 mL |
| 1½ tbsp | Sriracha, divided | 22 mL |
| 1 tbsp | creamy peanut butter | 15 mL |
| 1 lb | chicken tenders, patted dry | 500 g |
| 1¼ cups | chopped fresh pineapple | 300 mL |
| 4 cups | shredded coleslaw mix (shredded cabbage and carrots) | 1 L |
| 2 tbsp | freshly squeezed lime juice | 30 mL |
| ¼ cup | chopped fresh basil or mint | 60 mL |

1. In a large bowl, whisk together 3 tbsp (45 mL) brown sugar, ginger, 1 tbsp (15 mL) oil, 1 tbsp (15 mL) soy sauce, 1 tbsp (15 mL) Sriracha and peanut butter. Add chicken and toss to coat. Let marinate at room temperature for 15 minutes or cover and refrigerate for up to 6 hours.

2. Preheat broiler, with rack set 4 inches (10 cm) from the heat source.

3. Remove chicken from marinade, discarding excess marinade, and place on prepared pan, covering two-thirds of the pan and spacing evenly. Broil for 6 minutes.

4. Remove pan from oven and spread pineapple on remaining space on pan. Sprinkle pineapple with the remaining brown sugar. Broil for 3 to 5 minutes or until chicken is browned and no longer pink inside. Transfer chicken to plates.

5. Add coleslaw mix to pineapple on pan. Drizzle with lime juice and the remaining oil, soy sauce and Sriracha; toss to coat. Divide among plates with chicken and sprinkle slaw with basil.

# Chicken Sausages with Honey-Mustard Roasted Vegetables

**Makes 4 servings**

The sweet-savory combination of mustard and honey is inspired by German and Alsatian cuisine. The bold flavor livens up hearty roasted winter vegetables and chicken sausages.

**Tip**

Fully cooked turkey or pork sausages can be used in place of the chicken sausages.

- Preheat oven to 425°F (220°C)
- 18- by 13-inch (45 by 33 cm) rimmed sheet pan, lined with foil

| | | |
|---|---|---|
| 3 tbsp | olive oil, divided | 45 mL |
| 3 tbsp | liquid honey | 45 mL |
| 1 tbsp | Dijon mustard | 15 mL |
| ¾ tsp | salt | 3 mL |
| 4 | carrots, cut into 1-inch (2.5 cm) long pieces | 4 |
| 4 | parsnips, cut into 1-inch (2.5 cm) long pieces | 4 |
| 1 | large red bell pepper, cut into 2-inch (5 cm) pieces | 1 |
| 1 | small red onion, cut into 12 wedges | 1 |
| 4 | fully cooked chicken sausages (about 12 oz/375 g total) | 4 |

1. In a large bowl, whisk together 2 tbsp (30 mL) oil, honey, mustard and salt. Add carrots, parsnips, red pepper and onion, tossing to coat. Spread in a single layer on prepared pan. Roast in preheated oven for 25 minutes.

2. Remove pan from oven and gently stir vegetables. Nestle sausages among the vegetables, spacing evenly. Brush sausages with the remaining oil. Roast for 8 to 10 minutes or until vegetables are tender and sausages are browned and heated through.

# Roasted Turkey Breast with Thanksgiving Fixings

**Makes 4 servings**

Roasted turkey breast, assorted vegetables, dressing and cranberries mingle with butter and sage in this spectacularly easy, deconstructed Thanksgiving dinner. You may have to give thanks for this meal on many weeknights throughout the fall and winter months.

**Tip**

You can use 2 cups (500 mL) cubed peeled butternut squash in place of the sweet potato.

- Preheat oven to 425°F (220°C)
- 18- by 13-inch (45 by 33 cm) rimmed sheet pan, lined with foil and sprayed with nonstick cooking spray

| | | |
|---|---|---|
| 1 | bone-in skin-on turkey breast (about 2 lbs/1 kg), patted dry | 1 |
| 5 tbsp | unsalted butter, melted, divided | 75 mL |
| | Salt and freshly cracked black pepper | |
| 2 | large stalks celery, trimmed | 2 |
| 1 | large red onion, peeled | 1 |
| 1 | large sweet potato (about 1 lb/500 g), peeled | 1 |
| 8 oz | green beans, trimmed and halved crosswise | 250 g |
| 2 tsp | dried rubbed sage, divided | 10 mL |
| 2½ cups | cubed rustic-style bread | 625 mL |
| ½ cup | dried cranberries | 125 mL |
| ⅓ cup | ready-to-use chicken broth | 75 mL |

1. Gently loosen skin from turkey breast. Rub 2 tbsp (30 mL) butter under skin and all over outside of breast. Season generously, inside and out, with salt and pepper. Place on prepared pan. Roast in preheated oven for 20 minutes.

2. Meanwhile, cut celery, onion and sweet potato into 1-inch (2.5 cm) pieces. Place in a large bowl, along with green beans, 2 tbsp (30 mL) butter, 1 tsp (5 mL) sage, ¾ tsp (3 mL) salt and ½ tsp (2 mL) pepper; toss to combine.

3. Remove pan from oven and spread vegetables around turkey in a single layer. Roast for 25 minutes.

4. In the same bowl, toss together bread cubes, cranberries, the remaining sage, broth and the remaining butter. Remove pan from oven and tuck bread mixture around turkey and vegetables. Roast for 10 to 15 minutes or until vegetables are tender, turkey skin is crisp and golden brown and an instant-read thermometer inserted in the thickest part of the turkey breast registers 165°F (74°C). Remove pan from oven, cover loosely with foil and let rest for 10 minutes.

5. Carve turkey and serve with vegetables and stuffing.

# Turkey Meatloaf Minis with Skinny Fries

Transform a rich comfort food meal into a healthier — as well as faster and easier — choice with just a few alterations: use lean ground turkey, olive oil and fresh herbs, make the meatloaves miniature (to cook quickly) and then roast everything, fries included, on a single sheet pan.

## Tips

You can use fresh bread crumbs or ½ cup (125 mL) corn flakes cereal, crushed, in place of the panko.

Choose a barbecue sauce that is free of corn syrup and preservatives and has a short list of all-natural ingredients.

- Preheat oven to 425°F (220°C)
- 18- by 13-inch (45 by 33 cm) rimmed sheet pan, lined with foil and sprayed with nonstick cooking spray

| | | |
|---|---|---|
| 1½ lbs | russet potatoes, peeled and cut lengthwise into ¼-inch (0.5 cm) thick wedges | 750 g |
| | Hot (not boiling) water | |
| 2 tbsp | olive oil | 30 mL |
| 1 tsp | salt, divided | 5 mL |
| | Freshly ground black pepper | |
| 1 lb | lean ground turkey | 500 g |
| 1 | large egg, lightly beaten | 1 |
| ⅓ cup | finely chopped onion | 75 mL |
| ¼ cup | panko (Japanese bread crumbs) | 60 mL |
| 4 tbsp | barbecue sauce, divided | 60 mL |
| 2 tbsp | chopped fresh flat-leaf (Italian) parsley | 30 mL |

1. Place potatoes in a large bowl and add enough hot water to cover. Let stand for 10 minutes.

2. Drain potatoes, pat dry and return to dry bowl. Add oil, ¾ tsp (3 mL) salt and ⅛ tsp (0.5 mL) pepper; toss to coat. Spread in a single layer on one side of the prepared pan. Roast in preheated oven for 20 minutes.

3. Meanwhile, in the same bowl, combine turkey, egg, onion, panko, 3 tbsp (30 mL) barbecue sauce, the remaining salt and ¼ tsp (1 mL) pepper until blended. Form into 4 small loaves, each about 4 by 2 inches (10 by 5 cm).

4. Remove pan from oven and turn potatoes over. Place meatloaves on the other side of the pan, spacing evenly. Brush meatloaf tops with the remaining barbecue sauce. Roast for 20 to 25 minutes or until potatoes are golden and crisp and an instant-read thermometer inserted in the center of the meatloaves registers 165°F (74°C). Sprinkle potatoes with parsley.

# Crispy Baked Turkey Burgers

Liberate burgers from the unhealthy fast-food list by making them at home with lean ground turkey and baking them in the oven. The turkey is blended with thyme and green onions and then coated in panko, yielding crispy, uber-flavorful burgers.

**Tip**

You can use 2 cups (500 mL) corn flakes cereal, crushed, in place of the panko.

- Preheat oven to 375°F (190°C)
- 18- by 13-inch (45 by 33 cm) rimmed sheet pan, lined with parchment paper

| | | |
|---|---|---|
| 1¼ lbs | lean ground turkey | 625 g |
| ⅔ cup | finely chopped green onions (white and green parts) | 150 mL |
| 1 tsp | dried thyme | 5 mL |
| | Salt and freshly ground black pepper | |
| ½ cup | all-purpose flour | 125 mL |
| 2 | large eggs | 2 |
| 1¼ cups | panko (Japanese bread crumbs) | 300 mL |
| | Nonstick cooking spray | |
| 4 | hamburger buns or soft sandwich rolls, split | 4 |

**Suggested Toppings**

Barbecue sauce

Thinly sliced Swiss or provolone cheese

Lettuce or spinach leaves

Sliced tomatoes

1. In a large bowl, combine turkey, green onions, thyme, ¾ tsp (3 mL) salt and ⅛ tsp (0.5 mL) pepper until blended. Form into four ¾-inch (2 cm) thick patties.

2. In a shallow plate, combine flour and ¼ tsp (1 mL) salt. In a second shallow plate, whisk eggs until blended. Place panko in a third shallow plate. Working with one patty at a time, coat patty in flour, then egg, then panko. Place on prepared pan, spacing evenly. Lightly spray patties with cooking spray. Discard any excess flour, egg and panko.

3. Bake in preheated oven for 12 minutes. Remove pan from oven and, using a spatula, carefully turn patties over. Place buns, cut side up, around edges of pan. Bake for 5 to 8 minutes or until coating appears crisp and an instant-read thermometer inserted horizontally in the center of a patty registers 165°F (74°C).

4. Transfer patties to bottom halves of buns and layer with any of the suggested toppings, as desired. Cover with top halves of buns, pressing down gently.

# Thai Turkey Lettuce Wraps

Ground turkey, seasoned with fresh ginger, Thai curry paste and lime, is wrapped in butter lettuce leaves for a light and fun main dish that is personalized with an assortment of fresh and vibrant toppings.

## Tips

An equal amount of soy sauce can be used in place of the fish sauce.

You can use 2 tsp (10 mL) ground ginger in place of the fresh gingerroot.

- Preheat oven to 400°F (200°C)
- 18- by 13-inch (45 by 33 cm) rimmed sheet pan, sprayed with nonstick cooking spray

| | | |
|---|---|---|
| 2 tbsp | minced gingerroot | 30 mL |
| 4 tbsp | fish sauce (nam pla), divided | 60 mL |
| 1½ tbsp | Thai green curry paste | 22 mL |
| 2 tsp | finely grated lime zest | 10 mL |
| 1½ lbs | lean ground turkey | 750 g |
| 2 tbsp | packed light brown sugar | 30 mL |
| ⅛ tsp | cayenne pepper | 0.5 mL |
| ⅓ cup | freshly squeezed lime juice | 75 mL |
| 12 | butter or iceberg lettuce leaves | 12 |
| ½ cup | packed fresh mint or cilantro leaves | 125 mL |

**Suggested Toppings**

Fresh mint and/or cilantro leaves

Thinly sliced Thai red chile peppers

Chopped roasted peanuts

Bean sprouts

Grated carrots

1. In a large bowl, whisk together ginger, 2 tbsp (30 mL) fish sauce, curry paste and lime zest until blended. Add ground turkey, mixing gently with your hands or a wooden spoon until combined. Transfer turkey mixture to prepared pan, breaking it up into 1-inch (2.5 cm) pieces with a spoon and spacing evenly.

2. Bake in preheated oven for 10 minutes. Open oven door and stir, breaking up turkey with the spoon. Close door and bake for 6 to 11 minutes or until turkey is no longer pink.

3. Meanwhile, in a small bowl, whisk together brown sugar, cayenne, lime juice and the remaining fish sauce until sugar is dissolved.

4. Remove pan from oven and drizzle half the dressing over turkey; stir gently to combine.

5. Place 3 lettuce leaves on each of four plates, underside of leaves facing up. Spoon turkey mixture down the center of each leaf, then top with any of the suggested toppings, as desired. Serve with the remaining dressing on the side.

# Smoked Turkey Sausage, Potatoes and Green Beans

**Makes 4 servings**

Convenient smoked sausage is made special when coupled with thyme-scented potatoes and crisp green beans. The whole meal takes no more than 10 minutes of prep time!

## Tips

Fully cooked chicken or pork sausage can be used in place of the turkey sausage.

An equal weight of yellow-fleshed or red-skinned potatoes, cut into 1½-inch (4 cm) pieces, can be used in place of the baby potatoes.

- Preheat oven to 450°F (230°C)
- 18- by 13-inch (45 by 33 cm) rimmed sheet pan, lined with foil and sprayed with nonstick cooking spray

| | | |
|---|---|---|
| 1 | package (12 to 14 oz/375 to 400 g) fully cooked smoked turkey sausage | 1 |
| 1½ lbs | yellow-fleshed or red-skinned baby potatoes | 750 g |
| 3 tbsp | olive oil, divided | 45 mL |
| 2 tsp | dried thyme | 10 mL |
| ¾ tsp | salt | 3 mL |
| ¼ tsp | freshly ground black pepper | 1 mL |
| 12 oz | green beans, trimmed and cut in half crosswise | 375 g |

1. Cut sausage crosswise into 8 equal pieces. On prepared pan, toss together sausage, potatoes, 2 tbsp (30 mL) oil, thyme, salt and pepper. Spread in an even layer. Roast in preheated oven for 20 minutes.

2. Meanwhile, in a medium bowl, toss together green beans and the remaining oil.

3. Remove pan from oven and stir sausage and potatoes. Arrange beans evenly in between sausage and potatoes on pan. Roast for 8 to 12 minutes or until potatoes and green beans are tender and sausages are browned and heated through.

# Pork, Beef and Lamb Meals

# Herb-Crusted Pork Tenderloin with Butter-Dijon Parsnips

**Makes 4 servings**

Basil is a wonderful herb for adding sweetness to meats like pork tenderloin without relying on any added sugar. Here, it blends with crisp panko in a golden crust that matches the earthy sweetness of the parsnips.

**Tips**

An equal amount of flat-leaf (Italian) parsley can be used in place of the basil.

Fresh bread crumbs can be used in place of the panko.

- Preheat oven to 425°F (220°C)
- 18- by 13-inch (45 by 33 cm) rimmed sheet pan, lined with foil and sprayed with nonstick cooking spray

| | | |
|---|---|---|
| 1½ lbs | parsnips, cut into 2- by ½-inch (5 by 1 cm) pieces | 750 g |
| 3 tbsp | unsalted butter, melted | 45 mL |
| 1 tbsp | Dijon mustard | 15 mL |
| 1 tsp | salt, divided | 5 mL |
| ⅔ cup | packed fresh basil leaves, chopped | 150 mL |
| ½ cup | panko (Japanese bread crumbs) | 125 mL |
| 1 tsp | freshly ground black pepper | 5 mL |
| 3 tbsp | olive oil, divided | 45 mL |
| 1¼ lb | pork tenderloin, trimmed and patted dry | 625 g |

1. On prepared pan, toss parsnips with butter, mustard and ¼ tsp (1 mL) salt. Spread in a single layer. Roast in preheated oven for 10 minutes.

2. Meanwhile, reserve 1 tbsp (15 mL) of the basil. In a small bowl, combine panko, pepper, the remaining basil, the remaining salt and 2 tbsp (30 mL) oil.

3. Brush pork with the remaining oil and press crumb mixture all over tenderloin to coat.

4. Remove pan from oven, turn parsnips over and clear a space for the tenderloin. Place tenderloin in the cleared space. Roast for 19 to 24 minutes or until parsnips are browned and crisp and an instant-read thermometer inserted in the thickest part of the tenderloin registers 145°F (63°C) for medium-rare.

5. Transfer pork to a cutting board, tent with foil and let rest for 10 minutes before slicing across the grain. Sprinkle parsnips with the reserved basil just before serving.

# Black Pepper Pork Tenderloin with Parmesan Roasted Potatoes

**Makes 4 servings**

Go with pork tenderloin instead of chicken breasts any time you want lean protein but extra flavor. The flavor is pumped up further with a black pepper coating and a side of golden, parsley-flecked Parmesan potatoes.

## Tips

An equal amount of red or white wine vinegar can be used in place of the sherry vinegar.

In place of the parsley, you can use 2 tbsp (30 mL) chopped fresh dill.

- Preheat oven to 400°F (200°C)
- 18- by 13-inch (45 by 33 cm) rimmed sheet pan, lined with parchment paper or foil and sprayed with nonstick cooking spray

| | | |
|---|---|---|
| 2 lbs | yellow-fleshed potatoes, cut into 1-inch (2.5 cm) cubes | 1 kg |
| 4 tbsp | olive oil, divided | 60 mL |
| 1¼ tsp | freshly cracked black pepper, divided | 6 mL |
| ¾ tsp | salt, divided | 3 mL |
| 1 lb | pork tenderloin, trimmed and patted dry | 500 g |
| 1 cup | freshly grated Parmesan cheese | 250 mL |
| 1½ tbsp | sherry vinegar | 22 mL |
| ½ cup | packed fresh flat-leaf (Italian) parsley leaves, chopped | 125 mL |

1. On prepared pan, toss potatoes with 3 tbsp (45 mL) oil, ¼ tsp (1 mL) pepper and ½ tsp (2 mL) salt. Spread in a single layer. Roast in preheated oven for 15 minutes.

2. Meanwhile, cut six 1-inch (2.5 cm) slits, evenly spaced, across the top of the tenderloin. Brush pork with the remaining oil and season with the remaining pepper and salt. Using your hands, work the seasoning all over the tenderloin.

3. Remove pan from oven, stir the potatoes and clear a space for the tenderloin. Place tenderloin in the cleared space. Roast for 20 minutes. Open oven door and sprinkle potatoes with cheese and vinegar. Close door and roast for 5 to 8 minutes or until an instant-read thermometer inserted in the thickest part of the tenderloin registers 145°F (63°C) for medium-rare.

4. Transfer pork to a cutting board and let rest for 5 to 10 minutes before slicing across the grain. Sprinkle potatoes with parsley just before serving.

# Pork Tenderloin with Charred Corn Salad

Pork tenderloin is terrific for showcasing any number of flavors, but don't think you need to add them all at once. A simple rub of cumin, salt and pepper, for example, is outstanding. The charred corn salad alongside is based on the Mexican corn dish *esquites*. The word *esquites* comes from the Nahuatl word *ízquitl*, which means "toasted corn," and the dish is a popular street food throughout Mexico. In place of the typical creamy cheese sauce, this version gets a crumble of queso fresco.

## Tips

It will take about 4 to 5 large ears of corn to yield 3 cups (750 mL) corn kernels.

If fresh corn is out of season, use an equal amount of thawed frozen corn kernels. Thoroughly pat the kernels dry with paper towels before roasting.

An equal amount of cumin or regular chili powder, plus $\frac{1}{8}$ tsp (0.5 mL) cayenne pepper, can be used in place of the chipotle chile powder.

- Preheat oven to 400°F (200°C)
- 18- by 13-inch (45 by 33 cm) rimmed sheet pan, lined with parchment paper or foil and sprayed with nonstick cooking spray

| | | |
|---|---|---|
| 1 lb | pork tenderloin, trimmed and patted dry | 500 g |
| 2 tbsp | vegetable oil, divided | 30 mL |
| 1 tsp | ground cumin | 5 mL |
| | Salt and freshly cracked black pepper | |
| 3 cups | fresh corn kernels (see tips, at left) | 750 mL |
| 1 tsp | chipotle chile powder | 5 mL |
| 2 | green onions, thinly sliced | 2 |
| 1 | Hass avocado, diced | 1 |
| $\frac{1}{2}$ cup | packed fresh cilantro leaves, chopped | 125 mL |
| 2 tbsp | crumbled queso fresco or mild feta cheese | 30 mL |
| 1 tbsp | freshly squeezed lime juice | 15 mL |

1. Cut six 1-inch (2.5 cm) slits, evenly spaced, across the top of the tenderloin. Place on prepared pan. Brush with half the oil and sprinkle with cumin, $\frac{1}{4}$ tsp (1 mL) salt and $\frac{1}{4}$ tsp (1 mL) pepper. Using your hands, work the seasoning all over the tenderloin.

2. In a large bowl, toss corn with the remaining oil and chile powder. Season with salt and pepper. Spread in a single layer around pork.

3. Roast in preheated oven for 25 to 28 minutes or until corn is browned at edges and an instant-read thermometer inserted in the thickest part of the tenderloin registers 145°F (63°C) for medium-rare.

4. Transfer pork to cutting board and let rest for 5 to 10 minutes before slicing against the grain. Just before serving, add green onions, avocado, cilantro, queso fresco and lime juice to corn on pan, gently tossing to coat. Season to taste with salt and pepper.

# Oven-Fried Pork Chops with Lemony Broccoli and Cannellini

This sheet pan wonder pairs creamy cannellini and crisp-tender broccoli with juicy pork chops and lots of fresh lemon for an intensely aromatic and hearty meal.

## Tips

Chickpeas or any other white beans (such as Great Northern or navy beans) can be used in place of the cannellini beans.

Fresh bread crumbs can be used in place of the panko.

## Variation

Substitute an equal amount of cauliflower florets for the broccoli.

- Preheat oven to 450°F (230°C)
- 18- by 13-inch (45 by 33 cm) rimmed sheet pan, lined with foil and sprayed with nonstick cooking spray

| | | |
|---|---|---|
| 1½ cups | panko (Japanese bread crumbs) | 375 mL |
| ⅓ cup | mayonnaise | 75 mL |
| 2 tbsp | Dijon mustard | 30 mL |
| ¾ tsp | salt, divided | 3 mL |
| ¾ tsp | freshly cracked black pepper, divided | 3 mL |
| 4 | bone-in pork loin chops, about ½-inch (1 cm) thick, trimmed and patted dry | 4 |
| 4 cups | small broccoli florets | 1 L |
| 2 tbsp | olive oil, divided | 30 mL |
| 1 | can (14 to 19 oz/398 to 540 mL) cannellini (white kidney) beans, drained and rinsed | 1 |
| 1 tsp | finely grated lemon zest | 5 mL |
| 1 tbsp | freshly squeezed lemon juice | 15 mL |

1. Spread panko on a dinner plate. In a small cup or bowl, stir together mayonnaise, mustard, ½ tsp (2 mL) salt and ½ tsp (2 mL) pepper until blended.

2. Generously spread both sides of pork chops with mayonnaise mixture, then press into panko to coat. Place pork chops on prepared pan, spacing evenly. Discard excess mayonnaise mixture and panko. Roast in preheated oven for 10 minutes.

3. Meanwhile, in a medium bowl, toss broccoli with half the oil and the remaining salt and pepper.

4. Remove pan from oven and turn pork chops over. Arrange broccoli around pork chops. Roast for 7 to 10 minutes or until broccoli is bright green and an instant-read thermometer inserted in the thickest part of the pork, without touching the bone, registers 145°F (63°C) for medium-rare.

5. Remove pan from oven and transfer pork chops to plates. Add beans, lemon zest, lemon juice and the remaining oil to broccoli on pan, tossing to coat. Serve alongside pork.

# Paprika-Rubbed Pork Chops with Piperade

Sweet paprika, peppers and tomatoes share the spotlight with pork chops in this Basque classic, adding bold flavor and freshness to the dish.

## Tips

An equal amount of pimentón (smoked paprika) can be substituted for the sweet paprika.

Red, yellow or orange bell peppers can be used in place of the green bell peppers.

- Preheat oven to 400°F (200°C)
- 18- by 13-inch (45 by 33 cm) rimmed sheet pan, lined with parchment paper or foil

| | | |
|---|---|---|
| 4 | bone-in pork loin chops, about $\frac{1}{2}$-inch (1 cm) thick, trimmed and patted dry | 4 |
| 3 tbsp | olive oil, divided | 45 mL |
| $2\frac{1}{2}$ tsp | sweet paprika, divided | 12 mL |
| | Salt and freshly cracked black pepper | |
| 2 | green bell peppers, cut into $\frac{1}{2}$-inch (1 cm) strips | 2 |
| 1 | onion, thinly sliced horizontally | 1 |
| 4 | cloves garlic, minced | 4 |
| 2 cups | cherry or grape tomatoes | 500 mL |
| 1 tsp | granulated sugar | 5 mL |

1. Place pork chops on prepared pan. Drizzle with 2 tbsp (30 mL) oil, sprinkle with 2 tsp (10 mL) paprika and season generously with salt and pepper. Using your hands, rub the seasoning all over the chops, turning to coat. Move chops to one side of pan, spacing evenly.

2. Arrange green peppers and onion in a single layer on the other side of pan. Drizzle with the remaining oil and season with salt, pepper and the remaining paprika.

3. Roast in preheated oven for 10 minutes. Remove pan from oven and turn chops over. Add garlic, tomatoes and sugar to peppers and onions, tossing gently to combine. Roast for 15 to 20 minutes or until vegetables are tender and an instant-read thermometer inserted in the thickest part of the pork, without touching the bone, registers 145°F (63°C) for medium-rare.

# Rosemary Pork Chops with Roasted Pears and Red Onions

The bold flavors of rosemary and roasted pork meld with the red onions and pears, draping both in their combined aromas and flavors.

### Tip
You can substitute ¾ tsp (3 mL) dried rosemary, crumbled, for the fresh rosemary.

- Preheat oven to 425°F (220°C)
- 18- by 13-inch (45 by 33 cm) rimmed sheet pan, lined with foil and sprayed with nonstick cooking spray

| | | |
|---|---|---|
| 1 | large red onion, cut into 1-inch (2.5 cm) pieces | 1 |
| 3 tbsp | olive oil, divided | 45 mL |
| | Salt and freshly ground black pepper | |
| 4 | boneless center-cut pork loin chops (each 6 oz/175 g), trimmed and patted dry | 4 |
| 3 | pears (unpeeled), cut into eighths | 3 |
| 1 tbsp | liquid honey | 15 mL |
| 1 tbsp | balsamic vinegar | 15 mL |
| 1½ tsp | minced fresh rosemary | 7 mL |

**Suggested Toppings**

Chopped fresh flat-leaf (Italian) parsley
Crumbled blue cheese

1. On prepared pan, toss onion with 1 tbsp (15 mL) oil, ¼ tsp (1 mL) salt and ⅛ tsp (0.5 mL) pepper. Roast in preheated oven for 15 minutes.

2. Meanwhile, season both sides of pork chops with salt and pepper.

3. Remove pan from oven and stir onions. Nestle pears among the onions and drizzle pears with honey, vinegar and the remaining oil. Push aside onions and pears to make four spaces for the pork chops. Place pork chops in the spaces and sprinkle with rosemary. Roast for 17 to 22 minutes or until an instant-read thermometer inserted in the thickest part of the pork registers 145°F (63°C) for medium-rare.

4. Serve pork chops with pear mixture and the suggested toppings, as desired.

# Sheet Pan Pork Posole

My sheet pan version of this Mexican pork and hominy favorite is a departure from the traditional stew, but it's a delicious one. Plus, it is ready in less than 30 minutes. Serve with plenty of the suggested accompaniments for a fully authentic experience.

## Variations

*Red Pork Posole:* Replace the salsa verde with an equal amount of tomato salsa (not thick and chunky style).

*Sheet Pan White Chile:* Replace the hominy with two 14- or 15-oz (398 or 425 mL) cans of white beans (such as cannellini, navy or Great Northern), drained and rinsed. Increase the amount of salsa verde to 1 1/2 cups (375 mL).

- Preheat oven to 450°F (230°C)
- 18- by 13-inch (45 by 33 cm) rimmed sheet pan, sprayed with nonstick cooking spray

| | | |
|---|---|---|
| 1 lb | pork tenderloin, trimmed, patted dry and cut into 1-inch (2.5 cm) cubes | 500 g |
| 1 | large onion, halved lengthwise and sliced | 1 |
| 2 tbsp | vegetable oil | 30 mL |
| 1 tbsp | ancho chile powder or regular chili powder | 15 mL |
| 1 1/2 tsp | ground cumin | 7 mL |
| 1/2 tsp | salt | 2 mL |
| 1/8 tsp | freshly ground black pepper | 0.5 mL |
| 2 | cans (each 15 oz/425 mL) hominy, drained and rinsed | 2 |
| 1 1/4 cups | salsa verde | 300 mL |

**Suggested Accompaniments**

Lime wedges
Chopped fresh cilantro
Thinly sliced radishes
Thinly sliced or chopped jalapeño pepper
Corn tortillas, warmed

1. On prepared pan, toss together pork, onion, oil, chile powder, cumin, salt and pepper. Spread in a single layer. Roast in preheated oven for 15 minutes.

2. Remove pan from oven and stir pork and onion. Stir in hominy and salsa. Roast for 8 to 12 minutes or until just a hint of pink remains in pork, hominy is heated through and salsa has thickened slightly. Serve with any of the suggested accompaniments, as desired.

# Sheet Pan Fajitas

Fajitas are surprisingly quick and simple when all of the principle components are roasted on a sheet pan. Served with as many or few accompaniments as you like, this version is a guaranteed hit.

## Variation

Substitute an equal weight of boneless skinless chicken breasts or thighs for the pork tenderloin.

- Preheat oven to 450°F (230°C)
- 18- by 13-inch (45 by 33 cm) rimmed sheet pan, lined with foil and sprayed with nonstick cooking spray

| | | |
|---|---|---|
| 2 tsp | chili powder | 10 mL |
| 1½ tsp | ground cumin | 7 mL |
| 1 tsp | salt | 5 mL |
| ¼ tsp | cayenne pepper (optional) | 1 mL |
| 3 tbsp | vegetable oil | 45 mL |
| 1 lb | pork tenderloin, trimmed, patted dry and cut into 3- by ½-inch (7.5 by 1 cm) strips | 500 g |
| 3 | large bell peppers (1 each green, red and yellow), sliced | 3 |
| 1 | large onion, halved lengthwise and sliced | 1 |
| 8 | 6-inch (15 cm) flour or corn tortillas | 8 |

**Suggested Accompaniments**

Lime wedges

Sour cream

Fresh cilantro leaves

Queso fresco or mild feta cheese, crumbled

Hot pepper sauce

Guacamole or diced avocado

1. In a small bowl or cup, stir together chili powder, cumin, salt, cayenne (if using) and oil until blended.

2. On prepared pan, toss together pork, bell peppers, onion and oil mixture until coated. Spread in a single layer.

3. Roast in preheated oven for 10 minutes. Open oven door and stir pork mixture. Close door and roast for 5 minutes.

4. Wrap tortillas in a large sheet of foil so that they are completely enclosed. Place packet on top of pork mixture. Roast for 7 to 10 minutes or until vegetables are tender-crisp, pork is no longer pink inside and tortillas are warmed through.

5. Divide pork mixture among four plates and serve with warm tortillas and any of the suggested accompaniments, as desired.

# Lemon Parmesan Pork Meatloaves with Zucchini Chips

Crispy zucchini chips, coated in Parmesan and panko, serve as the side for lemon- and parsley-packed mini meatloaves in a bright, flavorful dinner that's ready in no time.

## Tip
Fresh bread crumbs can be used in place of the panko.

## Variation
Substitute lean ground lamb or turkey for the ground pork.

- Preheat oven to 450°F (230°C)
- 18- by 13-inch (45 by 33 cm) rimmed sheet pan, lined with foil and sprayed with nonstick cooking spray

| | | |
|---|---|---|
| 4 | small zucchini, cut into $1/4$-inch (0.5 cm) thick rounds | 4 |
| 2 tbsp | olive oil, divided | 30 mL |
| $3/4$ tsp | salt, divided | 3 mL |
| | Freshly cracked black pepper | |
| $1^1/_3$ cups | panko (Japanese bread crumbs), divided | 325 mL |
| 1 cup | freshly grated Parmesan cheese, divided | 250 mL |
| | Nonstick cooking spray | |
| 1 | large egg | 1 |
| 1 lb | lean ground pork | 500 g |
| 1 | small onion, grated | 1 |
| $1/2$ cup | packed fresh parsley leaves, chopped | 125 mL |
| 1 tbsp | finely grated lemon zest | 15 mL |

1. In a large bowl, toss zucchini with half the oil, $1/4$ tsp (1 mL) salt and $1/8$ tsp (0.5 mL) pepper.

2. On a large plate, stir together half each of the panko and cheese.

3. Dredge zucchini, one round at a time, in panko mixture, pressing gently to adhere. Place rounds in a single layer on prepared pan. Lightly spray with cooking spray. Roast in preheated oven for 10 minutes.

4. Meanwhile, in the same large bowl, lightly beat egg. Add pork, onion, parsley, lemon zest, $1/4$ tsp (1 mL) pepper and the remaining panko, cheese, salt and oil, gently blending until combined (be careful not to overmix or compact mixture). Shape into four football-shaped loaves, each about 4 inches (10 cm) long and $1^1/2$ inches (4 cm) thick.

5. Remove pan from oven and push zucchini aside to clear four spaces for the meatloaves. Place meatloaves in the cleared spaces. Roast for 20 to 25 minutes or until zucchini and meatloaves are browned and an instant-read thermometer inserted horizontally in the thickest part of the meatloaves registers 160°F (71°C). Let meatloaves rest for 5 minutes before serving with zucchini.

# Szechuan Pork Meatballs with Garlicky Green Beans

Sriracha and garlic meld into an addictive, piquant flavoring for roasted green beans, which are a terrific texture and taste contrast to the faintly sweet, spicy Szechuan meatballs that cook alongside.

**Tip**

Fresh bread crumbs can be used in place of the panko.

**Variation**

Replace the green beans with an equal weight of broccolini, trimmed.

- Preheat oven to 400°F (200°C)
- 18- by 13-inch (45 by 33 cm) rimmed sheet pan, lined with parchment paper or foil and sprayed with nonstick cooking spray

| | | |
|---|---|---|
| 1/3 cup | panko (Japanese bread crumbs) | 75 mL |
| 1 | large egg | 1 |
| 1/3 cup | milk | 75 mL |
| 1 lb | lean ground pork | 500 g |
| 1/2 cup | finely chopped green onions | 125 mL |
| 2 tbsp | hoisin sauce | 30 mL |
| 4 tsp | Sriracha, divided | 20 mL |
| 1 lb | green beans, trimmed | 500 g |
| 3 | cloves garlic, minced | 3 |
| 2 tbsp | vegetable oil | 30 mL |
| 1/4 tsp | salt | 1 mL |

1. In a large bowl, using a fork, combine panko, egg and milk. Let stand for 10 minutes.

2. Add pork, green onions, hoisin sauce and half the Sriracha to the crumb mixture, gently mixing to combine. Shape into 16 meatballs. Arrange on one-third of prepared pan, spacing evenly.

3. In another large bowl, toss together green beans, garlic, oil, salt and the remaining Sriracha. Arrange in a single layer on the remaining two-thirds of the pan.

4. Roast in preheated oven for 14 to 18 minutes or until green beans are beginning to brown and meatballs are firm to the touch and no longer pink inside.

# Kielbasa with Sweet-and-Sour Cabbage

## Makes 4 servings

Roasted kielbasa adds a contrasting savory, salty note to sweet-and-sour cabbage in this no-fuss dinner.

## Tips

Green cabbage can be used in place of the purple cabbage.

An equal amount of fennel seeds, crushed, can be substituted for the caraway seeds.

- Preheat oven to 450°F (230°C)
- 18- by 13-inch (45 by 33 cm) rimmed sheet pan, lined with foil and sprayed with nonstick cooking spray

| | | |
|---|---|---|
| 1 tbsp | packed brown sugar | 15 mL |
| 2 tbsp | balsamic vinegar | 30 mL |
| 1 | onion, halved crosswise and thinly sliced | 1 |
| 6 cups | thinly sliced purple or red cabbage | 1.5 L |
| 2 tbsp | olive oil | 30 mL |
| 1 tsp | caraway seeds, crushed | 5 mL |
| $\frac{1}{2}$ tsp | salt | 2 mL |
| $\frac{1}{4}$ tsp | freshly cracked black pepper | 1 mL |
| 1 lb | kielbasa or other smoked sausage | 500 g |
| $\frac{1}{4}$ cup | chopped fresh chives or green onions | 60 mL |

1. In a small cup, stir together brown sugar and vinegar.

2. On prepared pan, toss together onion, cabbage, oil, caraway seeds, salt and pepper. Spread in a single layer.

3. Cut sausage crosswise into a total of 8 pieces. Nestle sausage pieces among the cabbage mixture, spacing evenly.

4. Roast in preheated oven for 10 minutes. Open oven door and drizzle vinegar mixture over cabbage mixture, stirring to combine. Turn sausage pieces over. Close door and roast for 8 to 12 minutes or until cabbage is softened and sausage pieces are browned. Sprinkle with chives.

# Smoked Sausages with Oven-Fried Green Tomatoes

Here's a great recipe to showcase convenient smoked sausages, roasted and accompanied by fried green tomatoes. The latter is an iconic dish of the American South that typically involves a lot of breading and even more oil. This simplified version is "oven-fried," which allows the tart-sweet flavor of the tomatoes to shine.

## Tip

Regular firm-ripe red tomatoes can be used in place of the green tomatoes.

- Preheat oven to 400°F (200°C)
- 18- by 13-inch (45 by 33 cm) rimmed sheet pan, lined with parchment paper or foil and sprayed with nonstick cooking spray

| | | |
|---|---|---|
| 4 | green tomatoes, cut in half crosswise | 4 |
| 1 tbsp | cider vinegar | 15 mL |
| $\frac{1}{2}$ tsp | salt | 2 mL |
| $\frac{1}{4}$ tsp | freshly ground black pepper | 1 mL |
| 1 cup | panko (Japanese bread crumbs) | 250 mL |
| $\frac{1}{4}$ cup | freshly grated Parmesan cheese | 60 mL |
| 3 tbsp | unsalted butter, melted | 45 mL |
| 1 lb | smoked sausage (such as Polska kielbasa), cut crosswise into 4 sections, each piece halved lengthwise | 500 g |

1. Arrange tomatoes, cut side up, on prepared pan, spacing evenly. Brush with vinegar and season with salt and pepper.

2. In a medium bowl, combine panko, cheese and butter. Sprinkle onto cut sides of tomatoes, pressing to adhere.

3. Nestle sausage pieces among the tomatoes, spacing evenly. Loosely tent tomatoes and sausage with foil.

4. Roast in preheated oven for 25 minutes. Open oven door and remove foil. Close door and roast for 8 to 12 minutes or until sausages are browned, tomatoes are tender and panko mixture is golden brown.

# Italian Sausage and Pepper Supper

Could there be anything more comforting than a Sunday meat-and-potatoes dinner with friends and family? This sausage, pepper and potato meal is ready in no time, with minimal effort, saving you time over the stove.

## Tips

You can substitute 1 tsp (5 mL) dried rosemary, crumbled, or Italian seasoning for the fresh rosemary.

One or both of the bell peppers can be replaced by green bell peppers, if desired.

## Variation

*Italian Sausage and Pepper Subs:* Omit the potatoes. Serve the sausage, peppers and onions on 4 split soft Italian sub rolls.

- Preheat oven to 450°F (230°C)
- 18- by 13-inch (45 by 33 cm) rimmed sheet pan, lined with foil and sprayed with nonstick cooking spray

| | | |
|---|---|---|
| 2 | large red or yellow bell peppers (or 1 of each) | 2 |
| 1 | large onion | 1 |
| 1 lb | red-skinned or yellow-fleshed baby potatoes | 500 g |
| 3 tbsp | olive oil | 45 mL |
| 2 tsp | chopped fresh rosemary | 10 mL |
| $3/4$ tsp | salt | 3 mL |
| $1/4$ tsp | freshly cracked black pepper | 1 mL |
| 1 lb | sweet or hot Italian sausages, each cut crosswise into 4 pieces | 500 g |

1. Cut bell peppers in half lengthwise. Remove seeds and stem, then cut each half lengthwise into 4 wedges. Cut onion in half lengthwise, then cut each half into 6 wedges.

2. On prepared pan, toss together bell peppers, onion, potatoes, oil, rosemary, salt and pepper. Spread in a single layer. Nestle sausage pieces among the vegetables, spacing evenly.

3. Roast in preheated oven for 20 minutes. Open oven door and stir vegetables and sausages. Close door and roast for 10 to 15 minutes or until potatoes are fork-tender and sausages are lightly browned and juices run clear when pierced.

# Sausage- and Spinach-Stuffed Acorn Squash

**Makes 4 servings**

Treat your family to a cozy autumn meal of roasted golden-sweet acorn squash stuffed with hearty Italian sausage (it roasts in the oven, too!), Parmesan and spinach.

## Tips

Delicata squash can be substituted for the acorn squash.

Fresh bread crumbs can be used in place of the panko.

- Preheat oven to 425°F (220°C)
- 18- by 13-inch (45 by 33 cm) rimmed sheet pan, lined with foil and sprayed with nonstick cooking spray

| | | |
|---|---|---|
| 2 | acorn squash (each about 2 lbs/1 kg), halved and seeds removed | 2 |
| 3 tbsp | olive oil, divided | 45 mL |
| | Salt and freshly ground black pepper | |
| 8 oz | sweet or hot Italian sausages (about 2 to 3), each cut crosswise into 8 pieces | 250 g |
| 1 | package (16 oz/500 g) chopped frozen spinach, thawed and squeezed dry | 1 |
| 1 cup | freshly grated Parmesan cheese | 250 mL |
| 2/3 cup | panko (Japanese bread crumbs) | 150 mL |
| 1/3 cup | finely chopped green onions | 75 mL |

1. Brush insides of squash with 1 tbsp (15 mL) oil. Season with 1/4 tsp (1 mL) each salt and pepper. Place squash, cut side down, on prepared pan. Arrange sausage pieces around squash. Roast in preheated oven for 30 to 35 minutes or until juices run clear when sausages are pierced.

2. Remove pan from oven and transfer sausages to a cutting board. Return pan to oven and roast squash for 10 to 15 minutes or until tender.

3. Meanwhile, chop sausage and place in a large bowl. Add spinach, cheese, panko, green onions and the remaining oil. Season to taste with salt and pepper. Stir to combine well.

4. Remove pan from oven and preheat broiler to high.

5. Turn squash halves over and fill with sausage mixture. Broil for 2 to 5 minutes or until filling is golden.

# Salami, Basil and Tomato Pizza

**Makes 6 servings**

There's no need to order pizza once you learn how easy it is to make at home. This sheet pan recipe guides the way.

**Tip**

An equal weight of sliced pepperoni can be used in place of the salami.

- Preheat oven to 450°F (230°C)
- 18- by 13-inch (45 by 33 cm) rimmed sheet pan, sprayed with nonstick cooking spray

|         | All-purpose flour                                          |        |
|---------|------------------------------------------------------------|--------|
| 1 lb    | fresh or thawed frozen pizza dough                         | 500 g  |
| 1 tbsp  | extra virgin olive oil                                     | 15 mL  |
| 2 oz    | Genoa salami, cut into thin strips                         | 60 g   |
| 3       | plum (Roma) tomatoes, thinly sliced horizontally           | 3      |
| 1       | ball (about 6 oz/175 g) fresh mozzarella in water, drained and diced | 1 |
| ¼ cup   | freshly grated Parmesan cheese                             | 60 mL  |
| ½ cup   | packed fresh basil leaves, torn                           | 125 mL |

1. On a lightly floured work surface, press out dough into a 14- by 10-inch (35 by 25 cm) oval. Place on prepared pan and brush with oil. Top with salami, tomatoes, mozzarella and Parmesan.

2. Bake in preheated oven for 25 to 30 minutes or until crust is golden brown. Slide pizza onto a wire rack and let cool for 5 minutes. Top with basil.

# Roasted Gnocchi with Cauliflower, Tomatoes and Crispy Salami

Roasting shelf-stable gnocchi (a fantastic, versatile pantry item already) not only saves the step of boiling, but also browns the gnocchi as it cooks, yielding crispy, pillowy bites in one simple step. Everything else in the dish goes on the sheet pan as well, which means you have another great dinner at your fingertips.

### Tip

Look for shelf-stable gnocchi in the supermarket where dried pasta is shelved.

### Variation

*Roasted Gnocchi with Garlic and Greens:* Replace the cauliflower with 5 cups (1.25 L) chopped broccoli rabe (about 2 bunches) or chopped trimmed kale (tough stems removed). Add 3 cloves garlic, minced, with the oil in step 1. Omit the salami and replace the tomatoes with ¼ cup (60 mL) golden or dark raisins.

- Preheat oven to 425°F (220°C)
- 18- by 13-inch (45 by 33 cm) rimmed sheet pan, lined with foil and sprayed with nonstick cooking spray
- Large sheet of foil

| | | |
|---|---|---|
| 1 | package (16 oz/454 g) shelf-stable gnocchi | 1 |
| 4 cups | roughly chopped cauliflower florets (about 1 small head) | 1 L |
| ½ cup | ready-to-use chicken broth | 125 mL |
| 4 tbsp | olive oil, divided | 60 mL |
| | Salt and freshly cracked black pepper | |
| 4 oz | Genoa salami, cut into thin strips | 125 g |
| 2 cups | grape or cherry tomatoes | 500 mL |
| 1 cup | packed fresh flat-leaf (Italian) parsley, chopped | 250 mL |
| ½ cup | freshly grated Romano or Parmesan cheese | 125 mL |

1. On prepared pan, toss together gnocchi, cauliflower, broth, 3 tbsp (45 mL) oil, ½ tsp (2 mL) salt and ¼ tsp (1 mL) pepper until coated. Spread in a single layer. Cover tightly with a large sheet of foil, sealing the edges. Roast in preheated oven for 20 minutes.

2. In a medium bowl, toss together salami, tomatoes, the remaining oil and ⅛ tsp (0.5 mL) each salt and pepper.

3. Remove pan from oven, carefully remove foil and stir gnocchi mixture. Stir in salami mixture and spread evenly on pan. Roast for 10 to 14 minutes or until gnocchi and cauliflower are golden brown and tomatoes are just bursting. Serve sprinkled with parsley and cheese.

# Crispy Collard Green Ribbons with Ham and Black-Eyed Peas

This Southern-inspired supper packs a zesty punch: spicy, crisp-tender collard greens punctuated by salty-sweet ham, sprinkled with creamy, protein-rich black-eyed peas.

## Tip

Black beans, pinto beans or white beans (such as cannellini, Great Northern or navy beans) can be used in place of the black-eyed peas.

## Variation

Substitute 1 lb (500 g) smoked sausage, diced, for the ham.

- Preheat oven to 400°F (200°C)
- 18- by 13-inch (45 by 33 cm) rimmed sheet pan, lined with parchment paper or foil and sprayed with nonstick cooking spray

| | | |
|---|---|---|
| $1\frac{1}{2}$ lbs | collard greens | 750 g |
| 3 | cloves garlic, minced | 3 |
| 2 tsp | granulated sugar | 10 mL |
| $\frac{1}{2}$ tsp | salt | 2 mL |
| 2 tbsp | vegetable oil | 30 mL |
| 1 tbsp | cider vinegar | 15 mL |
| $1\frac{1}{2}$ tsp | hot pepper sauce | 7 mL |
| 2 cups | diced cooked ham | 500 mL |
| 1 | can (14 to 19 oz/398 to 540 mL) black-eyed peas, drained and rinsed | 1 |

1. Stack half the collard greens on a cutting board. Using a very sharp knife, cut away stems and tough portion of center ribs. Repeat with the remaining collard greens. Discard stems and ribs. Rinse and spin-dry leaves.

2. Stack half the collard leaves and roll up crosswise into a tight cylinder. Cut cylinder crosswise into $\frac{1}{4}$-inch (0.5 cm) thick slices. Repeat with the remaining leaves. Toss collard ribbons to uncoil.

3. In a large bowl, whisk together garlic, sugar, salt, oil, vinegar and hot pepper sauce. Add collard greens, ham and peas, tossing to coat. Spread in a single layer on prepared pan.

4. Roast in preheated oven for 10 minutes. Open oven door and stir vegetable mixture. Close door and roast for 5 to 10 minutes or until warmed through and collard ribbons begin to turn crispy at the edges.

# Egg, Ham and Cheese Bread Bowls

True, these thoroughly delectable egg and bread bowls, stuffed with ham and cheese, would be right at home for breakfast or brunch. But they are also exactly the dinner you want to cozy up to at the end of a long day.

## Tips

You need to use lunch-size bread rolls for this; small dinner rolls are too small.

Other varieties of thinly sliced deli meat, such as roast beef, roast turkey or salami, can be used in place of the ham. Do not skip the meat liner or the egg will soak into the bread.

Refrigerate or freeze the leftover bread for making fresh bread crumbs or croutons.

- Preheat oven to 350°F (180°C)
- 18- by 13-inch (45 by 33 cm) rimmed sheet pan, lined with foil

| | | |
|---|---|---|
| 4 | soft or crusty lunch-size bread rolls (about 3 inches/7.5 cm across) | 4 |
| 4 | small thin slices deli ham | 4 |
| 4 | large eggs, at room temperature | 4 |
| 1 cup | shredded Cheddar, Swiss or mozzarella cheese | 250 mL |
| 1 tbsp | minced fresh chives or parsley (optional) | 15 mL |

1. Using a serrated knife, cut off tops of rolls. Scoop out centers, reserving for another use. Place on prepared pan and press 1 slice of ham into each roll. Crack an egg into each roll and sprinkle with $\frac{1}{4}$ cup (60 mL) cheese. Sprinkle with chives (if using). Replace tops of rolls.

2. Lift foil on pan up and over rolls, crimping to enclose completely. Bake in preheated oven for 10 to 17 minutes (10 to 12 minutes for runny yolks; 13 to 15 minutes for firm, just-set yolks; 16 to 17 minutes for firm yolks). Remove from oven, unwrap and serve immediately.

# Roast Beef with Potatoes, Green Beans and Blue Cheese Mayo

Roast beef always makes an excellent centerpiece to dinner menus, any night of the week. This one, simply seasoned, is extra-perfect thanks to the smashing sides (green beans and potatoes) and blue cheese mayo in tandem.

## Tip

In place of the russet potatoes, you can use 1½ lbs (750 g) fingerling or yellow-fleshed baby potatoes, halved lengthwise.

## Variation

Replace the green beans with an equal amount of broccolini, trimmed.

- Preheat oven to 425°F (220°C)
- 18- by 13-inch (45 by 33 cm) rimmed sheet pan, lined with foil and sprayed with nonstick cooking spray

| | | |
|---|---|---:|
| ½ cup | crumbled blue cheese | 125 mL |
| ⅓ cup | mayonnaise | 75 mL |
| 1 | boneless beef rib-eye or top loin roast (about 2 lbs/1 kg) | 1 |
| | Salt and freshly cracked black pepper | |
| 2 | medium-large russet potatoes (about 1½ lbs/750 g total), cut lengthwise into 1-inch (2.5 cm) wedges | 2 |
| 2 tbsp | olive oil, divided | 30 mL |
| 12 oz | green beans, trimmed | 375 g |

1. In a small bowl, stir together blue cheese and mayonnaise until blended. Cover and refrigerate.

2. Place roast, fat side up, in center of prepared pan. Season all over with ¾ tsp (3 mL) salt and ½ tsp (2 mL) pepper. Roast in preheated oven for 20 minutes.

3. Meanwhile, in a large bowl, toss potatoes with 1 tbsp (15 mL) oil, ¼ tsp (1 mL) salt and ⅛ tsp (0.5 mL) pepper.

4. Remove pan from oven and spread potatoes evenly around beef. Roast for 20 to 25 minutes or until potatoes are just tender and golden brown and an instant-read thermometer inserted in the thickest part of the roast registers 130°F (55°C) for medium-rare, or to desired doneness.

5. Leaving oven on, transfer roast to a cutting board and tent with foil. Let rest for 15 minutes.

6. Meanwhile, in a medium bowl, toss together green beans and the remaining oil. Season with salt and pepper. Stir in with potatoes on pan. Roast for 10 to 15 minutes or until potatoes are crisp and green beans are just tender.

7. Slice beef across the grain and serve with potatoes, green beans and blue cheese mayo.

# Dry-Rub London Broil with Broiled Mushrooms and Chives

**Makes 4 servings**

Top round is an affordable and very flavorful cut that is available in most supermarkets. It is best broiled, "London broil" style, to maximize its flavor and to prevent overcooking. Broiled mushrooms and chives alongside turn it into Sunday supper in a snap.

## Tips

Top blade or flank steak can be used in place of the top round steak.

Reserve the mushroom stems for another use, such as making soups, broth or sauces.

Broiling the steak to medium-rare renders the most tender, juicy and flavorful steak for this cut, but you can broil to your desired level of doneness.

- 18- by 13-inch (45 by 33 cm) rimmed sheet pan, lined with foil and sprayed with nonstick cooking spray

| | | |
|---|---|---|
| 1 tbsp | chili powder | 15 mL |
| 1 tbsp | sweet paprika | 15 mL |
| 2 tsp | garlic powder | 10 mL |
| 1 tsp | salt, divided | 5 mL |
| | Freshly cracked black pepper | |
| 1½ lbs | top round steak, trimmed and patted dry | 750 g |
| 3 tbsp | olive oil, divided | 45 mL |
| 1 lb | cremini or button mushrooms, stems removed (see tip, at left) | 500 g |
| 1 tbsp | Worcestershire sauce | 15 mL |
| 2 tbsp | minced fresh chives | 30 mL |

1. In a small cup or bowl, combine chili powder, paprika, garlic powder, ¾ tsp (3 mL) salt and ½ tsp (2 mL) pepper. Place steak on prepared pan and rub all over with 2 tbsp (30 mL) oil and spice rub. Let stand for 15 minutes.

2. Preheat broiler, with rack set 4 to 6 inches (10 to 15 cm) from the heat source.

3. In a medium bowl, toss together mushrooms, Worcestershire sauce, the remaining oil, the remaining salt and ⅛ tsp (0.5 mL) pepper.

4. Broil steak for 5 minutes. Remove pan from oven and turn steak over. Arrange mushrooms, cap side up, evenly around steak. Broil for 5 to 6 minutes for medium-rare.

5. Transfer steak to a cutting board and tent with foil. Let rest for 10 minutes, then thinly slice across the grain. Serve with mushrooms and pan juices. Sprinkle with chives.

# Hanger Steak with Blistered Tomatoes

Blistered cherry tomatoes, balsamic vinegar and fresh Italian parsley give Italian allure to an all-American cut of beef. And with only three ingredients (other than pantry staples), this not-so-humble dinner keeps your sophistication level high and your grocery bill low.

**Tip**

Broiling the steak to medium-rare renders the most tender, juicy and flavorful steak for this cut, but you can broil to your desired level of doneness.

- Preheat broiler, with rack set 4 to 6 inches (10 to 15 cm) from the heat source
- 18- by 13-inch (45 by 33 cm) rimmed sheet pan, lined with foil and sprayed with nonstick cooking spray

| | | |
|---|---|---:|
| 1 | beef hanger steak (about $1^1/_2$ lbs/750 g), patted dry and center gristle removed | 1 |
| 3 tbsp | olive oil, divided | 45 mL |
| $1^1/_4$ tsp | salt, divided | 6 mL |
| | Freshly cracked black pepper | |
| 4 cups | cherry or grape tomatoes | 1 L |
| 1 tsp | balsamic vinegar | 5 mL |
| $1/_3$ cup | packed fresh flat-leaf (Italian) parsley leaves, roughly chopped | 75 mL |

1. Place steak on prepared pan and rub steak all over with 2 tbsp (30 mL) oil, 1 tsp (5 mL) salt and $1/_4$ tsp (1 mL) pepper. Broil for 6 minutes.

2. Meanwhile, in a large bowl, toss together tomatoes, the remaining oil, the remaining salt and $1/_8$ tsp (0.5 mL) pepper.

3. Remove pan from oven and turn steak over. Distribute tomatoes evenly around steak. Broil for 4 to 5 minutes for medium-rare.

4. Leaving oven on, transfer steak to a cutting board and tent with foil. Let rest for 10 minutes.

5. Meanwhile, return tomatoes to oven and broil for 2 to 5 minutes or until blistered.

6. Thinly slice steak across the grain. Drizzle vinegar over tomatoes and serve with steak. Sprinkle with parsley.

# Chimichurri Steak Sandwiches

Here's a one-pan meal that will transport you to Argentina, wherever you are: thinly sliced skirt steak, crusty baguette and iconic, emerald green chimichurri sauce make it happen.

## Tips

You can use all parsley or all cilantro (1¼ cups/300 mL packed), if desired.

A thicker, leaner piece of steak, such as boneless rib eye or strip loin (top loin), can be used in place of the skirt steak. Add 2 to 3 minutes of cooking time per side.

- Preheat broiler, with rack set 4 to 6 inches (10 to 15 cm) from the heat source
- 18- by 13-inch (45 by 33 cm) rimmed sheet pan, lined with foil and sprayed with nonstick cooking spray
- Food processor

**Steak**

| | | |
|---|---|---|
| 1½ lbs | beef skirt steak, trimmed and patted dry | 750 g |
| 1 tbsp | olive oil | 15 mL |
| 1 tsp | salt | 5 mL |
| ½ tsp | freshly ground black pepper | 2 mL |
| 1 | crusty baguette, cut crosswise into 4 equal pieces | 1 |

**Chimichurri**

| | | |
|---|---|---|
| 2 | cloves garlic | 2 |
| ¾ cup | packed fresh flat-leaf (Italian) parsley leaves | 175 mL |
| ½ cup | packed fresh cilantro leaves | 125 mL |
| ½ tsp | ground cumin | 2 mL |
| ½ tsp | salt | 2 mL |
| ½ tsp | freshly ground black pepper | 2 mL |
| ½ cup | olive oil | 125 mL |
| ⅓ cup | red wine vinegar | 75 mL |

1. *Steak:* Place steak on prepared pan. Rub steak all over with oil, salt and pepper. Broil for 5 minutes. Open oven door and turn steak over. Close door and broil for 5 to 7 minutes for medium-rare to medium.

2. Transfer steak to a cutting board and tent with foil. Let rest for 10 minutes.

3. Meanwhile, split each section of baguette. Place on same pan, cut side up. Broil for 30 to 45 seconds or until toasted.

4. *Chimichurri:* In food processor, combine garlic, parsley, cilantro, cumin, salt, pepper, oil and vinegar; process until blended and smooth.

5. Cut steak across the grain into ¼-inch (0.5 cm) slices. Divide among baguette sections and generously spoon chimichurri over meat. Serve sandwiches with the remaining chimichurri on the side.

# Chipotle Steak and Avocado Tacos

Here's a fun and fancy rethinking of beef tacos that's as easy as their ground beef cousins. Smoky chipotle steak, buttery avocados and assorted fixings equal a meal that is sure to satisfy.

## Tip

An equal amount of pimentón (smoked paprika) or ground cumin can be used in place of the chipotle powder.

- Preheat broiler, with rack set 4 to 6 inches (10 to 15 cm) from the heat source
- 18- by 13-inch (45 by 33 cm) rimmed sheet pan, lined with foil and sprayed with nonstick cooking spray

| | | |
|---|---|---|
| 8 | 6-inch (15 cm) flour or corn tortillas | 8 |
| 12 oz | boneless beef strip loin (top loin) or top sirloin steak, trimmed and patted dry | 375 g |
| 1 tbsp | olive oil | 15 mL |
| 1 tsp | chipotle chile powder | 5 mL |
| $\frac{1}{2}$ tsp | salt | 2 mL |
| 1 | firm-ripe Hass avocado, sliced | 1 |
| | Lime wedges | |

**Suggested Accompaniments**

Fresh cilantro leaves
Crumbled queso fresco or mild feta cheese
Sour cream or plain Greek yogurt
Thinly sliced red onion
Salsa

1. Wrap tortillas in foil and place on one side of prepared pan. Place steak on the other side of the pan. Rub steak all over with oil, chipotle powder and salt. Broil for 3 minutes. Turn steak and tortilla packet over. Broil for 3 to 5 minutes for medium-rare, or to desired doneness.

2. Transfer steak to a cutting board and tent with foil. Let rest for 5 minutes. Turn broiler off and keep tortillas warm in oven. Thinly slice steak across the grain.

3. Fill warm tortillas with steak and top with avocado. Squeeze lime juice over avocado and top with any of the suggested accompaniments, as desired.

# Sirloin, Mushroom and Cherry Tomato Kebabs

## Makes 4 servings

Kebabs aren't just for summer barbecues. They are a great way to combine meats and vegetables with fun, flavor and ease, as here, where beef sirloin, mushrooms and cherry tomatoes are broiled to perfection.

## Variation

Replace the onion with 1 large red bell pepper, cut into 16 pieces.

- 18- by 13-inch (45 by 33 cm) rimmed sheet pan, lined with foil and sprayed with nonstick cooking spray
- Four 10-inch (25 cm) metal skewers, or wooden skewers soaked in warm water for 30 minutes

| | | |
|---|---|---|
| 1 lb | boneless beef top sirloin, trimmed, patted dry and cut into sixteen 1-inch (2.5 cm) cubes | 500 g |
| 3 tbsp | olive oil, divided | 45 mL |
| 2 tbsp | soy sauce | 30 mL |
| 1½ tbsp | balsamic vinegar | 22 mL |
| 24 | cherry or grape tomatoes | 24 |
| 16 | cremini or button mushrooms, trimmed | 16 |
| 1 | small red onion, cut into 16 chunks | 1 |
| | Salt and freshly cracked black pepper | |

1. Place sirloin in a large sealable plastic bag and add 2 tbsp (30 mL) oil, soy sauce and vinegar. Seal bag, pressing out air. Gently squeeze bag to combine ingredients. Refrigerate for 30 minutes.

2. Preheat broiler, with rack set 4 to 6 inches (10 to 15 cm) from the heat source.

3. Remove beef from marinade, discarding marinade. Thread beef, tomatoes, mushrooms and onion chunks onto skewers. Place on prepared pan, spacing evenly. Brush vegetables with the remaining oil and season with salt and pepper.

4. Broil for 2 to 4 minutes. Open oven door and carefully turn kebabs over. Close door and broil for 2 to 4 minutes for medium-rare, or until beef is cooked to desired doneness, mushrooms are browned and tomatoes are beginning to burst.

# Middle Eastern Kefta and Sizzling Eggplant

This version of kefta – a type of seasoned ground meat found throughout the Middle East and North Africa – may be quick and easy, but it is still brimming with flavor: assorted spices, fresh herbs, onion and pepper. The eggplant alongside becomes tender and silky with broiling, a perfect side to the hearty meat patties.

**Tip**

Fresh bread crumbs can be used in place of the panko.

**Variation**

Substitute lean ground lamb or turkey for the ground beef. If using ground turkey, cook the patties until the thermometer registers 165°F (74°C).

- Preheat broiler, with rack set 4 to 6 inches (10 to 15 cm) from the heat source
- 18- by 13-inch (45 by 33 cm) rimmed sheet pan, lined with foil and sprayed with nonstick cooking spray

| | | |
|---|---|---|
| 1 lb | lean ground beef | 500 g |
| 1 | small onion, grated | 1 |
| 2/3 cup | panko (Japanese bread crumbs) | 150 mL |
| 1/2 cup | packed fresh cilantro leaves, chopped | 125 mL |
| 1/2 cup | packed fresh parsley leaves, chopped, divided | 125 mL |
| 1 1/2 tsp | ground cumin | 7 mL |
| 1/2 tsp | ground allspice | 2 mL |
| 1/4 tsp | ground cinnamon | 1 mL |
| | Salt and freshly ground black pepper | |
| 1 | globe eggplant, trimmed and cut crosswise into 1/4-inch (0.5 cm) thick slices | 1 |
| 3 tbsp | olive oil | 45 mL |

1. In a large bowl, gently combine beef, onion, panko, cilantro, half the parsley, cumin, allspice, cinnamon, 1/2 tsp (2 mL) salt and 1/4 tsp (1 mL) pepper. Shape into 8 patties, each about 2 inches (5 cm) in diameter.

2. Place patties on prepared pan, spacing evenly. Arrange eggplant slices around patties. Brush both sides of eggplant with oil and season with salt and pepper.

3. Broil for 5 minutes. Open oven door and turn patties and eggplant slices over. Close door and broil for 5 to 8 minutes or until eggplant slices are golden brown, kefta are no longer pink inside and an instant-read thermometer inserted horizontally in the center of the patties registers 160°F (71°C). Sprinkle with the remaining parsley.

# Streamlined Meatloaves with Cheddar Roasted Broccoli

This speedy take on meatloaf is loaded with flavor but light on fuss. Broccoli florets, roasted until crispy and then sprinkled with Cheddar cheese, complement the mini loaves for a meal that is 100% comfort.

**Tip**

Fresh bread crumbs can be used in place of the panko.

**Variation**

Substitute lean ground lamb or turkey for the ground beef. If using ground turkey, cook the meatloaves until the thermometer registers 165°F (74°C).

- Preheat oven to 450°F (230°C)
- 18- by 13-inch (45 by 33 cm) rimmed sheet pan, lined with foil and sprayed with nonstick cooking spray

| | | |
|---|---|---|
| 1 lb | lean ground beef | 500 g |
| 2 | cloves garlic, minced | 2 |
| ½ cup | chopped green onions | 125 mL |
| 1 cup | panko (Japanese bread crumbs), divided | 250 mL |
| ½ cup | freshly grated Parmesan cheese | 125 mL |
| 1 tsp | salt, divided | 5 mL |
| | Freshly ground black pepper | |
| 1 | large egg, lightly beaten | 1 |
| 6 tbsp | ketchup, divided | 90 mL |
| 5 cups | small broccoli florets (about 1 medium head) | 1.25 L |
| 3 tbsp | olive oil, divided | 45 mL |
| 1 cup | shredded sharp (old) Cheddar cheese | 250 mL |

1. In a large bowl, combine beef, garlic, green onions, half the panko, Parmesan, ½ tsp (2 mL) salt, ¼ tsp (1 mL) pepper, egg and 4 tbsp (60 mL) ketchup until blended (be careful not to overmix or compact mixture).

2. On prepared pan, shape meat mixture into 4 football-shaped loaves, each about 4 inches (10 cm) long and 1½ inches (4 cm) thick, spacing evenly. Brush tops with the remaining ketchup.

3. In a large bowl, toss broccoli with 2 tbsp (30 mL) oil, the remaining salt and ⅛ tsp (0.5 mL) pepper. Arrange broccoli around meatloaves. Roast in preheated oven for 15 minutes.

4. Meanwhile, in the same large bowl, toss together Cheddar cheese and the remaining panko and oil.

5. Open oven door and sprinkle cheese mixture evenly over broccoli. Close door and roast for 4 to 7 minutes or until cheese is melted, broccoli is tender-crisp and an instant-read thermometer inserted horizontally in the thickest part of the meatloaves registers 160°F (71°C). Let meatloaves rest for 5 to 10 minutes before serving with broccoli.

# Barbecue-Sauced Cheeseburger Sliders

**Makes 4 servings**

Here's some truly fast food: barbecue-sauced cheeseburger sliders, with your preferred fixings, that are ready in well under half an hour.

**Tip**

Choose a barbecue sauce that is free of corn syrup and preservatives and has a short list of all-natural ingredients.

- Preheat oven to 450°F (230°C)
- 18- by 13-inch (45 by 33 cm) rimmed sheet pan, lined with foil

| | | |
|---|---|---|
| 1½ lbs | lean ground beef | 750 g |
| ¾ cup | barbecue sauce, divided | 175 mL |
| ½ tsp | salt | 2 mL |
| ¼ tsp | freshly cracked black pepper | 1 mL |
| | Vegetable oil | |
| 8 | slider buns | 8 |
| 8 | small thin slices sharp (old) Cheddar cheese | 8 |

**Suggested Toppings**

Sliced plum (Roma) tomatoes

Spinach, arugula, baby kale or lettuce leaves

French fried onions (from a can)

1. Place prepared pan in oven for 10 minutes while preparing patties.

2. In a large bowl, combine beef, ½ cup (125 mL) barbecue sauce, salt and pepper until blended (be careful not to overmix or compact mixture). Shape into 8 small patties, each about ½ inch (1 cm) thick.

3. Remove hot pan from oven and grease foil with vegetable oil. Place patties close to the center, away from the edges. Immediately return pan to oven and roast for 5 to 10 minutes, placing buns around outer edge of pan during the final minute of baking, until patties are no longer pink inside and an instant-read thermometer inserted horizontally in the center of the patties registers 160°F (71°C).

4. Spread top halves of buns with the remaining barbecue sauce. Transfer patties to bottom halves and top with cheese and any of the suggested toppings, as desired. Cover with top halves, pressing down gently.

# Soy-Glazed Beef Patties with Roasted Snow Peas

Liven up ground beef with green onions and one of the best multipurpose seasonings you can keep in the refrigerator: miso paste. Roasted snow peas and a savory-sweet soy glaze make this a satisfying meal for everyone at the table.

**Tip**

An equal amount of white or red miso paste can be used in place of the yellow miso.

- Preheat broiler, with rack set 4 to 6 inches (10 to 15 cm) from the heat source
- 18- by 13-inch (45 by 33 cm) rimmed sheet pan, lined with foil and sprayed with nonstick cooking spray

| | | |
|---|---|---|
| 1 | large egg | 1 |
| 1 tbsp | yellow miso paste | 15 mL |
| 1¼ lbs | lean ground beef | 625 g |
| ⅔ cup | finely chopped green onions | 150 mL |
| ½ cup | panko (Japanese bread crumbs) | 125 mL |
| 12 oz | snow peas, strings removed, trimmed | 375 g |
| 1 tbsp | vegetable oil | 15 mL |
| ¼ tsp | salt | 1 mL |
| 3 tbsp | soy sauce | 45 mL |
| 2 tbsp | liquid honey | 30 mL |
| 1 tbsp | mirin or cooking sherry | 15 mL |

1. In a large bowl, whisk together egg and miso until blended. Gently mix in beef, green onions and panko until just blended (be careful not to overmix or compact mixture).

2. Shape beef mixture into 4 oval patties, each about ¾ inch (2 cm) thick. Place patties on one side of the prepared pan, spacing evenly. Broil for 15 minutes.

3. Meanwhile, in a medium bowl, toss snow peas with oil and salt.

4. In a small bowl, whisk together soy sauce, honey and mirin until blended.

5. Remove pan from oven. Using a metal spatula, turn patties over and press slightly to flatten. Spoon soy glaze over each patty. Spread snow peas in a single layer on the other side of the pan. Broil for 5 to 8 minutes or until snow peas are beginning to brown at the edges and patties are no longer pink inside and an instant-read thermometer inserted horizontally in the center of the patties registers 160°F (71°C).

# Lamb Chops with Olive Tapenade, Potatoes and Arugula

Roasted lamb chops get tender and tasty in the blink of an eye with the help of olive tapenade. A side of fingerling potatoes is gussied up with arugula and white wine vinegar.

## Tips

An equal amount of tender watercress, baby kale or baby spinach can be used in place of the arugula.

Sherry vinegar or red wine vinegar can be used in place of the white wine vinegar.

- Preheat oven to 400°F (200°C)
- 18- by 13-inch (45 by 33 cm) rimmed sheet pan, rubbed with olive oil

| | | |
|---|---|---|
| 1 lb | fingerling or yellow-fleshed baby potatoes, halved lengthwise | 500 g |
| 3 tbsp | olive oil, divided | 45 mL |
| | Salt and freshly cracked black pepper | |
| 4 tbsp | black or green olive tapenade | 60 mL |
| 8 | small lamb chops (each about 3 oz/90 g), trimmed and patted dry | 8 |
| 4 cups | baby arugula leaves | 1 L |
| 1 tsp | white wine vinegar | 5 mL |

1. On prepared pan, toss potatoes with 1 tbsp (15 mL) oil and ¼ tsp (1 mL) each salt and pepper. Spread in a single layer. Roast in preheated oven for 25 minutes.

2. Meanwhile, in a small bowl or cup, combine tapenade and 1 tbsp (15 mL) oil. Brush one side of each lamb chop with about half the tapenade mixture.

3. Remove pan from oven and stir potatoes. Nestle lamb chops, tapenade side down, among the potatoes, spacing evenly. Brush top sides of chops with the remaining tapenade mixture. Roast for 10 to 15 minutes for medium-rare, or until lamb is cooked to desired doneness and potatoes are fork-tender.

4. Transfer lamb to a serving platter or individual plates. Add arugula to the pan and drizzle with vinegar and the remaining oil. Season to taste with salt and pepper. Toss to coat and serve with the lamb chops.

# Spiced Lamb and Fresh Mint Turnovers

**Makes 4 servings**

Fresh mint is often used as a garnish or to enhance other flavors, but here it steals the spotlight as the dominant flavor in out-of-this-world lamb turnovers.

## Tip
An equal amount of ground cinnamon or pumpkin pie spice can be used in place of the allspice.

## Variation
Substitute lean ground turkey or beef for the lamb.

- 18- by 13-inch (45 by 33 cm) rimmed sheet pan, lined with foil

| | | |
|---|---|---|
| 1 lb | lean ground lamb | 500 g |
| 3 | cloves garlic, minced | 3 |
| ½ cup | packed fresh mint leaves, chopped | 125 mL |
| ⅓ cup | finely chopped green onions | 75 mL |
| ½ tsp | ground allspice | 2 mL |
| ½ tsp | salt | 2 mL |
| ¼ tsp | freshly ground black pepper | 1 mL |
| | All-purpose flour | |
| 1 | sheet frozen puff pastry (half a 17.3-oz/490 g package), thawed | 1 |
| 1 | large egg, lightly beaten | 1 |

**Suggested Accompaniments**
Plain yogurt
Mango chutney
Additional chopped fresh mint

1. In a medium bowl, combine lamb, garlic, mint, green onions, allspice, salt and pepper until blended.

2. Sprinkle work surface with flour. Unfold pastry sheet on surface and roll out into a 12-inch (30 cm) square. Cut into 4 equal squares. Brush edges of each pastry square with egg.

3. Spoon one-quarter of the lamb mixture into the center of each square. Fold each square over on the diagonal, pressing edges together to seal. Transfer turnovers to prepared pan, spacing evenly, and brush with the remaining egg. Cover loosely and refrigerate for at least 30 minutes or for up to 2 hours.

4. Preheat oven to 425°F (220°C).

5. Uncover and bake turnovers for 18 to 23 minutes or until deep golden brown. Let cool on pan for 5 minutes. Serve with any of the suggested accompaniments, as desired.

# Lamb Meatballs with Zucchini, Tomatoes and Yogurt Tahini Sauce

Combine spiced, minted lamb meatballs, zucchini, cherry tomatoes and a splash of olive oil on a sheet pan, put it in the oven and spend the next 25 minutes relaxing, waiting for this fresh, aromatic meal to finish cooking.

## Variation

Replace the lamb with lean ground beef or turkey. If using extra-lean beef or turkey, add 1 tbsp (15 mL) olive oil to the meat mixture to avoid dry meatballs.

- Preheat oven to 400°F (200°C)
- 18- by 13-inch (45 by 33 cm) rimmed sheet pan, lined with parchment paper or foil and sprayed with nonstick cooking spray

**Meatballs**

| | | |
|---|---|---|
| 1 lb | lean ground lamb | 500 g |
| 3 | cloves garlic, minced | 3 |
| 1/3 cup | finely chopped green onions | 75 mL |
| 4 tbsp | chopped fresh mint, divided | 60 mL |
| 1 tsp | ground cumin | 5 mL |
| | Salt and freshly cracked black pepper | |
| 3 | zucchini, halved lengthwise, then cut into 1 1/2-inch (4 cm) chunks | 3 |
| 1 1/2 cups | cherry or grape tomatoes | 375 mL |
| 2 tbsp | olive oil | 30 mL |

**Yogurt Tahini Sauce**

| | | |
|---|---|---|
| 1/2 cup | plain yogurt | 125 mL |
| 1/4 cup | well-stirred tahini | 60 mL |
| 2 tbsp | freshly squeezed lemon juice | 30 mL |

1. *Meatballs:* In a large bowl, combine lamb, garlic, green onions, half the mint, cumin, 3/4 tsp (3 mL) salt and 1/2 tsp (2 mL) pepper until just combined (be careful not to overmix). Shape into 1 1/2-inch (4 cm) meatballs. Arrange meatballs on prepared pan, spacing evenly.

2. In a large bowl, toss together zucchini, tomatoes and oil. Season with salt and pepper. Arrange vegetables around meatballs.

3. Roast in preheated oven for 23 to 28 minutes or until meatballs are browned and no longer pink inside, zucchini is tender and tomatoes are beginning to burst. Sprinkle with the remaining mint.

4. *Sauce:* Meanwhile, in a small bowl, whisk together yogurt, tahini and lemon juice. Season to taste with salt. Serve sauce with meatballs and vegetables.

# Sheet Sweets

# Easy as Pie Baked Apples

Baked apples are an old-fashioned autumn favorite. Cutting them up before baking slashes the baking time and delivers a result akin to apple pie filling. Leftovers are incredible for breakfast, solo or atop oatmeal.

## Tips

The apples are also wonderful for breakfast atop Greek yogurt or oatmeal.

An equal amount of ground ginger or 1 tsp (5 mL) cardamom or allspice can be used in place of the cinnamon.

## Storage Tip

Store the cooled apples in an airtight container in the refrigerator for up to 3 days. Serve cold, or warm in the microwave on Medium (70%) for about 1 minute.

## Variation

Add $\frac{1}{2}$ cup (125 mL) dried fruits, such as blueberries, cranberries, raisins, cherries or chopped apricots, with the apples in step 1.

- Preheat oven to 400°F (200°C)
- 18- by 13-inch (45 by 33 cm) rimmed sheet pan, lined with parchment paper or foil

| 6 | large tart-sweet apples (such as Braeburn, Gala or Fuji) | 6 |
|---|---|---|
| 2 tbsp | freshly squeezed lemon juice | 30 mL |
| $\frac{1}{3}$ cup | packed light brown sugar | 75 mL |
| 2 tsp | ground cinnamon | 10 mL |
| $1\frac{1}{2}$ tsp | cornstarch | 7 mL |
| $\frac{1}{4}$ tsp | salt | 1 mL |
| 4 tbsp | unsalted butter, cut into small pieces | 60 mL |

**Suggested Accompaniments**

Vanilla ice cream

Crisp butter cookies

1. Peel and very coarsely chop apples. Spread evenly on prepared pan and sprinkle with lemon juice.

2. In a small bowl, combine brown sugar, cinnamon, cornstarch and salt. Sprinkle sugar mixture and butter evenly over apples.

3. Roast in preheated oven for 20 to 25 minutes, stirring once, until apples are tender and juices are bubbling. Let cool on pan for at least 15 minutes before serving. Serve with the suggested accompaniments, if desired.

# Caramelized Bourbon Bananas with Vanilla Ice Cream

Brown sugar and bourbon dazzle up everyday bananas in this wickedly delicious, so-easy dessert. A scoop of vanilla ice cream finishes its presentation.

## Tips

Other spirits, such as brandy, whiskey, dark rum or orange liqueur, can be used in place of the bourbon.

For a kid-friendly version, replace the bourbon with apple or orange juice.

## Storage Tip

Store the cooled bananas in an airtight container in the refrigerator for up to 1 day. Serve cold, or warm in the microwave on Medium (70%) for about 1 minute.

- Preheat oven to 450°F (230°C)
- 18- by 13-inch (45 by 33 cm) rimmed sheet pan, lined with foil and lightly sprayed with nonstick cooking spray

| | | |
|---|---|---|
| 1/4 cup | packed brown sugar | 60 mL |
| 1/8 tsp | salt | 0.5 mL |
| 2 tbsp | unsalted butter, melted | 30 mL |
| 2 tbsp | bourbon | 30 mL |
| 4 | large firm-ripe bananas | 4 |
| | Vanilla ice cream | |

1. In a small bowl, combine brown sugar, salt, butter and bourbon.

2. Cut bananas in half lengthwise. Place banana halves, cut side up, on prepared pan, spacing evenly. Roast in preheated oven for 4 minutes. Remove pan from oven and drizzle bananas with sugar mixture. Roast for 3 to 4 minutes or until sugar mixture is bubbling and bananas are browned.

3. Cut each banana half crosswise into thirds. Serve bananas with ice cream, scooping any of the sugar mixture from the pan onto the bananas.

# Roasted Plums with Honey, Walnuts and Greek Yogurt

Honey gives a nuanced sweetness to the roasted plums and yogurt in this dessert. It's an ideal option after an otherwise rich meal.

## Tips

An equal amount of pure maple syrup or agave nectar can be used in place of the honey.

Apricots can be used in place of the plums.

## Storage Tip

Store the cooled plums in an airtight container in the refrigerator for up to 2 days. Store the walnuts in an airtight container at room temperature for up to 2 weeks. Serve the plums cold, or warm them in the microwave on Medium (70%) for about 1 minute.

- Preheat oven to 375°F (190°C)
- 18- by 13-inch (45 by 33 cm) rimmed sheet pan, lined with parchment paper

| | | |
|---|---|---|
| 9 | medium firm-ripe plums, halved | 9 |
| 2 tbsp | unsalted butter, melted | 30 mL |
| 5 tbsp | liquid honey, divided | 75 mL |
| ½ cup | walnut halves, coarsely chopped | 125 mL |
| 1 cup | plain Greek yogurt | 250 mL |

1. Place plums, cut side up, on one side of prepared pan, spacing evenly. Brush with butter and drizzle with 2 tbsp (30 mL) honey. Bake in preheated oven for 8 minutes.

2. Open oven door and scatter walnuts on the other side of the pan. Close door and bake for 6 to 8 minutes or until plums are soft and walnuts are lightly toasted.

3. Divide plums among six bowls, top each with a generous dollop of yogurt, sprinkle with walnuts and drizzle with the remaining honey.

# Berries and Cream Pavlova

Hello, gorgeous. This stunning dessert has multiple delightful layers: a crisp-pillowy meringue, a tangy whipped cream filling and fresh berries.

## Variation

Other diced fresh fruits, such as peaches, apricots, plums, mangos, blueberries or blackberries, can be used in place of the strawberries and raspberries.

- Preheat oven to 225°F (110°C)
- 18- by 13-inch (45 by 33 cm) rimmed sheet pan, lined with parchment paper

**Meringue**

| | | |
|---|---|---|
| 4 | large egg whites, at room temperature | 4 |
| ¼ tsp | cream of tartar | 1 mL |
| 1 cup | granulated sugar | 250 mL |

**Pavlova**

| | | |
|---|---|---|
| 1 lb | strawberries, quartered | 500 g |
| 1 cup | raspberries | 250 mL |
| 2 tbsp | granulated sugar, divided | 30 mL |
| 1 cup | heavy or whipping (35%) cream | 250 mL |
| ¼ cup | sour cream | 60 mL |
| | Fresh basil or mint leaves, thinly sliced (optional) | |

1. *Meringue:* In a large bowl, using an electric mixer on medium speed, beat egg whites until foamy, about 1 minute. Add cream of tartar and beat for 60 to 90 seconds or until soft peaks form. Gradually add 1 cup (250 mL) sugar, beating constantly. Increase mixer speed to medium-high and beat for 4 to 6 minutes or until meringue is glossy and stiff peaks form.

2. Spread meringue in a 10-inch (25 cm) circle on prepared pan, mounding it slightly higher at the outside edge to create a nest shape.

3. Bake in preheated oven for $2\frac{1}{2}$ to 3 hours or until firm and dry. Turn oven off and let meringue cool in oven for $1\frac{1}{2}$ to 2 hours or as long as overnight.

4. *Pavlova:* In a medium bowl, combine strawberries, raspberries and 1 tbsp (15 mL) sugar.

5. In another medium bowl, using an electric mixer on medium-high speed, beat cream, sour cream and the remaining sugar until soft peaks form.

6. Carefully transfer meringue to a serving plate. Top with whipped cream, berries and basil (if using). Serve immediately.

# Vanilla Rhubarb Crumble

This old-fashioned crumble has minimal preparation requirements, perfect for when you need to work on other menu items. The topping combines brown sugar, butter, oats and hazelnuts in delectable harmony.

## Tips

Frozen cut rhubarb can be used with success in this recipe. It will take 3 bags (each 16 oz/500 g) of thawed frozen rhubarb to yield the 12 cups (3 L) needed.

Other nuts, such as walnuts, pecans or almonds, can be used in place of the hazelnuts. Alternatively, omit the nuts altogether.

## Storage Tip

Store the cooled crisp, tightly covered in plastic wrap, in the refrigerator for up to 3 days.

## Variations

Replace 4 cups (1 L) of the rhubarb with halved strawberries.

Add 1 tsp (5 mL) ground cinnamon, ginger, allspice or cardamom with the flour in step 1.

- Preheat oven to 375°F (190°C)
- 18- by 13-inch (45 by 33 cm) rimmed sheet pan, lined with parchment paper and sprayed with nonstick cooking spray

**Crumble**

| | | |
|---|---|---|
| 2 cups | all-purpose flour | 500 mL |
| 1½ cups | packed light brown sugar | 375 mL |
| ¾ cup | large-flake (old-fashioned) rolled oats | 175 mL |
| ½ cup | chopped hazelnuts | 125 mL |
| ½ tsp | salt | 2 mL |
| ¾ cup | unsalted butter, melted and cooled slightly | 175 mL |

**Filling**

| | | |
|---|---|---|
| ⅔ cup | granulated sugar | 150 mL |
| ½ cup | all-purpose flour | 125 mL |
| ¼ tsp | salt | 1 mL |
| 1 tbsp | vanilla extract | 15 mL |
| 12 cups | sliced rhubarb (½-inch/1 cm slices) | 3 L |

1. *Crumble:* In a medium bowl, whisk together flour, brown sugar, oats, hazelnuts and salt. Stir in butter until moist and crumbly. Place in freezer for 15 minutes.

2. *Filling:* In a large bowl, whisk together sugar, flour, salt and vanilla. Add rhubarb and toss to coat.

3. Spread filling over prepared pan and sprinkle with crumble. Cover with foil.

4. Bake in preheated oven for 20 minutes. Remove foil and bake for 25 to 30 minutes or until browned and bubbling and rhubarb is tender. Let cool on a wire rack for 30 minutes. Serve warm or at room temperature.

# Rustic Apple Tart

Stacked ready-to-use pie crusts take the place of homemade pastry in this autumnal tart. Apricot preserves are a classic French finish to apple tarts, but you can use other varieties of preserves if you like.

**Storage Tip**

Store the cooled tart, loosely covered with plastic wrap, in the refrigerator for up to 1 day.

- Preheat oven to 350°F (180°C)
- 18- by 13-inch (45 by 33 cm) rimmed sheet pan, lined with parchment paper

| | | |
|---|---|---|
| 5 | large tart-sweet apples (such as Gala, Braeburn or Cortland) | 5 |
| 3½ tbsp | granulated sugar, divided | 52 mL |
| 2 tbsp | all-purpose flour | 30 mL |
| 1½ tsp | ground cinnamon | 7 mL |
| 3 tbsp | freshly squeezed lemon juice, divided | 45 mL |
| 1 | package (15 oz/425 g) refrigerated rolled pie crusts | 1 |
| 6 tbsp | apricot preserves, divided | 90 mL |
| 1 | large egg | 1 |
| 1 tbsp | water | 15 mL |

1. Peel and core the apples, then cut lengthwise into ¼-inch (0.5 cm) thick slices. In a large bowl, combine apples, 3 tbsp (45 mL) sugar, flour, cinnamon and 2 tbsp (30 mL) lemon juice.

2. On a lightly floured surface, stack one pie crust on top of the other. Roll out into one 16-inch (40 cm) circle. Transfer to prepared pan and spread with 4 tbsp (60 mL) preserves, leaving a 2-inch (5 cm) border.

3. In a small cup or bowl, whisk together egg and water.

4. Mound apples on crust, within the border. Fold crust border over apple mixture, pleating edge slightly and leaving filling exposed. Brush crust with egg wash and sprinkle with the remaining sugar.

5. Bake in preheated oven for 50 to 60 minutes or until crust is golden brown and apples are tender. Transfer to a wire rack to cool.

6. In a small saucepan, heat the remaining preserves and lemon juice over medium heat for 1 to 2 minutes or until melted. Brush over apples. Serve tart warm or at room temperature.

# Rustic Dried Fruit Tart

Orange marmalade adds sweetness and sheen to this understated but sophisticated tart.

## Tips

For the dried fruit, try a mixture such as apricots, cherries, figs and raisins.

This tart is best eaten immediately after baking. The puff pastry becomes soggy if left to sit.

- 18- by 13-inch (45 by 33 cm) rimmed sheet pan
- Large piece of parchment paper

| | | |
|---|---|---|
| 2 cups | assorted chopped dried fruit | 500 mL |
| 1½ cups | boiling water | 375 mL |
| ½ cup | orange marmalade | 125 mL |
| ⅔ cup | confectioners' (icing) sugar, divided | 150 mL |
| 1 | sheet frozen puff pastry (half a 17.3-oz/490 g package), thawed | 1 |

1. In a medium heatproof bowl, combine dried fruit and boiling water. Let stand for 30 minutes. Drain off any excess water and pat dry with paper towels. Stir in marmalade and refrigerate while preparing crust.

2. Preheat oven to 400°F (200°C).

3. Reserve 2 tbsp (30 mL) sugar. Place a large piece of parchment paper on work surface and generously sprinkle with some of the remaining sugar.

4. Unfold pastry onto the paper and sprinkle with some of the remaining sugar. Using a rolling pin sprinkled with sugar, roll out pastry into a 10-inch (25 cm) square. Spoon fruit filling into the center, leaving a 1½-inch (4 cm) border. Fold border over filling, pleating edge slightly and leaving filling exposed.

5. Transfer the paper with the tart onto the pan and sprinkle pastry with the reserved sugar.

6. Bake for 30 to 35 minutes or until pastry is golden brown and puffed. Let cool on a wire rack for 15 minutes. Cut into pieces and serve warm.

# Peanut Butter Cookie Tart with Raspberries

**Makes 8 servings**

Peanut butter takes a sophisticated turn, times two, in this fun dessert: first, as the key ingredient in an addictive cookie crust, and second, as the flavoring for a mousse-like cream on top. Crown all with plump, ruby raspberries for a dessert that guests of all ages will love.

## Variation

Other berries, such as blackberries, blueberries or sliced strawberries, or a combination, can be used in place of the raspberries.

- Preheat oven to 350°F (180°C)
- 18- by 13-inch (45 by 33 cm) rimmed sheet pan, lined with parchment paper

### Tart

| | | |
|---|---|---|
| ¾ cup | granulated sugar | 175 mL |
| 1 | large egg | 1 |
| 1 cup | creamy peanut butter | 250 mL |
| 1 tsp | vanilla extract | 5 mL |

### Peanut Butter Cream

| | | |
|---|---|---|
| ½ cup | heavy or whipping (35%) cream | 125 mL |
| 1½ tbsp | granulated sugar | 22 mL |
| 2 tbsp | creamy peanut butter | 30 mL |
| 1 tsp | vanilla extract | 5 mL |

### Topping

| | | |
|---|---|---|
| 2 cups | raspberries | 500 mL |
| 1½ tsp | granulated sugar | 7 mL |

1. *Tart:* In a medium bowl, using a wooden spoon, stir together sugar, egg, peanut butter and vanilla until blended. Spread in a 10-inch (25 cm) circle on prepared pan.

2. Bake in preheated oven for 8 to 12 minutes or until surface of cookie looks dry and edges are golden brown (it may look slightly underdone, but it will firm as it sets). Let cool completely on pan on a wire rack.

3. *Peanut Butter Cream:* In a medium bowl, using an electric mixer on medium-high speed, beat cream until soft peaks form. Beat in sugar, peanut butter and vanilla until blended.

4. Carefully transfer cookie to a serving plate. Spread peanut butter cream over cookie, leaving a 1-inch (2.5 cm) border.

5. *Topping:* Top tart with raspberries and sprinkle with sugar. Serve immediately or refrigerate for up to 4 hours.

# Angel Food Sheet Cake

Angel food cake in a sheet pan? It's heavenly. The ingredients are minimal, as usual, but prepping, filling and cleaning the pan is a snap. In addition, the baking time is dramatically slashed, which means you can (quite literally) whip this up for an impromptu dessert when the mood strikes.

## Storage Tip

Store the cooled cake, loosely wrapped in foil or plastic wrap, at room temperature for up to 3 days. Alternatively, wrap it in plastic wrap, then foil, completely enclosing it, and freeze for up to 6 months. Let thaw at room temperature for about 1 hour before serving.

- Preheat oven to 350°F (180°C)
- Sifter or fine-mesh sieve
- 18- by 13-inch (45 by 33 cm) rimmed sheet pan, lined with parchment paper

| | | |
|---|---|---|
| 12 | large egg whites, at room temperature | 12 |
| $\frac{1}{2}$ tsp | cream of tartar | 2 mL |
| $1\frac{1}{4}$ cups | granulated sugar, divided | 300 mL |
| 1 cup | all-purpose flour | 250 mL |
| $\frac{1}{4}$ tsp | salt | 1 mL |

1. In a large bowl, using an electric mixer on medium speed, beat egg whites and cream of tartar for 2 to 3 minutes or until soft peaks form. Gradually add $\frac{3}{4}$ cup (150 mL) sugar, beating until thick and glossy.

2. Using sifter or sieve, sift flour, salt and the remaining sugar over egg white mixture. Fold in gently until just combined, being careful not to deflate whites. Spread batter evenly on prepared pan.

3. Bake in preheated oven for 18 to 23 minutes or until golden and just set at the center. Let cool completely in pan on a wire rack. Slide parchment paper with cake off pan and cut cake into pieces. Peel pieces off parchment paper and serve.

# Vanilla Sour Cream Pound Cake

With a rich sour cream, butter and vanilla batter, plus a baking time under 45 minutes, this pound cake is a winner. It is endlessly variable: stir in chocolate chips, nuts or dried fruit, swap out or add in various flavorings or spices, or partner it with sauces galore, from chocolate to caramel to fruit.

### Storage Tip

Store the cooled cake, loosely wrapped in foil or plastic wrap, at room temperature for up to 3 days. Alternatively, wrap it in plastic wrap, then foil, completely enclosing it, and freeze for up to 6 months. Let thaw at room temperature for 4 to 6 hours before serving.

- Preheat oven to 325°F (160°C)
- 18- by 13-inch (45 by 33 cm) rimmed sheet pan, lined with parchment paper and sprayed with nonstick cooking spray

| | | |
|---|---|---|
| 3 cups | all-purpose flour | 750 mL |
| 1/2 tsp | baking soda | 2 mL |
| 1/2 tsp | salt | 2 mL |
| 3 cups | granulated sugar | 750 mL |
| 1 cup | unsalted butter, softened | 250 mL |
| 6 | large eggs, at room temperature | 6 |
| 1 cup | sour cream | 250 mL |
| 1 tbsp | vanilla extract | 15 mL |

1. In a medium bowl, whisk together flour, baking soda and salt.

2. In a large bowl, using an electric mixer on medium speed, beat sugar and butter for 3 to 5 minutes or until light and fluffy. Add eggs, one at a time, beating well and scraping bowl between each egg. Scrape sides and bottom of bowl with a spatula. Add flour mixture alternately with sour cream, beginning and ending with flour mixture, beating on low speed just until blended after each addition. Beat in vanilla. Spread batter evenly in prepared pan.

3. Bake in preheated oven for 35 to 40 minutes or until top is golden and a tester inserted in the center comes out clean. Let cool completely in pan on a wire rack.

### Variations

*Lemon Pound Cake:* Replace the vanilla with 1 tbsp (15 mL) finely grated lemon zest.

*Cardamom Vanilla Pound Cake:* Whisk 2 tsp (10 mL) ground cardamom into the flour mixture.

*Chocolate Chip Pound Cake:* Stir in 1 cup (250 mL) miniature semisweet chocolate chips after beating in the vanilla in step 2.

# Chocolate Ganache Cake

Designed to satisfy those diehard chocolate cravings, this excellent cake comes together easily (no mixer required!) for a variety of occasions. The ganache frosting makes it worthy of a fancy celebration or dinner party, or leave it off for a guaranteed lunchbox pleaser.

## Storage Tip

Store the frosted cake, loosely wrapped in foil or waxed paper, in the refrigerator for up to 5 days. Alternatively, wrap the cooled unfrosted cake in plastic wrap, then foil, completely enclosing it, and freeze for up to 6 months. Let thaw at room temperature for 4 to 6 hours before frosting and serving.

- Preheat oven to 350°F (180°C)
- 18- by 13-inch (45 by 33 cm) rimmed sheet pan, lined with parchment paper and sprayed with nonstick cooking spray

**Cake**

| | | |
|---|---|---:|
| 2 cups | all-purpose flour | 500 mL |
| ½ cup | unsweetened cocoa powder | 125 mL |
| 2 tsp | baking soda | 10 mL |
| 1 tsp | baking powder | 5 mL |
| ½ tsp | salt | 2 mL |
| 2 tsp | instant espresso powder | 10 mL |
| ½ cup | unsalted butter, cut into small pieces | 125 mL |
| 1 cup | boiling water | 250 mL |
| 2 cups | granulated sugar | 500 mL |
| 1 cup | buttermilk | 250 mL |
| ½ cup | vegetable oil | 125 mL |
| 2 | large eggs, lightly beaten | 2 |

**Ganache**

| | | |
|---|---|---:|
| 2 cups | bittersweet or semisweet chocolate chips (12 oz/375 g) | 500 mL |
| Pinch | salt | Pinch |
| 1 tbsp | light (white) corn syrup (optional) | 15 mL |
| 1½ cups | heavy or whipping (35%) cream | 375 mL |

1. *Cake:* In a large bowl, whisk together flour, cocoa powder, baking soda, baking powder and salt.

2. Place espresso powder and butter in a medium heatproof bowl and pour in boiling water. Whisk until butter is melted. Whisk in sugar, buttermilk and oil until blended.

3. Add the espresso mixture and eggs to the flour mixture, stirring until just blended. Spread batter evenly in prepared pan.

4. Bake in preheated oven for 22 to 27 minutes or until a tester inserted in the center comes out with a few moist crumbs attached. Let cool completely in pan on a wire rack.

5. *Ganache:* In a large heatproof bowl, combine chocolate chips, salt and corn syrup (if using).

6. In small saucepan, bring cream to a simmer over medium heat (do not let boil). Pour cream over chocolate chip mixture and let stand for 2 minutes. Whisk until completely melted and smooth.

7. Spread ganache over top of cooled cake. Let cool completely.

# Raspberry Peach Lazy Cake

This dessert is a cross between a cake, a crumble and a cobbler. It is loosely based on a popular dessert, made throughout the American South, that is best known as "dump cake" but is also called "lazy cake." This version embraces the latter name but eschews the usual cake mix in favor of a buttery, vanilla-enhanced crumble. It's terrific served warm, with a scoop of vanilla ice cream, but embrace the name and enjoy it any way you choose.

## Tips

It will take 2 bags (each 16 oz/500 g) of frozen peaches to yield the 8 cups (1 L) needed.

Frozen peaches work perfectly in this recipe, but stick with fresh raspberries. Frozen raspberries are too wet and will alter the consistency of the cake.

## Storage Tip

Store the cooled cake, tightly covered in plastic wrap, in the refrigerator for up to 3 days.

- Preheat oven to 350°F (180°C)
- 18- by 13-inch (45 by 33 cm) rimmed sheet pan, lined with parchment paper and sprayed with nonstick cooking spray

| | | |
|---|---|---|
| 1$\frac{1}{3}$ cups | all-purpose flour | 325 mL |
| 1$\frac{1}{4}$ cups | granulated sugar, divided | 300 mL |
| 2$\frac{1}{4}$ tsp | baking powder | 11 mL |
| $\frac{1}{4}$ tsp | salt | 1 mL |
| $\frac{3}{4}$ cup | unsalted butter, melted, divided | 175 mL |
| 2 tsp | vanilla extract | 10 mL |
| 8 cups | sliced frozen peaches, thawed | 2 L |
| 2 cups | raspberries | 500 mL |

### Suggested Accompaniment
Vanilla ice cream

1. In a medium bowl, combine flour, 1 cup (250 mL) sugar, baking powder and salt until blended. Stir in $\frac{1}{2}$ cup (125 mL) butter and vanilla until blended and crumbly.

2. Arrange peaches and raspberries in a single layer on prepared pan. Sprinkle with the remaining sugar. Sprinkle topping evenly over fruit. Drizzle with the remaining butter.

3. Bake in preheated oven for 45 to 50 minutes or until topping is golden brown and springs back to the touch. Let cool on wire rack for at least 10 minutes. Serve warm or at room temperature.

### Variations
Sprinkle 1 cup (250 mL) chopped nuts (such as pecans, almonds or walnuts) over the topping before drizzling with the remaining butter in step 2.

Add 1 tsp (5 mL) ground cinnamon, ginger, allspice or cardamom with the baking powder in step 1.

# Decadent Carrot Cake with Cream Cheese Frosting

Children, including those who claim an aversion to vegetables, are drawn to carrot cake. Perhaps it's because the carrots create a moistness that plays up the sweet spices of the cake, and accent the component everyone loves most: the tangy cream cheese icing.

## Tip

You can shred the carrots using the large holes of a handheld grater, or in a food processor using the large-hole grater/shredder attachment.

## Storage Tip

Store the frosted cake, loosely wrapped in foil or waxed paper, in the refrigerator for up to 3 days. Alternatively, wrap the cooled unfrosted cake in plastic wrap, then foil, completely enclosing it, and freeze for up to 6 months. Let thaw at room temperature for 4 to 6 hours before frosting and serving.

## Variations

Add 1 cup (250 mL) chopped toasted pecans or walnuts and/or ½ cup (125 mL) raisins with the carrots in step 2.

An equal amount of grated zucchini can be used in place of the carrots.

- Preheat oven to 350°F (180°C)
- 18- by 13-inch (45 by 33 cm) rimmed sheet pan, lined with parchment paper and sprayed with nonstick cooking spray

**Cake**

| | | |
|---|---|---|
| 2⅓ cups | all-purpose flour | 575 mL |
| 2½ tsp | ground cinnamon | 12 mL |
| 2 tsp | baking soda | 10 mL |
| 1½ tsp | ground ginger | 7 mL |
| ¾ tsp | salt | 3 mL |
| 2 cups | granulated sugar | 500 mL |
| 4 | large eggs | 4 |
| 1 | can (8 oz/227 mL) crushed pineapple, with juice | 1 |
| 1 cup | vegetable oil | 250 mL |
| 2½ cups | shredded carrots | 625 mL |

**Frosting**

| | | |
|---|---|---|
| 2 cups | confectioners' (icing) sugar | 500 mL |
| 1 lb | cream cheese, softened | 500 g |
| ½ cup | unsalted butter, softened | 125 mL |

1. *Cake:* In a medium bowl, whisk together flour, cinnamon, baking soda, ginger and salt.

2. In a large bowl, whisk together sugar and eggs until blended. Whisk in pineapple and oil until blended. Stir in flour mixture until just blended. Stir in carrots. Spread batter evenly in prepared pan.

3. Bake in preheated oven for 25 to 30 minutes or until a tester inserted in the center comes out with a few moist crumbs attached. Let cool completely in pan on a wire rack.

4. *Frosting:* In a large bowl, using an electric mixer on medium-high speed, beat confectioners' sugar, cream cheese and butter until smooth and creamy (do not overbeat). Spread frosting over top of cooled cake. Refrigerate until ready to serve.

# Sheet Pan Cheesecake

Who needs crust? The batter for this cheesecake is so simple to make, and an undeniable crowd pleaser. You'll be thinking about making it again – or perhaps one of the variations – before the last piece is eaten.

## Tip

If desired, you can add 1 tbsp (15 mL) vanilla extract or 1 tsp (5 mL) almond, orange or lemon extract with the sugar in step 1.

## Storage Tip

Store the cheesecake, loosely wrapped in foil or plastic wrap, in the refrigerator for up to 1 week. Alternatively, wrap cut pieces of cheesecake in plastic wrap, then foil, completely enclosing them, and freeze for up to 6 months. Let thaw at room temperature for 1 to 2 hours before serving.

- Preheat oven to 325°F (160°C)
- Stand mixer
- 18- by 13-inch (45 by 33 cm) rimmed sheet pan, lined with parchment paper and sprayed with nonstick cooking spray

| 1¼ cups | granulated sugar | 300 mL |
|---|---|---|
| 2½ lbs | cream cheese, softened | 1.25 kg |
| 5 | large eggs | 5 |

1. In a stand mixer fitted with the paddle attachment, beat sugar and cream cheese on medium speed for 3 to 5 minutes or until light and fluffy. Add eggs, one at a time, beating until just combined. Spread batter evenly in prepared pan.

2. Bake in preheated oven for 25 to 30 minutes or until center is almost set. Transfer pan to a wire rack and run knife around rim to loosen cake. Let cool completely on rack, then refrigerate for at least 4 hours. Cut into pieces and serve.

## Variations

*Chocolate Chip Cheesecake:* Fold in 1½ cups (375 mL) miniature semisweet chocolate chips after beating in the eggs.

*Toasted Coconut Cheesecake:* Sprinkle 2 cups (500 mL) sweetened flaked coconut over the batter before baking.

*Brown Sugar Cheesecake:* Replace the granulated sugar with an equal amount of packed dark brown sugar.

*Pumpkin Pie Cheesecake:* Reduce the cream cheese to 2 lbs (1 kg) and beat in 1 cup (250 mL) pumpkin purée (not pie filling), 1 tbsp (15 mL) vanilla extract and 2 tsp (10 mL) pumpkin pie spice after beating the sugar and cream cheese.

*Lemon Cheesecake:* Beat in 1 tbsp (15 mL) finely grated lemon zest and 3 tbsp (45 mL) freshly squeezed lemon juice after beating the sugar and cream cheese.

# Outrageous Brownies

**Makes 60 brownies**

These brownies showcase a perfect pairing of chocolate with more chocolate. Don't skip the coffee powder: you won't taste coffee, only a further intensification of chocolate. Ample amounts of butter and vanilla are the final guarantee of complete outrageousness!

## Tips

Be careful not to overbake; the center of the brownie will appear slightly underbaked when it is done. It will continue to set and become firm while cooling.

To make 60 bars, cut 10 rows by 6 columns.

## Storage Tip

Store the brownies in an airtight container in the refrigerator for up to 2 weeks or in the freezer for up to 6 months.

## Variation

Replace the cookies with 2 cups (500 mL) white, milk or semisweet chocolate chips.

- 18- by 13-inch (45 by 33 cm) rimmed sheet pan, lined with parchment paper or foil and sprayed with nonstick cooking spray

| | | |
|---|---|---|
| 2 cups | unsalted butter | 500 mL |
| 4 cups | semisweet chocolate chips (1½ lbs/750 g) | 1 L |
| 1¼ cups | all-purpose flour | 300 mL |
| 1 tbsp | baking powder | 15 mL |
| 1 tsp | salt | 5 mL |
| 2 cups | granulated sugar | 500 mL |
| 3 tbsp | instant coffee powder | 45 mL |
| 6 | large eggs | 6 |
| 2 tbsp | vanilla extract | 30 mL |
| 4 cups | coarsely chopped crème-filled chocolate sandwich cookies (such as Oreos) | 1 L |

1. In a large, heavy-bottomed pot set over medium-low heat, melt butter and chocolate chips, stirring until blended and smooth. Let cool for 15 minutes.

2. Preheat oven to 350°F (180°C).

3. In a small bowl, whisk together flour, baking powder and salt.

4. In a large bowl, whisk together sugar, coffee powder, eggs and vanilla until blended. Whisk in chocolate mixture and flour mixture until blended and smooth. Stir in cookies. Spread batter evenly in prepared pan.

5. Bake for 25 to 30 minutes or until a tester inserted 3 inches (7.5 cm) from the center comes out clean (see tip, at left). Let cool completely in pan on a wire rack.

6. Cover tightly with plastic wrap and refrigerate for at least 2 hours, until cold. Using paper or foil liner, lift brownie from pan onto a cutting board. Using a spatula, lift brownie off liner and discard liner. Cut into 60 bars.

# Sheet Pan Chocolate Chip Cookie Bars

Who needs round chocolate chip cookies? This bar version features everything you desire in the classic – brown sugary, buttery batter, loads of chocolate chips, a crisp-chewy texture – without all the scooping and multiple batches.

## Tip

To make 48 bars, cut 8 rows by 6 columns.

## Storage Tip

Store the bars in an airtight container at room temperature for up to 1 week, in the refrigerator for up to 2 weeks or in the freezer for up to 3 months.

## Variations

*Cranberry White Chocolate Chip Bars:* Replace the semisweet chocolate chips with white chocolate chips and add 1½ cups (375 mL) dried cranberries with the chips.

*Oatmeal Raisin Cookie Bars:* Reduce the flour to 3½ cups (875 mL) and add 1¼ cups (300 mL) rolled oats (large-flake/old-fashioned or quick-cooking) and 2 tsp (10 mL) ground cinnamon in step 1. Replace the chocolate chips with 2 cups (500 mL) raisins.

- Preheat oven to 350°F (180°C)
- 18- by 13-inch (45 by 33 cm) rimmed sheet pan, lined with parchment paper and sprayed with nonstick cooking spray

| | | |
|---|---|---|
| 4 cups | all-purpose flour | 1 L |
| 2 tsp | baking soda | 10 mL |
| 1 tsp | salt | 5 mL |
| 1½ cups | packed light brown sugar | 375 mL |
| 1 cup | granulated sugar | 250 mL |
| 1½ cups | unsalted butter, softened | 375 mL |
| 2 | large eggs | 2 |
| 1 tbsp | vanilla extract | 15 mL |
| 2 cups | semisweet chocolate chips (12 oz/375 g) | 500 mL |

1. In a medium bowl, whisk together flour, baking soda and salt.

2. In a large bowl, using an electric mixer on medium speed, beat brown sugar, granulated sugar and butter for 3 to 5 minutes or until light and fluffy. Beat in eggs and vanilla until combined. With mixer on low speed, beat in flour mixture until just combined. Using a wooden spoon, stir in chocolate chips. Spread dough evenly on prepared pan.

3. Bake in preheated oven for 20 minutes. Open oven door and rotate pan. Close door and bake for 20 to 25 minutes or until top is golden brown. Let cool completely in pan on a wire rack.

4. Using paper liner, lift cookie from pan onto a cutting board. Using a spatula, lift cookie off liner and discard liner. Using a serrated knife, cut into 48 bars.

# No-Bake Trail Mix Bars

You may never buy granola bars again once you make these uber-delicious trail mix bars. They are decadent enough for dessert, but nutritious enough to power you through a hike, bike ride or long day at work or school.

## Tips

To toast nuts or seeds, spread them on a sheet pan and bake in a preheated 350°F (180°C) oven for 8 to 10 minutes or until golden and fragrant. Alternatively, toast them in a large dry skillet over low heat, stirring constantly, for 2 to 4 minutes or until golden and fragrant. Spread nuts out on a plate to cool before chopping them.

The coconut oil is important for holding these bars together because it becomes very firm when chilled. For best results, do not use a substitute.

To make 60 bars, cut 10 rows by 6 columns.

Other varieties of creamy nut butter (such as almond or cashew) or seed butter (such as sunflower or hemp) can be used in place of the peanut butter.

## Storage Tip

Store the bars in an airtight container at room temperature for up to 1 week, in the refrigerator for up to 2 weeks or in the freezer for up to 3 months.

- 18- by 13-inch (45 by 33 cm) rimmed sheet pan, lined with parchment paper, leaving an overhang, and sprayed with nonstick cooking spray
- Large piece of parchment paper, sprayed with nonstick cooking spray

| | | |
|---|---|---|
| 6 cups | large-flake (old-fashioned) rolled oats | 1.5 L |
| 2 cups | crisp rice cereal | 500 mL |
| 1½ cups | chopped toasted nuts or toasted seeds (see tip, at left) | 375 mL |
| 1 cup | chopped dried fruit | 250 mL |
| 1 cup | packed light brown sugar | 250 mL |
| 1 cup | liquid honey or pure maple syrup | 250 mL |
| 2 tbsp | water | 30 mL |
| 1½ cups | creamy peanut butter | 375 mL |
| ½ cup | virgin coconut oil | 125 mL |
| 1 cup | candy-coated chocolate pieces or miniature semisweet chocolate chips | 250 mL |

1. In a large bowl, stir together oats, cereal, nuts and dried fruit.

2. In a medium saucepan, combine brown sugar, honey and water. Bring to a boil over medium-high heat, stirring. Reduce heat and boil, stirring, for 1 minute. Stir in peanut butter and coconut oil until melted and smooth. Pour over oat mixture, stirring until evenly coated.

3. Working quickly, press mixture into prepared pan with a spatula. Sprinkle with chocolate. Place coated side of parchment paper on top of mixture and press firmly to compact loaf. Refrigerate for at least 2 hours. Using parchment liner, lift bar from pan onto a cutting board. Using a spatula, lift bar off liner and discard liner. Cut into 60 bars.

## Variation

*Coconut Trail Mix Bars:* Replace the dried fruit with 1½ cups (375 mL) unsweetened flaked coconut.

# Browned Butter Rice Crispy Treats

In this recipe, everyone's favorite rice crispy treats are enhanced to new heights with the addition of one step: browning the butter. It adds a rich nuttiness that is unmatched!

## Tips

Watch the pot closely as the butter begins to darken; it takes only a moment of neglect for the butter to go from perfectly browned to burned.

The residual heat from the butter should be enough to melt the marshmallows, but if not, place the pot over low heat until they are melted.

To make 48 pieces, cut 8 rows by 6 columns.

## Storage Tip

Store the treats in an airtight container at room temperature for up to 1 week.

- 18- by 13-inch (45 by 33 cm) rimmed sheet pan, lined with parchment paper and sprayed with nonstick cooking spray
- Large piece of parchment paper, sprayed with nonstick cooking spray

| | | |
|---|---|---|
| 1 cup | unsalted butter, cut into small pieces | 250 mL |
| 1¼ lbs | marshmallows | 625 g |
| ¼ tsp | salt | 1 mL |
| 12 cups | crisp rice cereal | 3 L |

1. In a large pot, melt butter over medium-low heat. Allow butter to foam slightly, then, as it turns golden, stir frequently until it turns brown and smells nutty. Immediately remove from heat and stir in marshmallows and salt until melted and smooth. Stir in cereal until completely coated.

2. Working quickly, press mixture into prepared pan with a spatula. Place coated side of parchment paper on top of mixture and press firmly to compact treats. Let cool completely on a wire rack. Invert onto a cutting board, peel off parchment paper and cut into 48 pieces.

# Sheet Pan Shortbread

Isn't it terrific when the best version of a recipe is also easy? Case in point, these shortbread. The dough comes together in minutes, without appliances, because the butter is melted for easy mixing. A long chill before two spells in the oven (first uncut, then cut) renders absolutely perfect, teatime-worthy shortbread.

## Storage Tip

Store the cooled shortbread in an airtight tin at room temperature for up to 2 weeks or in an airtight container in the freezer for up to 6 months.

- 18- by 13-inch (45 by 33 cm) rimmed sheet pan, lined with parchment paper

| | | |
|---|---|---|
| ⅔ cup | granulated sugar | 150 mL |
| ¾ tsp | salt | 3 mL |
| 1½ cups | unsalted butter, melted (and warm) | 375 mL |
| 2 tsp | vanilla extract | 10 mL |
| 3 cups | all-purpose flour | 750 mL |

1. In a medium bowl, whisk together sugar, salt, butter and vanilla for 1 to 2 minutes or until sugar is somewhat dissolved. Stir in flour until blended (dough will be shiny).

2. Scrape dough onto prepared pan and use your fingertips to press it into a 12- by 10-inch (30 by 25 cm) rectangle of even thickness. Cover with plastic wrap and refrigerate for at least 2 hours, until firm, or for up to 24 hours.

3. Preheat oven to 300°F (150°C).

4. Bake shortbread for 45 minutes. Remove pan from oven, leaving oven on, and use parchment liner to lift shortbread from pan onto a cutting board. Using a long, heavy knife, cut shortbread into thirty 2-inch (5 cm) squares. Cut each square in half on the diagonal. Reline pan with a new sheet of parchment paper and transfer cookies to pan.

5. Bake for 10 to 15 minutes or until cookies are slightly golden at the edges. Transfer cookies to a wire rack and let cool completely.

### Variations

*Chocolate Chip Shortbread:* Let dough cool to room temperature at the end of step 1. Knead in 1½ cups (375 mL) miniature semisweet chocolate chips before shaping on pan.

*Lemon Ginger Shortbread:* Replace the vanilla with 1 tbsp (15 mL) finely grated lemon zest. Add 1 cup (250 mL) finely chopped candied ginger with the flour in step 1.

*Toasted Almond Shortbread:* Replace the vanilla with 1 tsp (5 mL) almond extract. Add 1 cup (250 mL) toasted sliced almonds, chopped, with the flour in step 1.

*Brown Sugar Pecan Shortbread:* Replace the granulated sugar with an equal amount of packed brown sugar (light or dark). Add 1 cup (250 mL) toasted pecan halves, chopped, with the flour in step 1.

*Spiced Shortbread:* Add 1½ tsp (7 mL) ground cardamom, cinnamon, allspice, ginger or pumpkin pie spice with the salt in step 1.

# Streamlined Rugalach

Ordinary pie crusts are dressed up for a special occasion with raspberry jam, cinnamon sugar and toasted walnuts for this simplified riff on rugalach.

## Tips

To toast the walnuts, spread them on a sheet pan and bake in a preheated 350°F (180°C) oven for 8 to 10 minutes or until golden and fragrant. Alternatively, toast them in a large dry skillet over low heat, stirring constantly, for 2 to 4 minutes or until golden and fragrant. Spread them out on a plate to cool before finely chopping them.

Other nuts, such as pecans, almonds or hazelnuts, can be used in place of the walnuts.

Other flavors of jam, preserves or marmalade can be used in place of the raspberry jam.

## Storage Tip

Store the cooled cookies in an airtight container at room temperature for up to 2 days or in the refrigerator for up to 1 week.

- Preheat oven to 350°F (180°C)
- 18- by 13-inch (45 by 33 cm) rimmed sheet pan, lined with parchment paper

| | | |
|---|---|---|
| 1/4 cup | granulated sugar | 60 mL |
| 1/2 tsp | ground cinnamon | 2 mL |
| 1 | package (15 oz/435 g) refrigerated rolled pie crusts | 1 |
| 1/2 cup | raspberry jam or preserves | 125 mL |
| 1/2 cup | finely chopped toasted walnuts (see tip, at left) | 125 mL |
| 1 | large egg | 1 |
| 1 tbsp | water | 15 mL |

1. In a small cup, combine sugar and cinnamon.

2. Unroll 1 pie crust on a flat surface. Spread half the jam over crust to within 1/4 inch (0.5 cm) of the edge. Sprinkle with half the walnuts and 1 tbsp (15 mL) cinnamon sugar. Cut crust into 16 wedges. Roll up each wedge, starting at the widest side. Place point side down on prepared pan, spacing evenly. Repeat with the remaining crust, jam and walnuts, and another 1 tbsp (15 mL) cinnamon sugar.

3. In another small cup or bowl, whisk egg with water. Brush cookies with egg wash and sprinkle with the remaining cinnamon sugar.

4. Bake in preheated oven for 25 to 30 minutes or until golden brown. Transfer cookies to a wire rack and let cool completely.

# Cinnamon Sugar and Butter Baked Churros

**Makes 36 churros**

Churros are deep-fried cinnamon sugar donuts found throughout Mexico and Spain. With the help of purchased puff pastry, you can make them in your oven in a flash. Beware: they will disappear fast!

**Tip**

An equal amount of ground cardamom, ginger or pumpkin pie spice can be used in place of the cinnamon.

**Storage Tip**

Store the cooled churros in an airtight tin at room temperature for up to 3 days.

- Preheat oven to 450°F (230°C)
- 18- by 13-inch (45 by 33 cm) rimmed sheet pan, lined with foil and sprayed with nonstick cooking spray

| | All-purpose flour (optional) | |
|---|---|---|
| 1 | package (17.3 oz/490 g) frozen puff pastry sheets, thawed | 1 |
| ⅓ cup | granulated sugar | 75 mL |
| 1 tsp | ground cinnamon | 5 mL |
| ¼ cup | unsalted butter, melted and cooled slightly | 60 mL |

1. If necessary, on a lightly floured surface, roll out each pastry sheet into a 9-inch (23 cm) square. Transfer to a cutting board. Cut each sheet in half lengthwise. Cut each half crosswise into 1-inch (2.5 cm) wide strips. Place strips on prepared pan, spacing evenly.

2. Bake in preheated oven for 10 minutes or until golden brown.

3. Meanwhile, in a shallow dish, combine sugar and cinnamon.

4. Remove pan from oven. Brush each pastry strip with butter and gently roll in cinnamon sugar. Transfer churros to a wire rack. Let cool for 5 minutes and serve warm, or let cool to room temperature.

# Chocolate Hazelnut S'mores

### Makes 12 small or 6 large s'mores

The distinct, rich flavor of hazelnuts adds a delicious twist to this recipe for s'mores.

## Tips

To more easily measure out the chocolate-hazelnut spread, lightly coat a metal kitchen spoon and $\frac{1}{2}$ cup (125 mL) measuring cup with nonstick cooking spray.

It is important to cover the graham crackers entirely with marshmallow fluff to avoid scorching them.

To toast chopped hazelnuts, spread them on a sheet pan and bake in a preheated 350°F (180°C) oven for 5 to 7 minutes or until golden and fragrant. Alternatively, toast them in a large dry skillet over low heat, stirring constantly, for 1 to 3 minutes or until golden and fragrant.

- Preheat broiler
- 18- by 13-inch (45 by 33 cm) rimmed sheet pan, lined with foil

| | | |
|---|---|---|
| $\frac{1}{2}$ cup | chocolate-hazelnut spread | 125 mL |
| 24 | graham cracker squares (or 12 graham cracker sheets) | 24 |
| 6 tbsp | toasted chopped hazelnuts (optional) | 90 mL |
| $1\frac{1}{2}$ cups | marshmallow fluff | 375 mL |

1. Spread chocolate-hazelnut spread over half of the graham crackers. Sprinkle with hazelnuts (if using).

2. Spread marshmallow fluff over the remaining graham crackers, making sure to cover the entire cracker. Place marshmallow-covered crackers on prepared pan, spacing evenly.

3. Broil for 30 to 60 seconds or until marshmallow is browned. Remove from oven and top with chocolate-hazelnut-covered crackers. Let cool slightly.

# Caramel Chocolate Pretzel Bark

**Makes 32 pieces**

This is the food gift your friends want: gooey, crunchy, salty, sweet and covered with chocolate. Don't tell them how easy it was to make!

## Storage Tip

Store the bark in an airtight container in the refrigerator for up to 2 months.

## Variations

Replace the pretzels with 1 cup (250 mL) chopped roasted salted nuts or seeds, such as almonds, cashews, green pumpkin seeds (pepitas) or sunflower seeds.

Replace the pretzels with 1 cup (250 mL) chopped dried fruit, such as apricots, cranberries, cherries or raisins.

Replace the semisweet chocolate chips with white chocolate chips.

- 18- by 13-inch (45 by 33 cm) rimmed sheet pan, lined with parchment paper

| | | |
|---|---|---|
| 2 cups | semisweet or bittersweet chocolate chips (12 oz/375 g) | 500 mL |
| 16 | small soft caramel squares, unwrapped | 16 |
| 1½ tbsp | water | 22 mL |
| 1½ cups | coarsely broken mini pretzels | 375 mL |

1. Place chocolate chips in a medium microwave-safe bowl. Microwave on High in 30-second intervals, stirring in between, until melted and smooth. Spread in prepared pan, leaving a 1½-inch (4 cm) border between the chocolate and the pan edges.

2. Place caramels and water in another medium microwave-safe bowl. Microwave on High in 30-second intervals, stirring in between, until melted and smooth. Drizzle in a zigzag pattern over the chocolate. Swirl the caramel and chocolate slightly with the tip of a knife. Sprinkle with pretzels.

3. Let cool at room temperature for 1 hour, then refrigerate for at least 1 hour to harden. Break into pieces.

# No-Bake Rocky Road Clusters

This handheld, no-bake cookie version of the beloved ice cream and fudge is great for lunch bags, potlucks and party buffet tables.

**Tip**

Other roasted salted nuts, such as cashews, almonds or mixed nuts, can be used in place of the peanuts.

**Storage Tip**

Store the clusters in an airtight container in the refrigerator for up to 1 month.

- 18- by 13-inch (45 by 33 cm) rimmed sheet pan, lined with parchment paper

| | | |
|---|---|---|
| 3 cups | crisp rice cereal | 750 mL |
| 2 cups | miniature marshmallows | 500 mL |
| 1 cup | roasted salted peanuts, coarsely chopped | 250 mL |
| 2 cups | semisweet chocolate chips (12 oz/375 g) | 500 mL |

1. In a large bowl, combine cereal, marshmallows and peanuts.

2. Place chocolate chips in a medium microwave-safe bowl. Microwave on High in 30-second intervals, stirring in between, until melted and smooth.

3. Pour the melted chocolate over the cereal mixture, scraping the sides of the bowl with a rubber spatula. Stir and fold until evenly coated.

4. Drop mixture in heaping 2-tbsp (30 mL) clusters onto prepared pan. Chill in the refrigerator for at least 30 minutes or until clusters are firm.

# Graham Cracker Toffee

**Makes 36 pieces**

While the buttery sweet crunch of this toffee is bewitching, the only magic is that it is crafted with incredible ease, with just a handful of pantry ingredients.

## Storage Tip
Store the toffee in an airtight container at room temperature for up to 2 months.

## Variations
*Chocolate Chip Toffee:* Sprinkle the toffee with 1 cup (250 mL) miniature semisweet chocolate chips immediately after baking.

*Coconut Toffee:* Replace the pecans with 1 ½ cups (375 mL) sweetened or unsweetened flaked coconut.

- Preheat oven to 350°F (180°C)
- 18- by 13-inch (45 by 33 cm) rimmed sheet pan, lined with parchment paper

| 36 | graham cracker squares (or 18 graham cracker sheets) | 36 |
|---|---|---|
| 1 cup | packed light brown sugar | 250 mL |
| 1 cup | unsalted butter | 250 mL |
| 1 cup | chopped pecans or almonds (optional) | 250 mL |

1. Arrange graham crackers, touching, side by side in a single layer on prepared pan, breaking or cutting some as needed to fit.

2. Place brown sugar and butter in a medium saucepan. Bring to a boil over medium-high heat, stirring constantly to dissolve the sugar. Boil, stirring constantly, for 2 minutes. Immediately pour over graham crackers, spreading with a spatula to cover. Sprinkle with pecans (if using).

3. Bake in preheated oven for 6 to 8 minutes or until topping is bubbly. Let cool completely in pan on a wire rack. Using paper liner, remove toffee from pan. Break or cut toffee into pieces.

# Index

Library and Archives Canada Cataloguing in Publication

Saulsbury, Camilla V., author
    200 best sheet pan meals : quick & easy oven recipes, one pan, no fuss! / Camilla V. Saulsbury.

Includes index.
ISBN 978-0-7788-0538-0 (paperback)

    1. One-dish meals. 2. Quick and easy cooking. 3. Cookbooks. I. Title. II. Title: Two hundred best sheet pan meals.

TX840.O53S29 2016          641.8'2          C2015-907951-9